TEACHING
NUMBER SENSE

GRADE 1

GRADE 1

1

TEACHING
NUMBER SENSE

CHRIS CONFER

Math Solutions Publications
Sausalito, CA

Math Solutions Publications
A division of
Marilyn Burns Education Associates
150 Gate 5 Road, Suite 101
Sausalito, CA 94965
www.mathsolutions.com

Library of Congress Cataloging-in-Publication Data
Confer, Chris.
    Teaching number sense, grade 1 / Chris Confer.
        p. cm.
    Includes index.
    ISBN 0-941355-59-4 (acid-free paper)
 1. Mathematics—Study and teaching (Primary) 2. Numeration.
3. Counting. 4. Arithmetic. I. Title.
    QA135.6.C654 2005
    372.7—dc22

                                                    2005010701

ISBN-10: 0-941355-59-4
ISBN-13: 978-0-941355-59-9

Editor: Toby Gordon
Production: Melissa L. Inglis
Cover & interior design: Catherine Hawkes/Cat and Mouse
Composition: Interactive Composition Corporation

Printed in the United States of America on acid-free paper
09 08 07 06 05   ML   2 3 4 5

A Message from Marilyn Burns

We at Math Solutions Professional Development believe that teaching math well calls for increasing our understanding of the math we teach, seeking deeper insights into how children learn mathematics, and refining our lessons to best promote students' learning.

Math Solutions Publications shares classroom-tested lessons and teaching expertise from our faculty of Math Solutions Inservice instructors as well as from other respected math educators. Our publications are part of the nationwide effort we've made since 1984 that now includes

- more than five hundred face-to-face inservice programs each year for teachers and administrators in districts across the country;
- annually publishing professional development books, now totaling more than fifty titles and spanning the teaching of all math topics in kindergarten through grade 8;
- four series of videotapes for teachers, plus a videotape for parents, that show math lessons taught in actual classrooms;
- on-site visits to schools to help refine teaching strategies and assess student learning; and
- free online support, including grade-level lessons, book reviews, inservice information, and district feedback, all in our quarterly *Math Solutions Online Newsletter*.

For information about all of the products and services we have available, please visit our Web site at *www.mathsolutions.com*. You can also contact us to discuss math professional development needs by calling (800) 868-9092 or by sending an e-mail to *info@mathsolutions.com*.

We're always eager for your feedback and interested in learning about your particular needs. We look forward to hearing from you.

A DIVISION OF MARILYN BURNS EDUCATION ASSOCIATES

Contents

Acknowledgments   ix
Introduction   xi

Numbers in Our World

1. Solving Real-World Problems   1
2. Making Classroom Decisions   6

Counting and Number Relationships

3. Estimate and Count   11
4. Containers: More and Less   17
5. Pattern Block Numbers   21
6. Spill and Compare   26
7. Guess My Number   35

Decomposing and Composing Numbers

8. What Do You See?   40
9. Snap It!   45
10. Mouse Count   52
11. Shake and Spill   61
12. Bead Boards: Six Birds   67
13. Roll and Add   73
14. Over in the Grasslands   80

Landmark Numbers

15. Bead Boards: Secret Numbers   87
16. Bead Boards: Story Problems   93

Moving Toward Place Value

17. Counting Buttons   97
18. A Candy Shop: How Many Candies?   101
19. A Candy Shop: Packaging Candy Bags   108

Blackline Masters

Estimate and Count Recording Sheet   119
More and Less Recording Sheet   120
Pattern Block Cutouts   121
Spill and Compare Recording Sheet   127
What Do You See? Cards   128
Shake and Spill: 5   131
Shake and Spill: 6   132
Shake and Spill: 7   133
Shake and Spill: 8   134

Index   135

Acknowledgments

Just as it takes a village to raise a child, it takes a community of learners to create a resource book that is helpful to teachers.

I have been extremely fortunate to be surrounded by, and learn from, the following teacher-researchers in the Tucson Unified School District's Title 1 Mathematics and Science Project: Heidi Aranda, Norma Badilla, Carol Brooks, Judy Darcy, Sharon Keown, Connie Lewis, Rosalie Milano, Lilia Olivas, Paul Ottley, Marco Ramirez, Kay Thill, Olga Torres, and Jackie Wortman.

The teachers and principals at two outstanding Tucson Unified School District schools, Mission View Elementary and Pueblo Gardens Elementary, have willingly contributed their expertise to this book, adding layers of complexity and practicality, and doing so with a clear vision of what is possible for young children to achieve in mathematics. Fortunate are the children who attend these schools!

Marilyn Burns, whose belief that children can and must make sense of mathematics, has changed the face of education, and has been an inspiration to me. Many thanks to Toby Gordon and Melissa Inglis, who cheerfully shepherded this book to completion. Thank you, also, to the teachers who read the manuscript and offered valuable suggestions: Bettye Braucher, Luis Carbonell, Kristin Garrison, Barbara Miller, Yolanda Sethi, Karolyn Williams, and Jackie Wortman. In addition to Marilyn Burns, I am also grateful to Kathy Richardson, Catherine Twomey Fosnot, and Paul R. Trafton, for the profound research they have done with young children, and for inspiring some of the activities presented in these chapters.

Special thanks to my niece, Ashley Klewer, whose trust in her mathematical abilities sparked my own interest in how young children learn to think about numbers.

And always, my love and appreciation to David, Jonathan, and Amanda, who make all things possible.

Introduction

Courtney, who had just turned four, sat on my lap. My niece laughed and stretched out a hand, showing me four fingers spread wide. "I'm this many!" she said happily.

"How many is that?" I asked her.

"I don't know," she answered, with a serious expression.

A few days later, Courtney's six-year-old sister, Ashley, and I were talking about the problem 7 + 6.

"I don't know seven plus six," she told me, "but I can figure it out. I know seven plus seven is fourteen, and six plus six is twelve, so seven plus six must be thirteen."

Ashley certainly has what we call "number sense." And Courtney will, too, someday. But what exactly *is* number sense? What is the path that Courtney will take toward developing it? And how can we teachers help children move forward in this?

Young Children and Numbers

Young children see math being used in their world, but it takes time for them to understand the purpose and thought behind what they observe. For example, they might see adults point at objects and count, saying, "One, two, three . . ." But they often believe that adults are naming things, in the way that individuals might point at people and say their names: "Fred, Sally, George . . ." Children often do not understand that the final number stands for the entire quantity.

Young children might count five buttons, and when the buttons are spread out more widely, think that the quantity has increased. This is because children trust their visual perception more than their newly developing sense of numbers. They think that by changing the arrangement, the quantity will change as well.

In the same way, children may count five buttons beginning with the green one, but when they count the same buttons beginning with the red one, they think a different number will result. Many young children are not bothered at all when they recount the same set of items and arrive at a different number.

The Importance of Number Experiences

It takes time for children to develop number understandings, and children come to first grade with widely varying number experiences. Some children have had few, others have had many. For example, Jason's mother consistently talks out loud about her mathematical thinking, and invites him into mathematical discussions.

She might say, "Jason, how many grapes do you think are in the basket?" As they eat, she'll make other observations. "I see three grapes in this cluster. Do you think there are more grapes in that cluster?" Later she might comment, "Oops! You ate one. Now how many are there?" or, "Uh oh! Your little sister wants a snack, too. You'll need to give half to her so it's fair. How many will each of you get?" Jason participates in conversations like this day after day, month after month, year after year.

Jason might have had an equally loving parent who only knew to say, "Jason, dear, come and eat."

The mathematical concepts and language that children bring to school reflect the mathematical interactions they have had in their lives. Mathematically proficient children have number capabilities not so much because they are "smart" or "gifted" but because their families participate in a multitude of mathematical experiences.

Our job as teachers is to recognize that children do the best they can. We need to create a mathematically literate environment at school that invites children to think mathematically. We need to invite them into mathematical discussions about what they think. We need to create safe environments that allow them to risk taking those first tentative mathematical steps, in the same way that we create child-safe physical environments in which toddlers can take their first wobbly steps. And just as we celebrate the milestones as our children learn to walk, skip, run, and throw a ball, we must celebrate our students' mathematical milestones whenever they occur.

The Complexity of Number

Numbers are so much a part of what we think about as adults that we have trouble remembering how nebulous they really are. Numbers don't truly exist in and of themselves but are instead an idea. They name an amount in relative terms. Three books is more than two books but fewer than five books. "Three" is small when we think of three paperclips but large when we think about three elephants.

Numbers are a way to describe an experience. They help explain the different way I feel when I go outside when it's 70 degrees and I feel the comfortable breeze, breathe in the cool air, and walk happily through the park, compared to when it's 110 degrees and I feel the oppressive heat that constricts my breathing, pushing me to seek shade, hurry inside, or cover my eyes against the intense light.

You can't *see* a number. Three apples may be in front of me. I may see the redness, smell the fruitiness, and eventually taste the flavor and experience the juiciness. But I don't see "three." Three is only an idea or a relationship that we construct.

Number usually tells us how many. We use number to decide if we have enough or too little or too much. Numbers arose from humans' need to describe quantity; the first shepherds had to make sure that the same number of sheep returned as went out into the pasture that morning. Children often need to determine quantity. Little Erin has one shoe on her foot and knows she needs the other before she can go outside.

Numbers have other roles as well. They are used to identify, such as in a Social Security number or a telephone number. Numbers can also be used to measure, or to identify an item in a sequence of other items, such when we say "the second chair."

What Number Sense Means

Children with well-developed number sense use numbers to solve problems. They make sense of numerical situations, and use what they know to figure out what they don't know. To have good number sense, children must understand the following basic concepts.

Counting

Counting is a complex idea, and foundational to other number concepts. In order to count, children must

- know the sequence of number names
- touch each item while coordinating the touching with verbal counting (one-to-one correspondence)
- keep track of which items have already been counted
- understand that the last number they say stands for the entire quantity and includes each of the other numbers they have said (inclusion)
- realize that the items can be rearranged and still be the same quantity (conservation)

Number Relationships

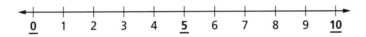

Children need to know how numbers relate to each other—for example, that five is one less than six, but three more than two. This includes the ideas of "more," "less," "the same," "how many more," "how many less," and the sequencing of numbers.

Decomposing and Composing Numbers

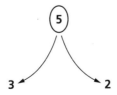

Children need to know that inside a number are other numbers, that they can break numbers apart and see what other numbers are inside. For example, they need to know that inside five is a three and a two. Children need to decompose flexibly, developing the habit of looking for possible combinations of numbers: for example, inside five, a one and four, and two and three. Children need many chances to decompose numbers five and ten. They will use what they know about these smaller numbers to decompose larger numbers.

Just as children decompose numbers, they need to know that when they recombine those two smaller numbers (such as three and two), the larger number (five) will be the result.

Landmark Numbers

Children get lost in the land of numbers in the same way that I get lost when I visit a new city. Children look for "landmark numbers" to make sure of where they are, just as last week I looked at the mountains around El Paso, Texas, to keep track of where I was.

The landmark numbers that first graders often use are five, ten, and twenty. Children need many experiences with the number five, because everything that they know about five will help them with ten. Later, children will use what they know about ten to help them with larger landmark numbers, such as twenty, fifty, and one hundred. I often encourage this kind of thinking by highlighting landmark numbers on the children's number lines or 1–100 charts.

Strategies for Computation

From all the above understandings, children develop strategies for computation. They use what they know to figure out what they don't know. And over time, children learn to compute quickly and efficiently.

Children develop various strategies for addition, such as:

- Counting all: For the problem 8 + 7, a child might make a group of eight objects and another group of seven objects, and then count each object, starting at one.
- Counting on: For the problem 8 + 7, a child might make a group of eight objects and another group of seven objects, and then touch the group of eight and count the rest, saying, "Eight—nine, ten, eleven, twelve, thirteen, fourteen, fifteen."
- Using doubles: For the problem 8 + 7, a child might say, "I know eight plus eight is sixteen, but it's one less, so the answer is fifteen."
- Making tens: For the problem 8 + 7, a child might say, "I'm going to take two from the seven and give it to the eight, so that I have ten plus five. That's fifteen."

Strategies for subtraction are related to strategies for addition. And since additive thinking is often easier than subtractive thinking, I spend more time helping children build number sense through addition. Children can develop the following types of strategies for subtraction:

- Counting what remains: For the problem 16 − 9, a child might make a group of sixteen objects, count out a group of nine objects from the original group, take them away, and count the remaining objects.
- Counting on: Many children, and adults too, add to subtract. For the problem 16 − 9, a child might count on from nine until he gets to sixteen, saying, "Nine . . . ten, eleven, twelve, thirteen, fourteen, fifteen, sixteen." As

the child counts on, he may put up one finger for each new number and then count those seven fingers.

A good visual model for this is the number line. Children may simply count each space between 9 and 16 to find the difference of seven. Children also learn to make "friendly jumps." For the problem $16 - 9$, a child with well-developed number sense might jump from 9 to 10 (since ten is a friendly number) and then jump six more spaces to 16. Then the child counts the jumps: $1 + 6 = 7$.

- Counting back: For the problem $16 - 9$, a child might count back from sixteen, saying, "Fifteen, fourteen, thirteen, twelve, eleven, ten, nine, eight, seven," while keeping track with his or her fingers.
- Using doubles: For the problem $16 - 9$, a child might say, "I know sixteen minus eight is eight, so sixteen minus nine has to be seven."
- Taking away ten: For the problem $16 - 9$, a child might say, "First I'll take away ten, because I know that's six. Then I'll add one more because I took away one too many. That makes seven."

Children use a wide variety of strategies. I learn from them as they compute in ways that make sense to them. Through experience, they develop knowledge of number relationships. As they become more mathematically proficient, they learn to trust in themselves.

Eventually children "just know" number facts, and that is an important goal. But I want all children to develop strategies. Children don't "just know" problems such as $25 + 19$. They will need ways to figure out challenging problems, ways that help them use what they know to figure out what they don't know, ways that require number sense.

The Importance of Making Sense of Numbers

We can't simply tell children about numbers and think that they will "know" them. Children will not develop number sense by merely circling answers and writing in workbooks. They have to construct these understandings and build these relationships in their minds, through experiences over time and through discussing with others the relationships they encounter.

Superficial experiences with number may produce a temporary veneer of competence. Children may have the appearance of understanding. But this veneer is likely to crumble in the child's upper elementary or middle school years. Many of us know middle school children who have trouble with fractions, who can't remember procedures for computation, who worry about word problems and say, "Do I add? Do I subtract? Just tell me what to do and I'll do it."

All children deserve the time that they need to construct understandings of number. Children who develop solid relationships with smaller numbers use them as tools for understanding larger numbers. What children know about five helps them understand ten, and then later twenty, fifty, one hundred, one thousand, and then ten thousand. The time invested in the early years to allow children to develop solid number understandings will pay off greatly in later years.

Thoughts About Organizing the Year

While counting is the basis of all number sense, other aspects of numerical understanding do not develop in a linear manner. Children can develop number relationships, decompose numbers, and develop strategies early on. A child who can count ten objects might decompose 4, and can compare numbers 1 through 8. As children gain control over larger numbers, they can decompose and develop number relationships with larger numbers. However, children's ability to count will always surpass their ability to decompose numbers. When Paula began first grade, she could count to 39, but could easily decompose numbers only up to 4. Hannah could count up to 109, but could decompose numbers only up to 5.

As a teacher, I need to have an idea of where each child is. I try to listen to each child count, compare numbers, and decompose numbers at the beginning of the year and in the middle of the year. This helps me develop a sense of the range of numbers in which each child needs to work when I'm highlighting specific aspects of number sense.

From the first day of school I include all children in interesting problem-solving activities, even with numbers that may be out of reach for some of them. We can never be sure of what each child knows; children often surprise us. Also, children learn a great deal from one another. Furthermore, all children need to participate in the beauty and complexity of mathematics. We don't wait until children master dribbling and chest passes before we let them play basketball. We read interesting chapter books to children who don't yet read independently at that level. In the same way, all children participate in problem solving, doing real mathematics, learning that mathematics is enjoyable and serves a purpose in their lives.

The Structure of the Lessons

In order to help you with planning and teaching the lessons in this book, each is presented in the same format, with the following sections:

Overview   To help you decide if the lesson is appropriate for your students, this is a nutshell description of the mathematical goal of the lesson and what the students will be doing.

Materials   This section lists the special materials needed, along with quantities. Not included in the list are regular classroom supplies such as pencils and paper. Worksheets that need to be duplicated are included in the Blackline Masters section at the back of the book.

Time   Generally the number of class periods is provided; sometimes the class period is divided into different time periods, reflecting several activities. It is indicated in the text that some activities are meant to be repeated from time to time.

Teaching Directions   The directions are presented in a step-by-step lesson plan.

Teaching Notes This section addresses the mathematics underlying the lesson and at times provides information about the prior experiences or knowledge students need.

The Lesson This is a vignette that describes what actually occurred when the lesson was taught to one or more classes. While the vignette mirrors the plan described in the teaching directions, it elaborates with details that are valuable for preparing and teaching the lesson. Samples of student work are included.

Extensions This section is included for some of the lessons and offers follow-up suggestions.

Linking Assessment and Instruction This section offers some ways to observe children and how you might interpret what you see children do. It relates children's responses to important mathematical understandings, how children represented their thinking, and what strategies they used.

Thoughts About Organizing Instruction

I often introduce a new investigation, activity, or game in a whole group with the class sitting in a circle on the rug. This way everyone can see the manipulatives I have laid out in front of me. Once the children know how to do the investigation, I often use it as part of math workshop time.

During math workshop, I provide children with a list of math activities from which they can choose. Children need to do math activities more than once; the first time they are just learning how to do the activity and what is expected of them. The real learning, connections, and language development occur when children repeat the activity. Children enjoy making choices and having control over their learning. And I appreciate being able to sit with an individual child or a small group of children during math workshop to hear their thought processes and support them in their thinking.

Children benefit from working with others, and I often have my first graders work with a partner. They work with the same partner, or math buddy, for several weeks at a time. During units on number, I frequently choose the partners ahead of time, based on the children's experience levels. When we study other topics in mathematics, I usually have the students draw colored cubes to create partners randomly. During whole group time, they sit on the rug with their math buddy, and from time to time I have the partners explain an idea or a word to each other. This keeps the children involved in the discussion, gives them a chance to use terminology, and helps them develop a better understanding of a concept. Math buddies also work at tables together, although each child usually records on his or her own paper. Math buddies help each other, talk to each other, and often teach each other as they work.

How to Use This Book

This collection of lessons is not intended to be a complete first-grade arithmetic curriculum. Instead I envision this book as a guide for first-grade teachers as they help their students build number sense. It presents a picture of the kinds of investigations, activities, and games that promote development of number sense. It describes the elements that make up the solid foundation in number understandings that children will draw upon as they encounter more complex mathematics in later years.

The first section of the book, "Numbers in Our World," presents lessons that show children how important mathematics is in their lives. These lessons help build a classroom culture for learning arithmetic and are to be used throughout the year, when mathematical opportunities naturally arise in the classroom. The second section, "Counting and Number Relationships," gives children opportunities to count and compare numbers and learn how numbers relate to each other. The third section, "Decomposing and Composing Numbers," helps children learn what happens when they break apart numbers and recombine them. The fourth section, "Landmark Numbers," provides some specific activities and models that focus on the numbers five, ten, and twenty. The last section, "Moving Toward Place Value," offers lessons that develop foundational place-value understanding.

I envision this book as the beginning of a conversation rather than a definitive statement of what teachers should do in first grade. Each child is unique, each learning situation different. I hope that teachers will hear my perspective and stories, but will make appropriate adjustments for their students. I hope teachers truly listen to what their children say, try to make sense of it, and change their teaching accordingly. As Marilyn Burns advises teachers, *"Do what makes sense to you . . . and persist until it does."*

Solving Real-World Problems

CHAPTER 1

OVERVIEW

Classroom life is brimming with opportunities for children to solve real-world problems that occur naturally. When teachers are aware of the mathematical possibilities, many kinds of investigations will emerge. In this lesson the children are asked to figure out how many cookies they need for a class treat.

MATERIALS

- counters, enough for the children who need to use them

TIME

- one class period

Teaching Directions

1. Tell the students you will be bringing cookies to class for a treat.

2. Ask them to figure out how many cookies you need to bring so that each student gets two. Let them know that they are free to use counters or any other classroom resource to solve the problem.

3. Ask them to record their thinking on paper.

4. Have several children share with the group their answers and how they went about solving the problem.

5. Come to a class consensus about the correct answer. Reflect on the results.

Teaching Notes

When I think back to my teaching over the years, one thing has certainly changed. The more mathematics I learn, the more I'm aware of the potential mathematical investigations that arise naturally on a daily basis. More and more, I'm building on these real-life situations in the classroom.

Some real-life mathematical investigations happen with regularity, while others do not. We encounter mathematics when we take attendance, do the lunch count, see who has brought back permission slips or library books. But other mathematical situations arise spontaneously. I try to take advantage of these situations, rearranging my teaching plans to include these powerful, real learning opportunities.

When children use mathematics to solve real classroom problems, they learn that mathematics is not just something to do for the teacher's sake, but it offers them important tools to shape their world.

In the vignette below, children at times express confusion. Many teachers are uncomfortable when children are confused. However, I prefer to witness children's misunderstandings and have students discuss them, rather than have them remain hidden. Many mathematical ideas are complex and therefore are difficult for first graders. When children grapple with real problems and encounter difficulties, they have a reason to do hard thinking and they are more likely to come to a resolution sooner than if the problem is an abstraction unrelated to their day-to-day lives. However, while some confusion can be a good thing, I don't want the children to cross the line and become truly frustrated, so I choose problems that are within children's capabilities and I do the best I can to intervene and provide support if children need it.

The Lesson

"Tomorrow is Children's Day," Sereslinda announced. "We should have a party."

"My mom says every day is Children's Day," commented Alfredo.

I remembered my mother saying the same thing, and I smiled.

"We go to movies, we eat pizza, we get to do lots of stuff," Alfredo explained.

"Tomorrow we could celebrate Children's Day in a small way," I said. "After we do math, we could have cookies. But I'll need to know how many cookies to bring."

"Bring lots," suggested Becky.

"Chocolate chip," added Carina.

"I'd be happy to bring two cookies for each of you," I continued. "But I'd like to know how many cookies to bring. What do we need to know to figure this out?"

"How many cookies?" asked Juanita doubtfully.

"Yes, that's what we need to know—how many cookies we need so that each of you can have two. Every child needs two cookies," I clarified. "Ashley needs two cookies, Jonathan needs two cookies, two for Becky, two for each of you." I pretended to give each child two imaginary cookies.

"How many children are there in our class?" I continued. The children agreed that there were twenty-two students. I wrote *There are 22 children* on the board. Then I added, *If each child gets 2 cookies, how many cookies do we need?* We read the problem together.

"You can draw pictures or use cubes or anything else in the room to figure it out," I said. "And you can work by yourself or with a partner or partners. Just make sure that if someone asks to work with you that you say 'yes!' Remember the rule that we use during recess, 'You can't say you can't play'? That goes for math time too."

I again reiterated the question that they were to think about: "How many children are in this room?" The children answered, "Twenty-two." I underlined *22 children*.

"And how many cookies does each one need?" "Two cookies," they said. I underlined *each child gets 2 cookies*.

"If I was you I'd get two cookies and then see if there's five, and it would go by twos," said Alfredo.

It wasn't clear to me what he meant. But that was okay. "You can figure it out any way you want," I

said. "Have the cubes be pretend cookies or draw pictures or do anything. Just find out how many cookies I need to bring. I want each of you to show your answer and how you figured it out on a piece of paper," I continued, placing a stack of blank papers on the table. "Try to use words, numbers, and pictures to show what you did."

As the children got to work I heard Sereslinda discussing the problem with Juanita. "We should draw the kids, and we're gonna write and put the cookies and put how much do we need." Lorena added, "We're gonna put circles."

Alfredo began drawing stick figures and two cookies next to each one. He clearly grasped that for every child, two cookies were needed. After two stick figures, he abandoned this idea. "It's too hard," he told me. "Can I start over?" He turned his paper over and began drawing sets of two cookies. Each pair of cookies had a slightly larger space between them. It seemed he was using the space to show that each child would get two cookies.

I checked in with Alejandrina, Navin, and Alicia, who were sitting on the rug. The girls had drawn pairs of cookies and had circled the pairs. They were counting to check that they had twenty-two pairs. Navin had written $2 + 2 + 2 + 2 \ldots$ and was counting by ones. "Forty-four!" he said triumphantly. *I conted them,* Navin wrote under his long equation.

Lorena made dots for her cookies. The pairs of cookies were clearly separated from each other. She counted them, drew some more, and recounted them from one to check how many cookies she had.

I moved on to Sereslinda, who had made circles for the cookies, all in a line, without any space separating the pairs of cookies. She stopped to count the cookies and came to sixteen. I wondered what she'd do next.

Alfredo had decided to circle his pairs of cookies. "These go together," he said. "It's two kids." It seemed that Alfredo had started to confuse what the circles represented: were they cookies or children? I decided not to intervene and see if he was able to sort this out himself. "I have to make the dots," he told me. "I'm making chocolate chips." (See Figure 1–1.)

Sereslinda had also begun to circle pairs of cookies, perhaps to show that each child got two cookies. She added a cookie at the end of the line. "That doesn't work," she said, and crossed out the last cookie. She went to the next line and began drawing pairs of cookies, which she circled. She periodically stopped to count the cookies. When she had twenty-two, she stopped.

She then began drawing stick people. She made ten and then began to write numbers to represent the other children in the class. Her numbers went up to twenty-two, but she had only drawn eleven stick figures and ten numbers. Sereslinda had miscounted, but I was interested in the way she had moved to a more efficient way of representing: using numbers rather than drawings.

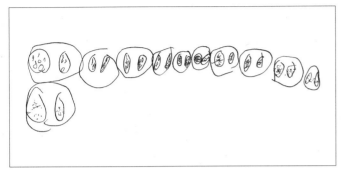

FIGURE 1–1 Even though he had circled pairs, Alfredo's paper showed twenty-two cookies, rather than twenty-two pairs of cookies.

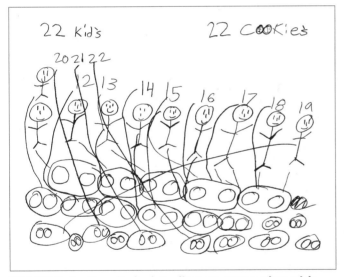

FIGURE 1–2 Sereslinda drew lines to connect her stick figures with pairs of cookies. The many lines on the drawing confused her, and she changed her answer from forty-four to twenty-two.

I watched as Sereslinda began to check that she had enough pairs of cookies for each child in the class. She traced lines to connect each stick person with cookie pairs or each number with a pair of cookies. But this became an unwieldy representational strategy. The lines crossed over each other and she was having difficulty determining if everything matched up (see Figure 1–2). Sereslinda was beginning to look frustrated. It was time to intervene. I decided to capitalize on the good strategy that she was using.

"Do you know what smart thing I see you doing, Sereslinda?" I asked her. "You're matching to check that you have two cookies for each person by drawing lines. That works great for smaller numbers, but gets hard with larger numbers like twenty-two. Can I offer you a suggestion?" She nodded. "You might try pointing to each pair of two cookies and see if you count twenty-two pairs, just like we have twenty-two kids." I demonstrated this for her and she continued counting on her own. "There's enough," she told me. I was pleased that this alternate strategy had proved helpful to her.

Lorena had made twenty-two pairs of cookies and began counting them from one in English. She miscounted partway through and somehow recognized her mistake. "You might want to count in Spanish," I suggested. When children are doing something difficult, they often have more success when using their first language. Even children who speak a second language fairly well can do more sophisticated thinking in their first language.

Lorena began counting over again in Spanish, counting on from two. She did this several times, making sure that she counted correctly. Lorena carefully wrote *44 cookies* at the top of her page, checking how I had written *cookies* on the board. (See Figure 1–3.)

I checked in with Sereslinda. Her paper had twenty-two pairs of cookies on it. "So how many cookies do we need to have?" I asked her. Sereslinda

FIGURE 1–3 Lorena drew twenty-two pairs of cookies, then counted by ones, in Spanish, to forty-four.

counted the groups of two. "We need twenty-two cookies," she announced. "So we have twenty-two children, and each child gets two cookies, and we need to bring twenty-two cookies?" I asked. Sereslinda nodded and wrote *22 cookies* at the top of her paper. She explained, "Two cookies for him, two cookies for him, two cookies for him." She clearly knew that the groups of two cookies matched each person. But when she answered the question, "How many cookies do I need to bring altogether?" she counted the groups of two and got twenty-two.

Alfredo nodded. "She's right," he said. But his paper had a very different representation: only twenty-two cookies, rather than twenty-two pairs of cookies.

I noticed Lorena circling her groups of two cookies to further emphasize that a pair of cookies was for each child.

Representing two cookies for each child is difficult, since there is a quantity of children that is relevant, and a quantity of cookies that does not match the first number but represents a doubling of that number. After representing these different quantities, the children need to remember and interpret which was which. Sereslinda was moving in and out of this understanding, while Lorena's understanding was more solid.

No matter their level of understanding, I want all first graders to grapple with this complex idea. Mistakes are always opportunities to learn something new. I planned to use the class discussion to further students' understanding.

A Class Discussion

I gathered the children on the rug. I had the children's papers in my hand, and I planned to have Alfredo and Lorena share their strategies, since their papers were typical of the class. I reminded the children of the problem. "What did you find out?" I asked the group. "How many cookies do I need to bring if there are twenty-two of you and each of you needs two cookies?"

I asked Alfredo to go first and I handed him his paper to share with the class.

"There's two kids here," Alfredo said, pointing to the two dotted circles that he had drawn to represent cookies. "And two kids here and two kids here. And that makes one, two, three, four, five, six, seven, eight, nine, ten, eleven, twelve, thirteen, fourteen, fifteen, sixteen, seventeen, eighteen, nineteen, twenty, twenty-one, twenty-two. And there's twenty-two kids and twenty-two cookies."

"So you think that if we have twenty-two cookies, there will be enough for each of you to have two cookies," I said, restating his contribution. Alfredo nodded.

Several of the children agreed with their classmate. "It's twenty-two," said Robert. "I counted it." He was experiencing the same confusion: did each circle stand for a cookie or for a child?

"How many of you agree that we need twenty-two cookies?" I asked. About a third of the children raised their hands. "Some of you think we need twenty-two cookies," I said. I wrote *22 cookies* on the board.

I asked Lorena to share next. "Be sure to listen to Lorena to see if you agree with what she says," I instructed.

"We need to see all twenty-two kids and count the cookies," Lorena said, pointing at the pairs of cookies she had drawn. "It's one, two, three, four . . ." She counted to forty-four, recognizing that each pair was made up of two cookies. "These are cookies," she said.

"That's not right," said Alfredo. "It's twenty-two. I counted them."

Navin was shaking his head. "It's forty-four," he said.

"Let's look at what Lorena drew. Where are the kids?" I asked her. She pointed to each pair of cookies, saying, "This is for me and this is for Sereslinda and this is for Heriberto . . ."

"You left a space between to show that the next pair of cookies was for a different person. And then you counted all the cookies?" I asked her. Lorena nodded. We counted all of the cookies that Lorena had drawn and got to forty-four. I wrote *44 cookies* on the board.

"So we don't agree," I said to the group. "Some of you think we need twenty-two cookies and some of you think it's forty-four. How can we find out for sure?"

"Give us the cookies," some of the children called out.

"But I don't have any cookies," I said. "I need to know how many to bring."

"We can use pretend cookies," said Carina.

"What can we use?" I asked.

"Cubes," suggested Heriberto.

We passed a bag of cubes around the circle, and I made sure that the children were frequently reminded of what the cubes represented. "Two cookies for Cristina, two cookies for Heriberto . . ." we chanted as each child removed two cubes.

"But Jennifer's not here," protested Robert. When I prompted him, he drew a face on the board to stand for the missing student, and put two cubes on the chalk tray. "Is that everyone?" I asked. The children nodded.

We put all the cubes in a line, keeping the pairs of cubes together. Then we counted the cubes from one. We ended with forty-four. "So we have twenty-two children and forty-four cookies," I said. I wrote *44 cookies* on the board.

"That's it," said Carina. "Bring forty-four."

"Can I get a drink?" asked Heriberto. It was clearly time to stop, but I planned to offer the children other chances to solve "real-life" problems throughout the year.

The next day I brought forty-four cookies, and the children were delighted to each get two. "We were right," observed Alfredo, happily munching on his treats.

Linking Assessment and Instruction

You may wish to make the following observations:

- How did the children represent the problem? Did they simply make a line of figures representing the cookies, or did they group the "cookies" in pairs, modeling the problem more specifically?

- Did the children remember that they needed to count *all* the cookies rather than the *sets of two* cookies? What to count was a source of confusion for several of the children, which is not unusual for first graders. With additional experiences, over time, children learn to remember what they are counting.

CHAPTER 2

Making Classroom Decisions

OVERVIEW

Daily classroom life is filled with chances for children to make decisions that require mathematical thinking. Children can participate in classroom decisions that affect them, such as what book the class should hear next, what kind of snack they should eat, or which activity to do next. In this vignette children vote to decide which books they should purchase to donate to their school's library. In the activity, the students make their decision through voting. They make a class chart that records their votes using tally marks. They must then assess the data, making sure that all tallies have been recorded (that everyone got a vote), and counting to see which elements got the most and the least votes.

MATERIALS

- chart paper
- 2 different-colored markers
- children's books

TIME

- one class period

Teaching Directions

1. Introduce the situation that requires the students to make a decision—in this case, which books to purchase for the school library.

2. Have the students identify possible choices, as well as their advantages and disadvantages.

3. Ask the students to vote for what they believe is the best decision.

4. Have the class count the votes and interpret the findings.

5. Have the class carry out the decision—for example, purchase and donate the books.

Teaching Notes

In this lesson, first-grade teacher Karolyn Williams involves her students in making a decision. The children collect money to donate books to their school library, an activity that will contribute to the school's rich learning environment. They vote on the books using mathematics as a tool to make a decision that truly matters to them.

The students use the mathematical representations of tallies and numbers. The children use their understandings about number relationships (which numbers are more and which numbers are less), as well as strategies for addition, to compare votes and make sure that everyone in the classroom voted.

The Lesson

Karolyn Williams's class had been collecting money to donate books to the school library. "We do this every year," she told me later. "It's important that the children get to contribute to their school."

The class had a jar that the children had been filling with pennies, nickels, dimes, and quarters. Robert and Victoria had each brought a dollar bill.

That morning, the children had counted and re-counted the coins until they were sure of what they had. "We have thirteen dollars and sixty-six cents to spend on books," Karolyn reminded the children, writing the amount on the board.

"And we can't forget this," she added, taking Robert's and Victoria's two dollar bills out of her pocket. "Now how much do we have? Everyone think." In real-life problems such as this one, there are many math opportunities. It's important to choose those that are appropriate for your specific group of children.

"It's thirteen sixty-eight," said Omar. "Two more."

Money can be confusing to young children, and understandably so. There are different units to consider: dollars, dimes, pennies, and so on. And the amounts that the coins represent are not immediately obvious to them.

"What did I take out of my pocket?" asked Karolyn. "Two pennies or two dollars?"

That was easy for Omar. "Two dollars," he answered.

Then Karolyn underlined the two 6s. "The numbers on this side are pennies." She underlined the 1 and the 3. "The numbers on this side are dollars. Which numbers need to get bigger?"

"It's fifteen sixty-six," Omar said, correcting himself.

The children had brought up to the front their favorite classroom books, which they thought the library would need. Eric Carle was clearly their favorite; they had brought *Dragons, Dragons*, *The Very Busy Spider*, *Thank You, Brother Bear*, and *Dream Snow*.

They talked about why they thought the library needed those books and which books the library already had. They removed *The Very Busy Spider* when Karolyn informed them that the library already had a copy.

"And what about *Heckedy Peg*?" added Karolyn. "We haven't talked about that book. I know the library doesn't have it, and you really enjoy it. Remember the mother kept saying, 'Don't open the door.' Don and Audrey Wood wrote that one. Should we consider buying that book?" The children agreed that they should.

Next, Karolyn and the children made a chart. Karolyn knows the value of having children participate in a chart's creation from the beginning. She guided them by explaining the important parts of the display. "This is the title," she said, pointing to "Books We Want to Buy for the Library!" "It tells people what the chart is about."

Karolyn also had the children use what they knew about sound-symbol relationships to help her spell the words in the book titles. They listed the titles under consideration, and numbered the titles from one to eleven.

Karolyn then invited the children to add any new titles to the list. Juan brought up *Salt in His Shoes*. "Yeah!" said Carlos. "Michael Jordan did it!" They removed *Bruno Bruin* from the list when Karolyn explained that the bookstore no longer had it, and Victoria wanted to add *Just Like Daddy*. "We read it and read it a lot," she explained.

The list looked like this:

Books We Want to Buy for the Library!

1. *Heckedy Peg*
2. *Just Another Ordinary Day*
3. *Dragons, Dragons*
4. *Dream Snow*
5. *Fire Race*
6. *Thank You, Brother Bear*
7. *Moon Lake*
8. *My Rotten Redheaded Older Brother*
9. *Koala Lou*
10. *Just Like Daddy*
11. *Little Penguin's Tail*
12. *Salt in His Shoes*

"Let's each choose two books that we want to vote for," suggested Karolyn. As the children stated their choices, Karolyn made a tally mark next to that title.

After six children had voted, Karolyn paused. She wanted the children to have a chance to interpret the data thus far, so that they would be prepared for the changes in number as they occurred.

"Look at what we have so far," she said.

"It's almost a tie," said Erin. "Two, two, two, one, one, two, and two."

"It's twelve," added Carina. "Two, four, six, seven, eight, nine, ten, eleven, twelve."

The next child voted for *Moon Lake*, which had only one vote before. "Oh!" the children exclaimed. "It's a tie!"

As the voting continued, the children spontaneously read the tallies and interpreted the data. "Cool!" "*Fire Race* is the most!" "Five and five—it's a tie!"

Karolyn paused again partway through to let the children consider the new data. "How many votes does *Salt in His Shoes* have?" she asked. The tally showed this:

卌 ||||

"It's nine," said Cristina. And she counted each tally from one.

"You can do this," explained Carina. "Five—six, seven, eight, nine. It's counting on."

"*Salt in His Shoes* has the most," Robert commented.

"And *Koala Lou* hasn't got any," added Armando.

When everyone had voted, Karolyn and the children totaled each book's tallies.

The final chart looked like this:

Books We Want to Buy for the Library!

1. *Heckedy Peg* | | | |

2. *Just Another Ordinary Day* | | |

3. *Dragons, Dragons*   卌 |

4. *Dream Snow* | | | |

5. *Fire Race*   卌 | | |

6. *Thank You, Brother Bear* | | | |

7. *Moon Lake* | |

8. *My Rotten Redheaded Older Brother*

9. *Koala Lou* |

10. *Just Like Daddy* |

11. *Little Penguin's Tail*   卌 |

12. *Salt in His Shoes*   卌 | | | |

"Which book got the most tallies?" Karolyn asked.

"The shoe book got the mostest," said Omar.

"*Fire Race* didn't got so many," said Victoria.

"That's true. *Fire Race* got fewer votes than *Salt in His Shoes*," agreed Karolyn.

Karolyn not only used words of comparison such as *most*, *least*, *more*, and *fewer*, but she had the children think about *how many more votes* and *how many fewer votes* different books had received.

She helped the children compare *Fire Race*, which got eight votes, and *Dragons, Dragons*, which received six. "How many more votes did *Fire Race* get? How many extra votes did it receive?" Karolyn knows that the phrase *how many extra?* is a good clarification of "*how many more?*" She helped the children compare six tallies and eight tallies. "You can just cover the six tallies that are in the eight," she explained. "That way you can see how many extra tallies it has."

Then Karolyn asked, "How many fewer votes did *Dream Snow* receive, compared with *Thank You, Brother Bear*?" The children looked puzzled, but then Jennifer laughed. "Zero! It's the same!"

"Which book is in first place?" Karolyn now asked, switching to ordinal comparison. The children labeled the books that were in first place, second, third, and fourth place. There was a tie for third place and a three-way tie for fourth place.

"I have to know what books to buy," said Karolyn. "This vote helped me some. For example, I know that I don't need to look for *Just Another Ordinary Day*, *Moon Lake*, *Koala Lou*, *Just Like Daddy*, and *My Rotten Redheaded Older Brother*. But there are a lot of ties, and it could be that the store will be out of some books."

"Do you have any advice for me?" she asked, pausing.

"Let's vote again," said Jennifer.

"First take off the ones we don't need," suggested Carlos.

So Karolyn crossed off the books that got the fewest votes. "I'll get another color marker to keep this vote separate," she said, modeling the use of color-coding as a tool for organization.

This time each child could vote for only one book. Again Karolyn stopped periodically to let the children interpret the data. The children's interest in the activity remained high. *Salt in His Shoes* got more and more votes, topping out at nine. "Yes!" said Omar when the final tally went to that book.

"Before we see which books were most popular, let's see if we all voted. What do we need to do?" Karolyn asked the children.

"How many are we?" asked Jennifer.

They tried to count heads, but it was difficult to keep track of who was counted and who wasn't.

"Juanita and Brittney are absent," said Luis thoughtfully.

"How many children are usually here?" Karolyn asked. The children count during attendance every day. "It's twenty-six, but do we have twenty-four votes?" asked Navin. He had mentally subtracted two from twenty-six.

Karolyn took this opportunity to write a series of numbers across the chart, representing the tallies that each book got:

$$6 + 1 + 4 + 3 + 2 + 8$$

"How can we find out how many votes we have in all?" she asked.

Some children counted on their fingers, but others used a different strategy.

"There's a ten. Six and four!" said Sereslinda.

"And two and eight makes ten," Omar noted. "Ten and ten is twenty."

Karolyn represented their thinking this way:

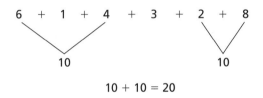

"And twenty plus one is twenty-one," said Luis.

"Then twenty-two, twenty-three, twenty-four," finished Erin. "Everyone voted!"

Karolyn wrote:

$$20 + 1 = 21$$
$$21 + 3 = 24$$

"Is there another way we can think about these numbers to add them?" Karolyn asked, encouraging the children to look for another strategy. She wrote the number string once again.

"I see five," offered Carina.

"And there's another five," said Omar. "That makes ten."

Karolyn wrote:

6 + 1 + 4 + 3 + 2 + 8

5   5

5 + 5 = 10

"Now what can we do?" Karolyn asked. A few hands went up, but she waited. Karolyn wanted more children to have a chance to think. There were many

different ways to proceed, from counting on to more sophisticated strategies.

"The eight could give a four to the six and it would make another ten," said Alejandrina. "And then you'd have twenty, and four more makes twenty-four."

Karolyn wanted to make Alejandrina's thinking more apparent for the other children. "Do you mean that you split the eight into four and four?" she asked, "And then you gave a four to the six?" Alejandrina nodded. Karolyn circled the 4 and the 6.

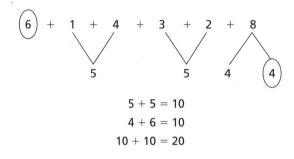

"Then you added that last four and got twenty plus four equals twenty-four." Karolyn wrote that equation. "Twenty-four votes. We all voted."

The children then checked the totals. The shopping list they made for Karolyn had *Salt in His Shoes* first, *Heckedy Peg* second, *Dream Snow* third, *Fire Race* fourth, *Thank You, Brother Bear* fifth, and *Dragons, Dragons* sixth.

"This is very exciting," Karolyn said with a smile. "I'll go shopping tonight and bring the books I find tomorrow. Then we can sign our names in them and take the books to the library."

Linking Assessment and Instruction

You may wish to make the following observations:

- Which children contributed ideas for solving the problem? Did the ideas work or did they have to be modified in some way?
- How did the children manage the numbers?

  - Did they count correctly by ones? Children will use this beginning strategy until deeper number understandings help them develop more efficient strategies.
  - Did they count on?
  - Did they use doubles or make friendly numbers such as five and ten?

- Did they split any numbers to make a friendly number? Alejandrina used this sophisticated strategy.

- How did the children interpret number representations such as tally marks?

  - Did they immediately recognize the groupings of five and ten or did they count each tally mark?

- Did they count on from groups that they immediately recognized?

- Did the children show evidence of number understandings when they compared vote totals? What language did they use to make number comparisons? Did they use standard language such as "most, least, how many more, how many fewer"?

Estimate and Count

CHAPTER 3

OVERVIEW

In this activity, children estimate the length of a ribbon in cubes, or the number of cubes in a container, and record their guesses on a recording sheet. Then the children measure the ribbon using cubes, or count the cubes in the container, and record the actual number.

MATERIALS

- small zip-top bags containing 10 ribbons of various lengths (3–14 inches), 1 bag of shorter ribbons and 1 bag of larger ribbons per group of 4 students working with ribbons

- containers, such as yogurt containers, half-pint milk cartons, small cottage cheese containers, film canisters, pudding containers, cardboard cartons cut to different heights, small jewelry boxes, and plastic cups, 1 set of 10 smaller containers and 1 set of 10 larger containers per group of 4 students working with containers
- Unifix cubes or wooden cubes, about 100 per group of 4 students working with ribbons or small containers; more cubes for larger containers
- *Estimate and Count* Recording Sheet, cut in half horizontally, 3–4 half-sheets per student (see Blackline Masters)

	Estimate _____
	Count _____
	Estimate _____
	Count _____

TIME

- one class period

Teaching Directions

1. Prepare bags of ribbons: Cut ribbons 3 to 6 inches in length for children thinking about smaller numbers and 7 to 14 inches for children thinking about larger numbers. Label the ribbons by stapling a small piece of paper marked with a different capital letter, A through J, on each. Use blue labels for the shorter ribbons and red labels for the longer ribbons; this makes it easy to distinguish the bags and adjust the activity for students as necessary.

2. Prepare containers: Label each container with a capital letter, A through J. Label the smaller containers in blue marker and the larger containers in

red; this allows you to adjust the difficulty of the task for specific children as necessary.

3. Show the students a ribbon and hold up a cube. Wonder aloud how many cubes long the ribbon is. If children have trouble making estimates, offer possible estimates such as, "Could it be one hundred cubes long? Could it be two cubes long? So how many cubes long *could* it be?"

4. Show the students the recording sheet. Record the ribbon's letter in the square box. Then write an estimate on the recording sheet.

5. Explain to the students that they are going to find out how many cubes long the ribbon piece really is. Emphasize that the actual number will probably be different from the estimate. Measure the ribbon with cubes. Stop partway through and ask the children to think about whether the estimate will turn out to be close. Remind the children that an estimate is our best guess and will probably be different from the actual number. Write the actual count on the recording sheet. Explain that partners will share the materials to be measured, but that each student will record on his or her own recording sheet.

6. Hold up a container and ask how many cubes will fill it. Ask the children to make estimates. Then fill the container and figure out the answer. Explain that the children will use either containers or ribbons during this investigation.

7. After the investigation, have the students discuss their strategies for making good estimates.

Teaching Notes

These investigations invite children to develop meanings for numbers and number relationships through different contexts. After doing this lesson as a whole group, it becomes an important part of math workshop time, which children do several times a week (see Introduction, page xvi). During math workshop, children make choices about how they will investigate a mathematical idea. I find that when children make choices they have a bigger investment in what they do.

Be sure to maintain the problem-solving aspect by having the children predict their answers first. Help the children recognize that the actual count will differ from the estimate. Always have the children record their estimates, as well as what they actually find out.

While the children work I have the chance to observe them and offer support or increase the complexity of the task as necessary. Support may include directing the child's attention to a helpful resource, such as a number line, that can aid a child in making numbers. Or if children are having difficulty counting, I might offer assistance or have them work with smaller numbers. Sometimes I will select two specific children to work together so they can help each other.

When a child finds an investigation too easy I adapt the exercise to include larger numbers, perhaps by having the child measure with smaller, centimeter cubes or by using larger containers or ribbons. Sometimes I increase the complexity by having the child put items in order from smallest to largest. Or I ask the child to measure two items and find out how many cubes altogether (adding) or how many more cubes a larger container holds than a smaller container (subtracting). There are many ways to have children with different experience levels use the same materials by shifting the mathematical focus.

Since children work at different paces, I don't expect them to complete the same number of pages. At the end of the lesson, I staple each child's pages together to make a booklet to take home.

I often have the children do this lesson in the fall, but I repeat it throughout the year during math workshop. Sometimes I vary the materials by bringing in sticks for the children to estimate and count or small boxes for them to fill. Children sometimes invent their own variations. Erin had the idea of estimating and measuring the spines of books, and when we did a unit on plants we estimated and measured the length of leaves.

The Lesson

I showed the class a ribbon that was about 4 inches long. "What do you notice about my piece of ribbon?" I asked.

"It's yellow," Erin said.

"I've got that ribbon on my folklorico dress," Laura said.

Then I held a Unifix cube next to the ribbon. "If I wanted to cover my piece of ribbon from one end to the other, without leaving any spaces, how many cubes do you think I'd need?" I asked.

The children now focused on the ribbon's length. Several children began pointing at the ribbon, counting imaginary cubes.

"Maybe six?" asked Omar tentatively.

"It could be six," I affirmed. "We don't know for sure, do we? But six *is* a possible number. Does anyone else have a different estimate?"

"It's four," said Amanda. "I counted like this and like this and like this and like this." She held up the finger and thumb of one hand, as if holding a cube, and pretended to measure the ribbon.

"Four is a good estimate too," I answered. "We're just estimating right now. We don't know for sure. When you estimate you make the best guess that you can, and it will probably be different from the actual answer. Let's choose Amanda's estimate for now."

I showed the children the recording sheet. "We have ribbon *C* so we'll write *C* in the square. And Amanda thinks it might be four cubes long so we'll write a four by the word *Estimate*. We don't know whether the ribbon really is four cubes long," I said, "but this way we can remember what we thought at first."

"Now we'll find out how many cubes long the ribbon really is," I continued. As I laid the cubes side by side I could feel the children's intense focus on my actions. We found out that five cubes matched the ribbon's length.

"I was right," commented Laura.

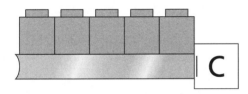

"Some of our estimates matched the actual count, but all of our guesses were close," I commented. "Most of the time your estimate will be different from the number you count." I wanted to move the discussion away from "right" and "wrong." I wrote *5* next to the word *Count*. "You and your partner can share

the ribbons," I said, "but you each need to write on your own paper. When you fill one paper, you can get another. At the end of the period, we'll staple them together to make a booklet."

I reminded the children to write their names on their recording sheet. Then I introduced the containers. "You can choose to do the same thing with containers," I said, holding up a yogurt container. "How many cubes do you think this container could hold if we fill it even with the top?"

The guesses were varied. "Maybe a hundred," said Cristina. "Or sixty," said Robert. "Sixteen or twenty," said Alejandrina. We recorded the letter of the container, our estimate, and then our final count. "Remember to fill the container as close to the top as you can. But no mountains of cubes," I said, showing the children how the cubes should be level with the top of the container.

I told the children that they could work in partners or by themselves. "The ribbons with blue labels have smaller numbers and the ribbons with red labels have larger numbers," I explained. "You can choose either one." I placed a baggie of small ribbons and a baggie of large ribbons at two tables, and two sets of containers, one large, one small, at two other tables.

The children took turns selecting their activity. Some pairs of children chose containers, but the ribbons seemed to be the more popular choice. Luis and Heriberto were too late; the ribbons were gone. "It looks like you'll be investigating the containers today," I told them, "but there's a good chance that you'll get to investigate the ribbons during our next math workshop." Soon everyone was sitting down.

During the Investigation

As they worked, I circulated among the children, observing their strategies and offering various kinds of support.

"It's ten!" said Gerardo excitedly. "I thought it was ten and it *was*!"

"Your estimate matched the actual count," I affirmed, using the mathematical language that over time I expected the children would adopt. "That happens sometimes," I said.

Alicia and Cristina had chosen the ribbons with red labels and were having trouble with the larger numbers. "Why don't you try the shorter ribbons with blue labels," I suggested. They seemed to do fine with the smaller numbers. I like being able to adapt the investigations as necessary. I find that when children work with numbers that are neither too easy nor too difficult, they stay interested in the tasks.

Alejandrina and Amanda were sharing their baggie of ribbons, singing softly as they worked. "How much did you get for the white one?" asked Alejandrina. "I got eight." They compared numbers and saw that they both had gotten eight. I didn't see this as "copying," as I might have when I first began teaching. Instead I saw children verifying their thinking. If the numbers had been different I would have encouraged them to both check to see which number best matched the actual count of the ribbon.

Luis and Heriberto were in a heated exchange, so I stood by, waiting to see how or whether they would resolve it themselves.

"It can't be twenty-five!" said Luis. "No way!"

"Yeah, huh!" answered Heriberto.

"Can *not*," retorted Luis.

"Can *so*," replied Heriberto angrily.

I decided to intervene. "I think each of you should explain what it could be and why you think that. And remember, it's an estimate or a guess. It doesn't have to turn out to be the number that you guess."

I waited as the boys settled down. "It can't be twenty-five, 'cause the last one was twenty and it's more bigger," said Luis, pointing to a cup that was taller than the container he held. "I think it's fifteen." Heriberto then nodded and wrote a *15* in the estimate column. Was he swayed by Luis's reasoning or did he just give up? I wasn't sure and I didn't have a chance to find out—Laura was calling me from across the classroom. "Mrs. Confer!"

"How do you make a seven?" she asked when I approached. I wanted to help Laura develop a strategy for independently answering her question. "How can you find out for yourself?" I asked. Laura shrugged. "Does anyone at your table know how?" Laura shrugged again. It looked like Brittney and Laura were sitting side by side but not working together. "Your partner can help you with questions like that," I said. Then I pulled Brittney into the conversation. "Brittney, Laura needs help making a seven. What can she do?"

"It's like this," answered Brittney, drawing a 7 on the bottom of her paper.

"If you need help making a number you can ask someone at your table," I said, "or you can check the number line or the calendar." I indicated to her the number line, which was in their pencil basket at all times. "How can you find the seven?" I asked her. I watched as she touched each number starting from 1 and counted aloud. When she touched the 7 she knew

that was the number she wanted to make, and she carefully copied it. I watched as she worked with the next ribbon and used the number line in the same way. She now had a resource that would help her answer her questions independently.

I came to Navin and Gerardo, who seemed to find the activity easy. I decided to increase the difficulty by helping them focus on number relationships. "How long was the orange ribbon?" I asked.

"Twelve," Gerardo answered.

"So if the orange ribbon is twelve cubes long, how long do you think the blue ribbon will be?"

The boys immediately responded by making a shift in their thinking, and held the two ribbons side by side.

"The blue one is longer," Navin said. "It's probably fifteen."

"Maybe sixteen but it's probably fifteen," added Gerardo.

"Oh," I said, "Since the orange ribbon is twelve cubes long, you estimate that the blue ribbon is three cubes longer, or fifteen. I wonder if that is the actual count." I watched as the boys counted to fifteen, then did the class "silent cheer" as they found their estimate to be accurate.

I noticed that Becky and Victoria were having difficulty counting. "I'd like to hear you count the cubes together," I said. Becky pointed to one cube at a time. They counted together but after ten their counting sequences were clearly different. "It's like this," said Victoria. "You say eight, nine, ten, eleven, twelve."

"Let's count together," I suggested. We did this several times for practice.

Alejandrina was laughing. "I got eight again! I keep getting eight!"

"Are your ribbons the same length?" I asked. Alejandrina placed them side by side. The orange ribbon was longer. Alejandrina looked perplexed; she knows that a number expresses magnitude, and expects that ribbons of the same length will have the same number. I watched as Alejandrina recounted her ribbons and found that the purple ribbon was actually thirteen cubes long.

Jonathan had just written an estimate for the orange ribbon. "Why did you choose sixteen for your estimate?" I inquired.

"Well," he answered, "it's a lot longer than the fat one. And the fat ribbon was ten, so I guessed sixteen." Jonathan was making connections, using number relationships to complete the activity.

"I like this," said Alejandrina. "Can we do it again tomorrow?"

"Well," I answered, "tomorrow we're going to learn a new activity. The next time we do math workshop you can choose this as your activity." I then made a booklet for Alejandrina and Amanda, by stapling each girl's record sheets together.

A Discussion

The children sat with their partners on the rug. Today I wanted to discuss with the class their strategies for estimating.

I held up a ribbon and a container. "You made a lot of estimates today. You looked closely at a ribbon or a container and you made a good guess about how long the ribbon is or how many cubes the container holds. I'd like you to think about how you chose your estimates. What if you needed to estimate how many cubes long this ribbon is so your mom could know if she could use it? How do you decide on an estimate?"

I paused to give the children a chance to think. Several children pointed at the ribbon with their finger and counted in the air, whispering as they went.

"I'd like to talk about how you choose a number to guess," I said. "Is it a hundred cubes long?"

Alejandrina laughed. "No, it's too too big. It's not a hundred."

"How about three cubes long?" I inquired.

Heads were shaking. "It can't be three. It would be one, two, three, and then some more," Javier told us.

"So if three is too few and one hundred is too many," I said, "what *is* a good guess? And how do you decide on a number?"

"Well," said Mark, "you have to choose a number that's not too big or too small. It has to be just right."

"You can use your finger and touch it," said Victoria. She came up and showed how she touches the ribbon over and over, spacing the touches like the width of the cubes. "Does this work?" I asked, touching the ribbon at the beginning and the end, saying "One, two." "Or does this work?" I asked, touching the ribbon many times close together, counting very fast.

"No," Victoria said, laughing. "You can't do that."

"Who can explain why that doesn't help make an estimate?" I asked, drawing the group into the conversation.

Robert raised his hand. "You have to touch it like the cubes."

"So you imagine the cubes laid out on the ribbon and you count the imaginary cubes?" I asked. Robert nodded.

"That's an interesting strategy," I said. "Did anyone make estimates a different way?"

Jonathan wanted to share. "You can remember what the other ribbon is and put them together and see what the number can be."

"You mean that if you know the white ribbon is three cubes long, you can hold it next to the blue one?" I said, lining up the two ribbons. "How can that help you?" I asked. "What do you know about the blue ribbon?"

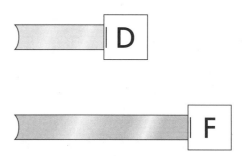

"It's bigger," said Luis.

"It's more than three," said Victoria. "Maybe six."

"Like seven," said Luis. "You could have another three and one more. That makes seven." He counted from one on his fingers to check.

"I just like to guess," said Erin.

"Many of you like to use what you know to figure out what you don't know," I said. "You know about how long a cube is and you measure with your finger. Or you can use what you know about one ribbon to estimate a new ribbon. An estimate is a good guess that you make after thinking about it."

Before we ended I wanted to remind the children about resources in the room that could help them. "What if you forget how to make a number, like a six or a fourteen? Where could you look?" Alicia explained about how she used the number line. Becky reminded us that both numbers were on the class calendar. "That's right," I affirmed. "And larger numbers are on the hundred charts that are at each table. You won't have to ask anyone; you can just find the numbers yourself."

Linking Assessment and Instruction

As the children work, you may make the following observations:

- Were children's estimates reasonable or unreasonable? This is a good indication of their number sense.

- How did the children make estimates? Did the children visualize cubes to make estimates? Did they use what they knew about one ribbon or container to make estimates for others? Using what you know to figure out what you don't know is an important habit of mind for developing number sense.

- How did the children count? What numbers did they find manageable? Did they remember the sequence of number names? Did they count each item once and only once, while coordinating the number name with touching the cube? Did they use a strategy for keeping track of what they already counted? Did they count confidently and consistently?

- Did the children just know how to make the numerals? If not, did they use a classroom resource, such as looking at the calendar, a number line, or a 1–100 chart? My goal is for children to become as independent as possible.

Containers

MORE AND LESS

CHAPTER 4

OVERVIEW

In this lesson, children explore a collection of containers: First they select two containers and predict which container holds more and which holds less; they then compare how many cubes each one holds. After the children find out which container actually holds more, they record what they discover on a recording sheet.

MATERIALS

- containers, such as yogurt containers, cream cheese containers, cottage cheese containers, film canisters, pudding containers, half-pint milk cartons cut to different heights, small boxes, and plastic cups: 2 sets of about 12 containers each (one set that holds up to about 15 cubes and another set that holds more) per group of 4 students
- interlocking cubes or wooden cubes, 30–40 per student
- *More and Less* Recording Sheet, cut in half horizontally, 3–4 per student (see Blackline Masters)

Container _____ holds _____ cubes.

Container _____ holds _____ cubes.

Which container holds more?

Which container holds less?

Or are they the same? _____

TIME

- one class period

Teaching Directions

1. Prepare containers: Label each container with a capital letter. Label the smaller containers in blue and the larger containers in red; this allows you to adjust the difficulty level for specific children as needed.

2. Show a small group of students two different-shaped containers that are not easy to compare visually. Have them discuss which container they think holds more and which holds less, and why they think that.

3. Ask a student to fill one of the containers with cubes. Discuss what "full" means, and that the cubes should not pile high above the edge of the container. Remove cubes one at a time from a container and snap them together to make a train. Count the cubes in the train. On the recording sheet, write the container's letter label and how many cubes it held. Do the same for the other container.

4. Compare the numbers of cubes and discuss which number is larger. Position the trains side by side, to visually see which set contains more cubes. On the record sheet, write the letter labels for the containers that actually held more and less, or write *yes* if they held the same amount.

5. Explain that after the students compare one set of containers, they should replace the containers and cubes, select another pair of containers, and get a new recording sheet.

6. Have the students decide whether to do this activity individually or in partners. Explain that if they work in partners, they will share containers but each student should record on his or her own recording sheet. When the students finish, staple their recording sheets together to make individual booklets.

Teaching Notes

Children enjoy using common household objects in new ways. They like predicting and then filling containers with cubes, finding out which holds more and which holds less.

The children work individually or in partners. As they work, I make observations and support their counting and comparing abilities. It's important to have resources available to the children that they can use when they forget how to make a number, or when they need help figuring out which number is more and which is less. That's why I keep laminated cards with number lines as well as laminated 1–100 charts right at each table for children to use when necessary.

This activity can be revisited throughout the year. It is interesting to see children develop in their counting and number-sense understandings. As they become more proficient, I increase the numbers that the children investigate by including larger containers. Another way I raise the level of difficulty is by having students measure with smaller, centimeter cubes.

The Lesson

"We're going to explore containers today," I told the children. I brought out the tub of small containers, each labeled on the side with a red capital letter. We talked about what the children noticed about the containers. As we did so, I used the letters to name the containers. I knew they would need this information to record on the recording sheet.

"This one's so little," said Alicia, holding the cream cheese container next to the yogurt container. "That's right," I responded. "Container F is shorter than container H." I showed them the letter labels on the side.

The children picked up each container and read its capital letter.

"What else do you notice?" I asked them.

"This one's got strawberries," said Erin. "This is the best. Not the pineapple one." She made a face.

"You could bring this for lunch," said Robert, holding up the sandwich container.

"What could fit in it?" I asked him.

"Pizza," he said.

Luis shook his head. "Not pizza, it's too little."

Robert reconsidered. "Well, maybe the little square kind."

"I'm going to choose two containers," I said, introducing the activity. I selected a yogurt container and a margarine container, which were not easy to visually compare. We checked their capital letters.

"Which container do you guess holds more, I or E?" The children offered their responses all at once. "Let's hear your predictions one at a time," I suggested.

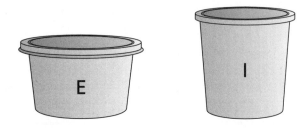

Alicia had an idea. "E holds more," she said. "I is taller but E's got bigger sides and that one has little sides."

Both containers were round. "I see what you're saying," I agreed. "E has a bigger circumference than I. It's bigger around." I use mathematical terminology when I feel it is appropriate. I don't require first graders to use words such as *circumference*, but such words should be part of their environment. I returned to the conversation at hand. "What else do you see?"

"This one's bigger," said Robert, indicating the height of container I.

Luis had an idea. "I holds more, 'cuz if you put too much in it it'll fall down and if you don't put in too much it won't fall." He seemed to be combining two ideas—that the yogurt container could hold more and that containers can be overfilled.

"What Luis is saying makes sense to me," I agreed. "When you fill the containers with cubes, try to make sure that the cubes don't stick up high. See if you can get them as close as possible to the top but not much over."

The children continued talking. Luis and Robert thought the yogurt container would hold more, and

Alicia and Erin thought the margarine container would hold more. I privately agreed with the girls, because I knew how changing the circumference affects volume. But I could also understand how the boys were thinking.

"When you play by yourself, you'll guess which has more, just like we did," I reminded the children. "Now let's find out."

But Robert suddenly changed his mind. "The E is more fat and it's bigger."

"And that's OK," I said. "In math, when you hear a new idea, it might make sense to you, and then you get to change your mind. Let's find out now," I said.

"You can put cubes in it to see what holds more?" Luis inquired.

"That makes sense," I said.

The children worked to fill the containers with cubes. Alicia began to push her cubes in hard. "Remember that you don't need to push hard," I told the group. "Just fill it up to the top. No mountains," I said.

"I got the orange ones," said Luis. He filled the container with orange cubes, mounding them high. "Is that enough?" he asked.

"It looks like a mountain to me," I said. "What do you think?"

Luis eyed the container and Erin took some off the top.

"Now it's got holes," he protested, putting some cubes back.

The children adjusted the containers and then spilled the contents of one container on the table. "Let's get the extra cubes out of the way," I suggested, and the children returned them to the bag. Alicia began counting the cubes. The cubes were scattered randomly and Alicia missed a few and counted some cubes twice. However, she did say the number names and their order correctly.

"Twenty-one," Alicia announced.

"You think there are twenty-one cubes," I said. "Let Robert count and check to see if he agrees."

"Let's do this," Robert said, connecting the cubes into a line.

"That might help," I agreed. "That way you can make sure that you count one cube at a time."

Robert counted correctly, counting each cube once and only once, and saying one number as he touched each cube. Interestingly enough, he also found twenty-one cubes. I suggested to Alicia that she recount the line of cubes that Robert made. Meanwhile, I showed Robert where to write *E* and *21* on the record sheet.

The children then spilled and counted the cubes from container I.

"Ooh," Luis exclaimed, feeling the tension build.

"Seventeen," the children cried. "E's more!" said Alicia.

Erin connected the cubes into a second train and then held the two trains side by side to compare. "It's longer," she agreed.

"There's three, no four, extra," Robert said, pointing to the part that extended beyond.

I helped the children finish filling in the recording sheet. "Container E held more, so you write that letter here," I said. "The less goes here," explained Alicia, pointing to that space.

Container _____E_____ holds _____21_____ cubes.

Container _____I_____ holds _____17_____ cubes.

Which container holds more?

Which container holds less?

Or are they the same? _____

Later in the Year

I reintroduced *Containers: More and Less* as part of math workshop. Several children needed practice counting and comparing small numbers. Other children were ready to work with larger containers, which would challenge them to manage larger numbers.

Omar and Gerardo chose two large containers, and I had given them small wooden centimeter cubes. "There's the biggest!" Omar said, hugging the container that he thought was larger.

"We're going to investigate which container holds more. People won't win and lose and containers won't win and lose either," I said. "We just want to find out which container holds more." I wanted to move the boys away from competitive thinking.

Gerardo carefully filled his sandwich container, stacking the cubes in piles of two. "I could get more," he said, showing the spaces that were left inside.

Omar looked over at what Gerardo was doing and spilled out the contents of his container. "I'm gonna do that too," he said.

"Why?" I asked.

"It's gonna hold more," he told me. "They fit together."

The boys were thinking about efficiency in packing three-dimensional shapes. Gerardo joined Omar in filling container A tightly with cubes. When done, the boys eyed their work.

"How many is it?" wondered Gerardo, and he dumped the contents of his container onto the table.

Omar did likewise. Gerardo examined Omar's pile. "I'm gonna put mine in tens," he said. He carefully laid out a row of ten cubes. Then he made more rows of the same length. "Ten, twenty, thirty, forty, fifty, sixty," he said, counting five rows of ten and then counting an extra single cube that had accidentally got mixed in as "sixty." Gerardo was still making sense of counting by groups.

"Let's count the cubes together, slowly," I suggested.

"Ten . . . twenty . . . thirty . . . forty . . . fifty . . . What do we do with this one?" I pointed to the single cube.

"Sixty . . . no, sixty-one . . . no, fifty-one!" Gerardo said.

"Hey, that's mine," said Omar, grabbing the single cube back.

"Fifty!" Gerardo said, smiling.

I moved away to check on some of the other children, and when I returned Omar and Gerardo had made two rows of ten. Gerardo started connecting more cubes to the rows of ten, and Omar began making different lengths of rows.

Gerardo looked at their work. "It's not gonna work," he said. "This has too much and this doesn't got enough." Gerardo then began counting by tens, even though he touched groups of more than ten as well as single cubes.

I felt some support would be helpful, so I held up a row of ten and a single cube. "How many are here?" I asked.

"Ten, twenty—" Gerardo halted. "That's not twenty!" he said. "It's ten and one more's eleven."

Both boys were still constructing place-value understandings, that we can count a group of ten or we can count single items, and that we count differently depending on the situation. My quick question seemed to do the trick. The boys went back to work, making consistent rows of ten cubes.

"Now I count them," announced Omar when they were finished. He began counting by tens: "Ten, twenty, thirty, forty, fifty, sixty, mmm, seventy . . ." He paused before counting the individual cubes that remained. "Seventy," he repeated, concentrating hard. "Seventy-one, seventy-two, seventy-three, seventy-four, seventy-five, seventy-six!"

Linking Assessment and Instruction

* How did the children count? Did they remember the sequence of number names? Did they touch each item once and only once, while coordinating the names with the touching? Did the children use strategies for keeping track of what they already counted, such as moving cubes or arranging the cubes? Did they know that the last number to which they counted stood for the entire quantity of cubes?

* How did the children make predictions about which containers held more and fewer cubes? On what aspects of the containers did they focus?

* How did the children decide which amount of cubes was more and less? Did they just know by thinking about the numbers? Did they make trains of the numbers and compare their lengths? Or did the children find the numbers on a calendar, a number line, or a 1–100 chart?

* Did the children just know how to make the numerals? Or did they use a resource in the room to help them?

Pattern Block Numbers

CHAPTER 5

OVERVIEW

In this lesson, children use a specific number of pattern blocks to create designs. To record these designs, they use paper cutouts in the shape of the blocks and glue them on construction paper. The children write or dictate sentences that describe their design, such as "8 blocks can be a kite." The teacher compiles the pages into a class book, which provides the children with opportunities to count the shapes and guess the designs.

MATERIALS

- pattern blocks, about 120 per group of 4 students
- Pattern Block Cutouts (see Blackline Masters)
- glue sticks, 1 per student
- 11-by-9-inch pieces of black construction paper, 1 per student
- 3-by-8½-inch pieces of copy paper, 1 per student

TIME

- one class period

Teaching Directions

1. Prepare the pattern blocks ahead of time: Reproduce the Pattern Block Cutouts (see Blackline Masters) on the color of paper that matches the block color. Cut out the shapes and place each kind of shape in a different envelope or container.

2. Choose a number that you want the students to explore, or let the students choose a number.

3. Ask them to take out that number of pattern blocks, for example, eight.

4. Ask the students to arrange the pattern blocks to make designs. For example, one student might use eight blocks to make a flower, while another might arrange eight different blocks to make a star. (It is fine for the children to put back and take out new blocks, as long as the total remains the target number.)

5. In a small group, discuss the students' designs. Then count the blocks together, or have the children describe the various parts of their design and how many blocks are in each part.

6. Ask the students to use the paper pattern cutouts to reproduce their own designs on black construction paper.

7. Have students describe their designs using the sentence frame, ____ *blocks can be a* ____. (As in, *8 blocks can be a kite.*) Write the sentence on the paper under the design, or have the students write the sentence, if they're able.

   Optional: Have students describe the small groups of blocks they see within the arrangement, such as "two orange blocks and four green blocks and one yellow block make seven blocks." The students, or you, then write the number sentence that describes their words: $2 + 4 + 1 = 7$.

8. Compile the pages into a class book.

9. Read the book with the students from time to time. As you read, have them count the blocks and identify the designs. Or, if you've written number sentences, have students identify the small numbers of blocks inside the larger designs.

Teaching Notes

The basis of number sense is the ability to count and visualize quantities. Children need many chances to create and interpret smaller numbers, as smaller numbers help children make sense of larger numbers.

Children love using pattern blocks. They enjoy making arrangements and discovering that a single quantity of blocks can be arranged in many different ways. Children enjoy doing this activity over and over again, and as they do so, they develop their understanding of conservation of number, and obtain a sense of the magnitude of numbers.

I often let children select a number to explore. At times, however, I have all the children explore the same number to reinforce that the same number of items can have many different appearances.

Some children need to focus simply on counting during this activity. Other children come to first grade with more number experiences, and I adjust the level of difficulty to reflect this. I might ask these children to describe the small groups that they see inside their design, to identify, for example, the four trapezoids, two hexagons, and two squares they used in their design. Then I might invite the child to write the number sentence that describes this picture: $4 + 2 + 2 = 8$.

The Lesson

"We're going to think about the number eight today," I told a small group of children sitting with me around a table. On the table was a tub of pattern blocks.

"My sister is eight," Brittney told us.

"I got eight aliens and I fight them with the Lion King," Heriberto explained. Children's minds seem to be wired to make connections!

"Right," I said. "Eight can be how old someone is, or a number of toys. Today we're going to use pattern blocks and make eight in many different ways. Let's get some blocks out," I said.

I took out a handful. Together we counted out five. "How many more blocks do I need to make eight?" I asked.

Brittney recounted the first five blocks and then took out one more block at a time while counting on to eight. "Here they are," she said.

"How many more did you have to take out?" I asked her. I wanted to challenge her to think about this smaller quantity, three, that resides within the larger quantity, eight.

Brittney counted the new blocks. "Three," she answered.

"I wonder what you can make by using any eight pattern blocks," I continued. "I'd like each of you to get any eight blocks and see what design you can make with them."

Jennifer took out two handfuls of pattern blocks. She counted them, counting some blocks twice or even three times. "Some children find that it helps to put the blocks in a line, so it's easy to keep track," I said. Jennifer did this, and counted ten blocks successfully.

Heriberto counted his blocks and found eleven. "It's too much," he said, and took two away. He counted nine. "I need eight," he said, and took one away.

As the children worked, different strategies emerged. Alicia and Brittney each chose eight blocks and then arranged them into pictures. Cristina and Erin took out a few blocks, arranged them, and repeated this process until they had a design of eight blocks.

Juanita was making an elaborate design with many more than eight blocks. "Sometimes you can make anything you want," I said. "Today I'd like you to make something with only eight blocks." This constraint gave the activity a specific mathematical focus. But I made a mental note to put out the pattern blocks again during math workshop time so that Juanita and others could simply build.

"I'm gonna make something else," Heriberto said after making one design.

He put back his assortment of eight pattern blocks and counted out eight hexagons. Heriberto carefully arranged them on the table. "I made a robot hand!" he said, delighted. Then he looked at it from another perspective and saw a numeral in his shape. "Like this, it's a four," he said. This perceptual flexibility would later help Heriberto decompose numbers with ease.

Brittney looked at her design. She shook her head. "I take two," she said, "and put two back." Brittney substituted two new blocks for two old blocks. She looked at her new design and shook her head. "Two away and two back," she said to herself, again exchanging two blocks. Brittney was exploring equivalence: any number minus two, plus two, equals the original number. Algebraically it could be stated: $n + 2 - 2 = n$. What a significant discovery!

"Is that always true?" I asked her. "Can you take away two and put two back and it will still be that number?" Brittney shrugged, but I decided this idea would be interesting to share during a class discussion.

"Lookit, binoculars!" said Jennifer. She was pleased at what she had designed. But then she pushed the blocks back together. "What else?" she asked herself, and began a new design. When she'd finished, I said, "You had eight blocks in your binoculars. You didn't get any new blocks. How many blocks are in your flower?" She wasn't sure and counted the blocks. "There's eight," she told me. The new physical arrangement looked different to her, and so she thought the number might have changed. Jennifer was not yet conserving eight.

"I'm finished," said Erin, showing me a street sign she had made of two hexagons and six blue rhombi.

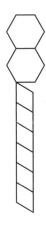

"How many yellow hexagons do you have?" I asked her. When she answered "Two," I asked her, "Then how many blue rhombi did you use to make eight?" She counted them. "There's six," she told me. Since Erin is good at counting, I'm trying to move her to part–whole thinking, decomposing the smaller numbers that are inside larger numbers. Eventually she'll have so much experience with number that she'll just know the answer.

"Where are the green ones?" asked Juanita, sorting through the container of blocks to finish her design.

"How many do you need?" I asked her.

"One, two, three, four, five, six." She counted the blocks she had already used. Then she continued counting with her fingers, "Seven, eight. Two more."

The children had by this time finished several designs. "I'd like you to finish the design that you're working on. When you have it, I'd like you to talk to someone else who's finished. Please check their design to see if they have eight blocks in it," I said. Not only would this encourage the children to independently check their work, but it would also give them more chances to count.

Then I commented, "Look around the table at all the different designs we made. And they're all eight! Eight blocks can look many different ways." I was reinforcing the idea of conservation of number. "What does your design of eight blocks remind you of?" I continued.

Each child showed his or her design to the group while the others guessed what it could be. The children looked at Cristina's design.

"A flower!" guessed Alicia.

"It could be a kite," thought Brittney.

"No, it's a balloon," she told us.

"How many blue rhombi did Cristina use to make the balloon's string?" I asked. We counted five.

"And how did Cristina make the balloon part?" I asked.

"With two red things and a hexagon," answered Heriberto.

"Hmm," I said, pointing to each part. "Five and two and one makes eight." I again encouraged the children to think about how the number eight can be decomposed.

We then looked at Heriberto's arrangement.

"It's like a boat. Here's the sail," guessed Alicia.

"Nope," said Heriberto.

"A bear?" asked Brittney.

"Nuh-uh," answered Heriberto.

"A balloon?" asked Cristina.

Heriberto shook his head.

"I give up," said Alicia. "It's something weird."

"It's not weird. It's a fire-breathing dragon," protested Heriberto.

"Well, it's not so real," explained Brittney.

"That's OK," I said. "We can imagine all kinds of different things when we look at pattern blocks. Tell us about the parts that make up the dragon," I said, encouraging Heriberto to look at the elements comprising his design of eight blocks.

"See, here's the head and this is the tail," he explained. "You have to think the fire."

"So the fire part is in your imagination," I said.

"You pretend it," Heriberto answered.

I moved on to a new discussion. "Brittney noticed something," I said. "She had eight blocks." I took out eight orange squares. "She got out two more blocks." I took out two squares. "Then she put back two blocks." I put back two squares. "She had eight, she got two more, then put back two. How many blocks did she have then?"

Alicia leaned over and counted. We all joined in and found eight.

"This is the story of what she did," I said. I wrote: $8 + 2 - 2 = 8$. "We started with eight and ended with eight. What do you notice about the numbers?"

"There's eight and eight," said Cristina.

"And two and two," said Jennifer.

"Does that always work?" I wondered aloud. "Can you take a number, add two and take away two, and get that same number?"

Some children seemed to understand my question. Others clearly didn't.

"You put them and you took them away," commented Alicia. She got three blocks, and then put them back. "Now it's zero," she said.

"Let me do it," said Heriberto. He put two hexagons on his fire-breathing dragon, and then put them back. "There's the dragon," he said.

"It's eight and eight," said Erin.

"You have the eight and then you don't and then you do," explained Heriberto.

"We could do an investigation of this some other time," I said. "What if you take any number, add two, then take away two? Will you get the same number?" This investigation into equivalence could be interesting, I thought.

Recording with Paper Cutouts

"You can keep your design or make a new one," I said to the children. "When you have a design that you want to keep, you'll use the paper pattern blocks to make a copy on the black paper." I showed the children the envelopes, each containing a different kind of paper pattern blocks. "Glue your design on the paper with glue sticks," I explained.

As the children finished their block designs, each got a piece of black paper and the pattern block cutouts. This next task was easy for some children but difficult for others. Some children obviously had more spatial experiences in the past, perhaps through building with blocks or Legos.

Some designs were more difficult to copy than others. Heriberto had a particularly difficult arrangement of rhombi and hexagons. It lacked symmetry and the rhombi were pointing in different directions, making it difficult for him to keep track of what he was doing. But Heriberto persisted. His final copy didn't match his original design perfectly, but was pretty close.

Brittney looked at her design carefully. She counted the numbers of each pattern block and then got out the same number of corresponding paper cutouts. Then she arranged one part, checked her design, arranged another part, checked her design, and kept going until she was satisfied. "It's the same," she told me. "What can eight blocks be?" I asked her, modeling the language pattern that our book would use.

"A flower," she told me.

On the white strip of paper that she glued to her design, I wrote: *8 blocks can be a flower.* (See Figure 5–1.)

Erin had also made a flower, but out of hexagons. Two were piled on top of each other in the middle so that her flower could have six petals and she could use all eight blocks. When she transferred this to her paper copy, the hidden block was no longer evident. "How will people know where the eighth block is?" I asked her. Erin drew a shaky arrow pointing to the hidden block. (See Figure 5–2.)

When all the children were done, we compiled the pages into a class book that we titled *Eight Blocks.*

FIGURE 5–1 Brittney made a design with eight blocks.

FIGURE 5–2 Erin's arrow pointed to the hidden hexagon.

We read our book over and over during class story time, and it was a popular book during independent reading as well. When we discussed the book I supported mathematical thinking in the following ways: Sometimes we counted the blocks in each design, sometimes we guessed what design the author had made, and sometimes I encouraged the students

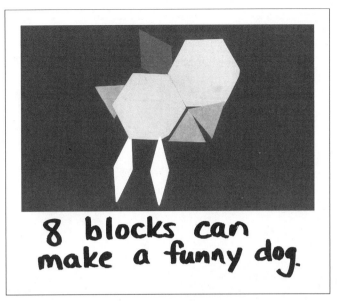

FIGURE 5–3 Laura's funny dog pleased the students.

to decompose numbers by asking how many of each kind of block made up the design. The students are delighted by representations that are clear as well as those that are unexpected (see Figure 5–3).

Linking Assessment and Instruction

You may wish to make the following observations:

- How did the children count? For example,

  - Did they know the sequence of number names?
  - Did they use one-to-one correspondence?
  - Did they have a way to keep track of which blocks they had already counted?

- Did the children realize that if they rearranged a certain number of blocks, the number would stay the same? This is called conservation of number.
- If the children decided to put back some blocks, did they know to take out the same number of blocks? This is evidence of good number sense.
- If the children decided to put back some blocks, did they randomly take out more blocks, and then count to check?
- Did the children easily reproduce their designs with the paper shapes? This indicates good spatial sense.
- Did the children easily describe what their arrangement looked like? Were they able to describe it in more than one way, as Heriberto did? This indicates that the children flexibly relate the block shapes with real—or imaginary—things in their world.

CHAPTER 6

Spill and Compare

OVERVIEW

This four-day investigation encourages children to compare numbers, record and interpret tallies, and consider odd and even numbers. Children use their hands to spill various numbers of two-color counters onto a workspace. They decide whether more counters are red, more are yellow, or if they have the same number of reds and yellows. The children later investigate patterns in even and odd numbers.

MATERIALS

Day 1

- two-color counters, 6 per pair of students
- $8\frac{1}{2}$-by-11-inch pieces of felt or paper, 1 per pair of students
- *Spill and Compare* Recording Sheet, 1 per pair of students (see Blackline Masters)

Names: _____		Our Number ☐
More Reds	More Yellows	The Same Number of Reds and Yellows

Days 2 and 3

- two-color counters, about 10 per pair of students
- 3-by-5-inch index cards, each labeled with a number, 2 through 12, with duplicate cards showing 6, 7, 8, 9, and 10, 1 set for the class

- *Spill and Compare* Recording Sheet, 4 per pair of students

Day 4

- 1 set of completed *Spill and Compare* Recording Sheets, exploring each number, 2 through 12
- 12 two-color counters
- 1 piece of 42-by-24-inch butcher paper
- 1 red marker and 1 yellow marker

TIME

- four class periods

Teaching Directions

Day 1
Introducing the Investigation

1. Ask one student to be your partner to demonstrate the game using the target number six. Share one *Spill and Compare* Recording Sheet, and write your names at the top, as well as the numeral 6 in the Our Number box.

2. Take six counters, cup them in your hands, and spill them onto the felt or paper workspace. Remind students to spill the counters quietly and carefully, keeping the counters on the workspace.

3. Ask students whether more reds, more yellows, or the same number of reds and yellows came up. Count the red counters and then the yellow counters to check.

4. Show the children the recording sheet. Make a tally under the section corresponding with the configuration of colors that was thrown. Remind

the children how to make tally marks in groups of five.

5. Spill, compare, and record the counters several times.

6. Ask the students to spill and record, taking turns with their partner, until the recording sheet shows twenty tallies.

7. Give partners six counters and a recording sheet to share. Have them work together, taking turns shaking and spilling the counters and recording their data.

8. Gather the students on the rug to interpret the data from several of their recording sheets. Reproduce a sample recording sheet on the chalkboard, using a pair of students' data. For example, the board might look like this:

9. Have the class interpret the information on the board. Have them practice reading the tallies and explaining how they knew the number of tallies. Some children will count all the tallies. Others will figure out the number without having to count every single tally. (For example, a student might say that the five grouping shows that the quantity is five. They don't have to count every tally mark. A five grouping and two more tallies allows them to count on from five: "Five: six, seven." Two five groupings make ten tallies altogether.)

10. For each section on the sample chart, record the total number. Then examine the chart to see which section had more: *More Reds*, *More Yellows*, or *The Same Number of Reds and Yellows*. Put a star next to the section with the most tallies.

11. Do the same with another recording sheet, to give the students practice interpreting tally marks.

Days 2 and 3
Investigating New Numbers

1. Ahead of time, prepare the index cards labeled 2 through 12. To ensure that there are enough cards for each pair of children, include duplicate cards for the numbers 6 through 12.

2. Remind students how they spilled the counters and filled in their charts the day before. Explain that they will be doing the same thing today, but that they will choose their own number card, picking a number to explore. Remind the students that they will again shake and spill twenty times. Then they will write the number of tallies in each section, and put a star in the section that receives the most tallies.

3. Have partners play the game. As the students work, invite different children to explain how the counters looked for different tally marks. For example, if a student placed a tally mark in the *More Reds* section and the student had seven counters, there could have been four red and three yellow, five red and two yellow, six red and one yellow, or seven red and zero yellow.

4. When they finish, ask the partners to return their number cards to the box. Ask them to choose a new number to explore, until all the numbers have been investigated. Save the recording sheets for the Day 4 discussion.

Day 4
Investigating New Numbers and Discussing Odd and Even

1. Ahead of time, prepare a wall chart for the class discussion. Use a marker to write the numbers *2* through *12* vertically on the left-hand side of a piece of butcher paper. (This will become a poster for the classroom. Leave space at the top for a title.)

2. Gather the students on the rug for a discussion. Examine the last section of each recording sheet, *The Same Number of Reds and Yellows*. Begin by having a pair of math buddies examine the chart for number 2, to see if there are any tallies in that section of the chart. Write *Yes* on the poster if the number 2 does have tallies in the last section, and write *No* if 2 has no tallies there.

3. Have other pairs of math buddies examine the recording sheets for numbers 3, then 4, then 5, and so on, each time writing *Yes* on the poster if

the number has tallies in the last section, and *No* if it doesn't.

4. Ask the students to discuss the pattern that they see in the list. (There should be a pattern of *Yes*, *No*, *Yes*, *No*, according to whether the number is odd or even.)

5. Give twelve counters to each pair of students. Ask the students to use the back of their charts as a workspace. For each number, have them place the counters on the paper to show how the counters looked when the same number of reds and yellows was thrown. Write equations to show these combinations of doubles next to each number. Use a red marker to show the number of red counters and a yellow marker to show the number of yellow counters. Circle the even numbers. The list will look like this when you're finished:

②	Yes	1 + 1
3	No	
④	Yes	2 + 2
5	No	
⑥	Yes	3 + 3
7	No	
⑧	Yes	4 + 4
9	No	
⑩	Yes	5 + 5
11	No	
⑫	Yes	6 + 6

6. Add red and yellow circles to illustrate how the counters looked for even numbers. (See page 34 for an example.) Write the title *Even Numbers* at the top of the poster. Ask the students to explain what even numbers are. Write the students' explanations at the bottom of the poster. Place the poster in the classroom environment. Refer to this poster throughout the year when you see the same pattern developing in other contexts, such as "Number of feet that people have" or "Numbers of tires on a bicycle."

Teaching Notes

This activity allows first graders to visit and revisit the concepts of "more," "less," and "the same." Its probability context encourages children to wonder, "What

will happen this time?" which motivates them to play again and again.

The children repeat this investigation with different numbers on different days. Then they are ready for a discussion about which numbers can have the same number of reds and yellows, and which numbers cannot. In this way children are introduced to the idea of odd and even numbers.

It's important to have a number of children explain their idea of what even numbers are. Through hearing various explanations, more children will have a way to understand this new idea of how we classify numbers.

I like to make a permanent chart of the numbers we found that do make two even groups, so that we can refer to it when we encounter even numbers or doubles in different contexts throughout the year. In this way the classroom mathematical environment reflects what the children have learned, and it becomes a resource for the children to use throughout the year.

The Lesson

Day 1

I showed the children the two-color counters that they were going to use. "What do you know about these counters?" I asked them.

"There's red on one side and yellow on the other," answered Robert.

"That's true," I said. "I can toss them and see what colors come up. You'll be tossing six counters today, but I want you to spill them very carefully, so that they don't fall on the floor or roll onto someone else's workspace. Please spill them onto the felt workspaces. What are some words that describe how you're going to toss the counters?"

"Softly," said Victoria.

"So lightly that you can't hardly hear it," added Brittney.

I asked Armando to show us how he might gently toss six counters. He did so and I drew the children's attention to the four red counters that came up. "How many yellow counters are there?" I asked. Becky held up six fingers, put down four, and then said, "There's two."

Next I asked the children to think about which color we had more of. "Don't say a word, but raise your hand when you decide: Did we get more red counters, more yellow counters, or the same number of red and yellow?" Hands waved in the air as I paused to give all the students time to think. Then I asked Juanita to answer. She said, "More reds 'cause four is more bigger." I asked the other children whether they agreed that four was more than two. Heads nodded.

"We can show more reds by putting a tally mark on this recording sheet," I said, holding up the *Spill and Compare* Recording Sheet. "How would we do that?"

Armando explained that we should put a line in the section labeled *More Reds*. I put a red dot next to this section, and a yellow dot next to the *More Yellows* section, to remind the children what each section stood for. Then I drew the tally mark as Armando had suggested.

I reminded the children about making tallies in groups of five. "Remember how we make tallies for our lunch choices?" I asked them. "You make four tallies in a row," I said, drawing four vertical lines, side by side. "And then how do I make tally number five?" I asked.

"You make it like this," said Robert, holding a hand diagonally.

"That's right," I agreed, drawing a diagonal line across the group of four to make five. "But who can explain it in words?"

I encourage children to use mathematical language as often as possible.

"It goes sideways," said Lorena.

"Right, we make a diagonal line," I continued. "That way you can tell at a glance that it's a group of five."

"You'll shake and spill the counters twenty times," I said. We did this twice more and recorded the tallies on the recording sheet. "I wonder whether more reds will come up more often, or more yellows, or the same number of reds and yellows," I mused aloud.

"You'll get red a lot," Robert stated. "It's always the most."

"Why do you think that?" I asked him.

"It just is," he told me confidently.

"Red's my favorite color," Armando informed us.

"Maybe it's like heads and tails with pennies," said Victoria. "It's like when you throw a penny." Victoria was making an important connection.

"I'd like you to work with your math buddy," I told the children. I invited the first several pairs of children to go to a table. I had the others watch as these children took six counters, wrote their names on their paper, and began tossing the counters gently. In this way I labeled my expectations for the other children.

The Children at Work I circulated to watch the children work. "I got more yellows!" Miguel told his partner enthusiastically. I watched him make a tally in the *More Yellows* section. Minutes later things had apparently changed for Miguel. "We went two more times already. There's more reds a lot," he told me, concerned.

"Interesting," I replied. "I wonder if you and Joaquin will keep getting more reds." I turned their attention to the total number they needed to roll. I asked, "How many tallies do you have so far?" Joaquin counted from one and told me he had sixteen. "How many more do you need to get twenty tallies?" I asked. Joaquin shook his head. Miguel counted on from sixteen using his fingers: "Seventeen, eighteen, nineteen, twenty. Four more."

Becky was busy shaking and spilling the counters while Alejandrina recorded. Once she got all reds, and put a tally in the section marked *The Same Number of Reds and Yellows*. "Why did you mark that section?" I asked her.

"They're all the same," she told me, pointing at the six counters showing red.

"I see what you're thinking," I answered. "But that section of the chart means that you had the same number of reds and yellows, like three reds and three yellows. How many reds did you get?" I asked.

"Six," she answered.

"How many yellows did you get?" I asked.

"Zero," Becky said.

"So," I asked, "do you have more reds or more yellows?"

"More reds," she said, and reached for an eraser.

I came to Cristina and Jennifer, who seemed unsure how to continue. I knew that counting even small numbers was still hard for Cristina. I suggested that they start with four counters.

Cristina counted out four counters and put the rest back in the container in the center of the table. That told me she knew four is inside the larger number six. I had thought that she might not see the relationship of the numbers, and would put all the counters back before counting out four. Cristina carefully spilled the counters and saw three red and one yellow.

"Which is more, the red or the yellow?" I asked her.

"Is it red?" she asked me tentatively. I made a graph with the counters, placing the red counters in a line vertically with the yellow one lined up at the side. "Does the red look bigger, like it's more?" I asked.

"The red ones is more bigger," Cristina answered.

"That's right," I said. "The red line is longer and that shows it has more." The visual arrangement seemed to help her understand. The girls proceeded with the activity independently.

Heriberto and Gerardo were excitedly playing together, hoping to get more reds each time. Heriberto spilled the counters and Gerardo did the recording. "I'm doing the sticks," Gerardo told me. I wanted to make clear to Heriberto what the tally marks meant, so I pointed to one. "What does that line stand for?" I asked. Heriberto answered confidently, "It means this time when I tossed the counters I got more reds." He showed me how his counters had looked. It's important to make this explicit connection with young children, since the tally mark is used to represent a relationship between a quantity of counters, and this relationship looks nothing like the tally mark itself. I talked to several other children to help make this connection clear.

Lorena laughed as I approached. "We got it again!" she said.

"Got what?" I inquired.

"Me and Carina got four red and two yellow again!" she answered, then corrected herself. "Oops! This time it's four yellow and two red. But it's kind of the same," she added.

"That's true," I said. "You got four and two again, but this time it was four yellow instead of four red." I was pleased that she was looking for connections. This is a habit of mind I try to develop in all the children. And Lorena had discovered the commutative property of addition, that $4 + 2 = 2 + 4$.

Later Lorena called me over again. "Now we really keep getting the same thing again. Carina got four reds and two yellows two times and I got four reds and two yellows two more times."

"That seems to surprise you," I said. "Do you think you should get different numbers?" She nodded.

"Where will you put your tally mark?" I asked.

"More reds, 'cause four gots more," Carina answered.

I watched how the children determined which number was "more." Sereslinda had placed her counters in a pattern of "red, yellow, red, yellow, red, yellow." But when she finished, she looked perplexed.

"Do you have more red or more yellow?" I asked her.

"I don't know," she answered.

"Is there another way you could arrange them?" I asked her.

Sereslinda selected a red circle and placed a yellow next to it. One at a time she paired red and yellow circles until she could see that each had a partner. "It's the same," she told me, and carefully made a tally mark in that section of her paper.

Several children had placed their tally marks in a long string. I helped them rearrange their string of eight tally marks into the conventional grouping of five and three.

I had several children count the tallies that they had made so far. Then I asked them how many more they needed to make to get twenty tallies. Most of the children counted the tallies from one by ones. But Alejandrina made use of the five groupings, saying, "Five, ten, twenty—I mean, five, ten, fifteen, twenty, twenty-one, twenty-two, twenty-three." Then she explained why she had gone past twenty. "I want to tie them, keep going so that I have the same number of tallies," she said. The fact that she changed the rules didn't bother me. I was pleased that she had challenged herself in an interesting way, trying to make the numbers match.

As children finished, I had them total the tally marks in each section. Then I asked them to explain which they got more often: more reds, more yellows, or the same number of reds and yellows. Most children interpreted their recording sheets accurately. Some children asked to do another page of *Spill and Compare* with a new number, and others chose to read a book for a few minutes.

It was time to gather for a short discussion, so I asked for the children's attention. I said, "I'd like you and your partner to see how many tallies you have in each section. For example, see how many tallies you have in *More Reds* and write the number there. Remember that tallies are in groups of five; you don't have to count each line to figure out the total. Then please put away your materials and come to the rug."

A Short Discussion   I made a copy of their chart on the chalkboard, and gathered the children on the rug.

"I like to throw the circles," Heriberto said.

"I was the thrower," Lorena said. "And Carina did the marks."

"Did other pairs of you divide up the work that way?" I asked.

"Me and Heriberto did," answered Gerardo.

"You certainly worked together well," I told them. "I have your papers here. Let's see what you found out."

I showed them Heriberto and Gerardo's recording sheet, and reproduced the chart on the board so they all could see.

Names: _____		Our Number	6

More Reds	More Yellows	The Same Number of Reds and Yellows
ⵑⵑⵑ ‖	ⵑⵑⵑ ‖‖‖	‖‖‖

"What does this tally mean?" I asked, pointing to the first section.

"It's more reds," Brittney explained. "It could be four reds and two yellows."

"Or five reds and one yellow," added Jennifer.

"How many times did they get more reds?" I asked, showing them the tallies:

ⵑⵑⵑ ‖

"Seven," the children answered.

"How do you know?" I asked.

"It's easy: one, two, three, four, five, six, seven," answered Fernando.

"It's true, you can count all the tallies," I said. "Is there another way that you can find out without having to count each tally?"

"Well you know it's five," said Navin, "'cause there's the sideways one, and then it's six, seven."

"So you don't have to count that first set, you just know it's five because of the diagonal line?" I asked Navin. He nodded.

"You can count on from five," I said. "That seems faster: five, six, seven." I wrote 7 under that section.

We practiced reading the other tallies from each section. Each time we talked about counting on, and I wrote the total number below the tallies. Then we looked at all three sections. "Which section got more tallies?" I asked. We agreed that yellows came up the most, and I put a star in the *More Yellows* section.

We did the same thing with Lorena and Carina's data. "Tomorrow we'll play the game again with different numbers," I said.

Days 2 and 3
Investigating Different Numbers
Ahead of time I had prepared small cards labeled with the numbers 2 through 12. I reminded the children

about how we had done the activity the previous day. We practiced a bit, to make sure that they remembered what to do. Before the partners began, they selected a card and took out that number of counters. I reminded the children how they would finish. "Today, be sure to do twenty tallies. When you're done, write the total number of tallies in each section."

The children settled into their work quickly. I circulated among them to offer support and to hear how they were interpreting their tally marks.

Juanita and Omar were working with ten counters. Omar guessed, "There're more reds." "Let me see," said Juanita. She lined up the counters, pairing them to compare more easily. "One, two, three, four, five, six," she said, counting the reds, and "One, two, three, four," counting the yellows. "Six is more than four," she said. "The stick goes there," she advised Omar, pointing to the *More Reds* section.

Fernando and Navin were investigating twelve. "I'll count the yellows," Navin directed, and found six. "There's six reds too!" said Fernando excitedly. "It's the same!"

I noticed that Becky and Brittney had eight tally marks in a section. I wanted to see whether they would count on from five. "How many tallies do you have in *More Reds*?" I asked. "One, two, three, four, five, six, seven, eight," counted Becky.

"I see," I said. "Is there another way you can find out how many without having to count all the tallies?"

"If you want you can say 'five' for this, and six, seven, eight," said Brittney.

"How do you know there's five in that part?" I inquired.

"Well it's got the swoosh stick," she said, swishing her hand diagonally.

Miguel and Joaquin were exploring five. I noticed that they had a tally in *The Same Number of Reds and Yellows*. I pointed to that tally. "How did your counters look when you got that?" I asked them.

Miguel began turning over the counters. "I can't find it," he said.

"Let me," Joaquin told him, moving the counters closer. "We need another," he told me.

"Do you think you made a mistake with this tally mark?" I asked. "Maybe it goes here," Joaquin said, pointing to the *More Yellows* section. He picked up an eraser.

I heard some counters spill on the floor. Gerardo stooped to gather them up. "You'll want to make sure that the number of counters that you have matches your number card," I suggested. This would be necessary for our odd and even data to be accurate.

Alejandrina and Erin returned to spilling their counters industriously. "Last time it was more yellow," Alejandrina said. "This time it'll be more reds." She spilled more yellows, figured this out with a glance, and said, "Maybe it's not gonna be more reds this time." Alejandrina read the tallies in each column: "Five and five and zero." She rolled two more times, added a tally to each of the first two columns, and said, "Six and six and zero. Weird."

"What's weird?" I asked her.

"I never get the same," she explained.

"I wonder why?" I asked. I knew this was because seven is an odd number. I wondered whether she could articulate this idea. Alejandrina shrugged. "I don't know," she answered.

I noticed that Heriberto and Gerardo were nearly finished. They were working with the number ten. When Heriberto tossed the last set of counters I brought his attention to the two reds that he had. "How many yellows do you think there are?" I asked him. Heriberto thought a minute and then said, "There's eight." "How do you know?" I asked him. "Well," he answered, "it's two here, then it goes three, four, five, six, seven, eight." He counted on with his fingers.

"As you play you both might try just counting one color and then figuring out the other color in your head," I suggested.

Day 4
Discussing Odd and Even Numbers

The children were seated on the rug next to their math buddies. "Please put your recording sheets on the floor in front of you," I said.

I listed the numbers *2* through *12* vertically on a large sheet of butcher paper. I wrote the numbers on the far left side, leaving some space at the top for a title. "These are the numbers we've been exploring. Let's see what happened to the section that we marked when we had the *same* number of reds and yellows," I said.

I held up one of the recording sheets. "The last section shows *The Same Number of Reds and Yellows*. As I walked around I noticed that some charts had tallies there and some didn't. Look at your sheet and see if you have tallies in the last section," I said.

Dianna looked at hers. "Seven doesn't got any."

Heriberto noticed the same thing. "Neither does eleven," he said.

"Twelve does," Navin told us.

"Let's look and see what numbers *did* get the same number of reds and yellows," I suggested. "If they did, we can write *Yes* on the board next to that number. If it didn't, we can write *No.*"

The children checked their recording sheets and reported to the group on the number they had investigated. When we finished, the poster looked like this:

2	Yes	
3	No	
4	Yes	
5	No	
6	Yes	
7	No	
8	Yes	
9	No	
10	Yes	
11	Yes	No (Two pairs of children had investigated this number. One chart had tallies, the other didn't.)
12	Yes	

"What do you notice?" I asked the group.

"It's a pattern," several of the children called out together. These children had worked with patterns a lot in kindergarten, developing the habit of mind to look for them. But Carina noticed an inconsistency. "It's got yes, yes, yes at the end," she said. "And eleven is weird."

"Let's check all the numbers and investigate how the counters could have looked to have a 'yes,'" I said. I put two counters on a sheet of white paper in front of me. Then I placed piles of counters in front of every four children in the circle. In this way counters would be accessible to all of them.

"I'd like you to work with your math buddy. Turn your recording sheet over on the back so you have a workspace to share. One buddy needs to get two counters, and the other buddy can show us how two counters look when you get the same number of red and yellow." This seemed to be easy for the children. They turned the counters to show one yellow and one red.

"One and one," said Nazario. I wrote *1 + 1* next to the 2 on the chart, using the red marker for the red counter and the yellow marker for the yellow counter. Then I drew a red circle and a yellow circle next to the 1 + 1.

"Now the buddies trade jobs. The other buddy gets another counter so you have three. And the buddy who didn't arrange the counters before gets a turn. How can we have the same number of reds and yellows with three?"

The children got another counter. They turned their counters over and over. "I can't do it," said Carina finally. "It's if we have another counter it's OK but not with three."

"You have that one all by itself," said Carlos doubtfully.

"There's no way," Alejandrina announced confidently.

"Let's look at four," I suggested. "How would four counters need to look to have the same number of reds and yellows? Trade jobs again. Get four counters and see if they can have the same number of each."

The children leaned over their counters. Robert said, "Two and two."

"Do you agree?" I asked the rest. They nodded. "Look, you can put the counters in a line and see that they're the same," I said. The children lined up their counters, two red and two yellow.

I drew this configuration on the poster. Next to the 4 I wrote *2 + 2*. "This will show us how the counters would look," I said.

"What if I have five counters?" I continued. "Just think for a minute. How would they need to look to have the same number of each? Everybody think and then raise your hand."

I paused. Only a few hands were up, and many children looked puzzled.

"It's really hard," Heriberto said. "I don't think you can do it."

A realization seemed to be dawning on many of them.

Luis spoke up. "See, there's four and one more is five and he doesn't got a partner to be with. It can't be the same."

"Oh?" I asked. "What do the rest of you think?"

Brittney had an explanation. "With five you have to get one more, so it's six, and it has the same."

"Let's find out," I said. "Buddies trade jobs, get another counter, and find out."

We checked 6 on our chart. It had tallies in *The Same Number of Reds and Yellows*.

"What would six look like if it had the same number of each?" I asked.

Luis turned over his counters somewhat randomly but eventually found a way. "Three and three," he said. The other children found it too. I put *3 + 3* on the chart and drew the corresponding circles.

"Let's try seven," I said, and I added a red counter to one of the lines.

"Now can we have the same number of each?"

"But it could be yellow," protested Jennifer, looking at my lines of counters. So I picked up the last red counter I had added, turned it over, and put it in the yellow line. The lines were still uneven. "Try your counters," I suggested. "See what you find out."

"See, there's no partners," said Luis.

Alejandrina spoke up. "If there's two here and two here, then you could put one more in each and have three and three." She pointed to the leftover and said, "Someone would have three and the other would have four. That's not even."

We checked the chart for 7—there were no tallies in *The Same Number of Reds and Yellows* section.

"What do I have to do to get 'the same' again?" I asked.

"Put another one," the children said, nearly in unison.

"What would eight have?" I asked. "How many of each color?"

"Four and four," many of the children said.

"Check with your counters," I suggested. I added a counter to my own lines. "What do you think?"

"That's it," Jennifer said.

"Eight is an 'even' number," I said. "Can you see why we say 'even'?"

"The lines is even," Carlos told the group.

"Four and four is fair. It's like even," Victoria explained.

"And nine?" I asked.

"You can't," said Luis. "It can't match. It doesn't got no partners anymore."

"That's right," I said, "and we say nine is an 'odd' number. It's not even, it's odd."

We did the same for the number ten. Then I said, "We had different ideas about eleven. Some of us found the same number of reds and yellows and some of us didn't. Why don't you get eleven counters and see if you think it's possible to get 'the same.'"

The children tried and tried.

"Ten did, and now we have an extra. It's only 'no.' You can't do it," said Jennifer.

The others agreed. "Maybe there was a mistake," Carlos said. I crossed out the *Yes* on the chart.

When we finished working with twelve, we looked at our poster again. "Let's circle the numbers that did get the same number of each." Our poster looked like this:

②	Yes	1 + 1	●○
3	No		
④	Yes	2 + 2	●● ○○
5	No		
⑥	Yes	3 + 3	●● ○○ ...
7	No		
⑧	Yes	4 + 4	
9	No		
⑩	Yes	5 + 5	
11	No		
⑫	Yes	6 + 6	

I continued. "What is the special name for the numbers that can have the same number of reds and yellows?"

"Even," some of the children responded. "That's right," I said. I wrote *Even Numbers* at the top of our poster.

"Why do we call them 'even'?" I asked.

"Like the lines are even," said Armando.

At the bottom of the chart, I wrote what Armando had said: *The lines are even.* "Who else can explain what even numbers are?" I asked. I wrote the other children's contributions at the bottom of the chart: *The parts match; It makes the same number; They have partners;* and *It's like they're holding hands.*

The children helped me tape the poster to the wall. I like giving them the opportunity to participate in changing the classroom environment. This way, they are more likely to use the poster as a resource during the year.

Linking Assessment and Instruction

You may wish to make the following observations:

- Did the children identify more and less at a glance, or did they count? Did they line up the counters evenly in order to make a visual comparison? This observation gives you a sense of children's understandings of number relationships.
- If the children counted, did they say the sequence of number names correctly? Did they use one-to-one correspondence as they counted? Did they keep track of what they already counted so that items weren't counted more than once?
- Could the children answer the "how many more" question when you posed it?
- Did the children record with tally marks in the standard manner? Could they look at a tally mark and explain what it stood for?
- How did the children read the tally marks? Did they count each tally from one without making use of the five-grouping? Or did the children quickly recognize "five" or "ten" and count on from that quantity?
- Could the children explain how the counters could have looked for a specific tally mark? For example, if a child had five counters and placed a tally in *More Reds*, could he or she discuss the possible configurations, such as three reds and two yellows, four reds and one yellow, or five reds? This investigation helps children decompose numbers.
- Could the children explain what an odd number and an even number is? Did they apply this concept by identifying odd and even numbers in other contexts?

Guess My Number

CHAPTER 7

OVERVIEW

This number-guessing game helps children develop number relationships. The game is played on a number line showing the numerals 0 to 20. To begin, one individual thinks about a secret number from 0 to 20, and the others take turns guessing what the number is. After each guess, the person who knows the number offers one of two clues: either "your guess is too big" or "your guess is too small," and tapes a corresponding triangle on the number line over the guess, a large triangle if the guess is too big, and a small triangle if the guess is too small. The triangles are moved to reflect each guess, narrowing the possibilities until the secret number is revealed. This is a good activity to do at the beginning of the math period or when there is some spare time during the day. Revisit the lesson again and again, giving children repeated experiences with number relationships.

MATERIALS

- 1 36-by-3-inch strip of paper, such as adding-machine paper, with numerals from 0 to 20 written in alternating bold colors and spaced so that they are distinct from each other
- 2 paper triangles, inverted, a large one labeled *Too Big* and a small one labeled *Too Small*
- 3-by-5-inch index cards or pieces of paper, 1 per student

TIME

- fifteen minutes

Teaching Directions

1. Gather the students on the rug, seated next to their math buddies. Tape the number line on the board.

2. Read the numbers with the students. Ask them what they know about the numbers that they see. You may discuss things such as which number is largest, which is smallest, which side has the bigger numbers, and which side has the smaller numbers.

3. Tell the students that you are thinking of a number and that you'd like them to guess what it is. Write the secret number on an index card and then fold the card over so the number is hidden.

4. Have the students take turns guessing. As they guess, say "[the number] is too big," or "[the number] is too small." If the guess is too large, tape the large triangle above it so that it points to the guess. If the guess is too small, tape the small triangle over it. Explain what the triangles mean.

5. As they guess, ask students to explain why they think their number is a good guess. You may also ask them to discuss with their math buddies what a good next guess might be.

6. Continue the game until a student guesses the number. Show students the number you initially wrote on the index card, to check that this is the secret number.

7. Let a student choose a secret number. Have the student write the number on an index card. If necessary, help the child respond to the guesses, offer clues, and move the triangles correctly.

Teaching Notes

Students invariably enjoy this guessing game, and it's always informative to me as a teacher as well. I like seeing whether children use the clues and, if so, how. Even though there may be a large triangle pointing to 8 and I say, "Eight is too big," a child may next guess ten. That child is either learning basic number relationships, or is misinterpreting the words in the clue. I like to have children explain why they made a specific guess, which helps the "guesser" consider his or her reasoning. This also helps less-experienced children see the number sense behind appropriate guesses.

This activity, while on the surface simple, deals with different aspects of number sense. Children first need to have a sense of quantity, and understand what numbers mean. Only then can they know what "too big" or "too small" refers to. This understanding develops through many experiences with counting real objects for real purposes.

As the children develop this kind of complex thinking, they also develop the language to explain their thinking. When I ask children to explain what they know so far, or why they think their guess could be right, I'm encouraging their use of mathematical language.

The activity also helps children see how the number line can be a tool for comparing numbers. Eventually this same tool will help children develop strategies for computation.

The Lesson

Introducing the Game

I showed the children a number line that I had made from a long strip of paper, with numbers from 0 to 20. "We're going to play a game," I explained. "We'll use this number line. It will help us think about larger numbers and smaller numbers." I taped the number line to the board and asked the children what they noticed about the numbers.

Luis began to read the numbers along the line beginning with zero, and the other children joined in.

"Here's one, two, three, four, five, six, seven, eight, and nine too," said Lorena, pointing to the ones place in the teen numbers.

"What's the smallest number on the number line?" I asked. They answered, "Zero."

"It's not nothing," explained Jennifer.

"You're right, zero means nothing at all," I said, modeling standard grammar. I placed my hand on the 0 and slowly began to move my hand to the right. "What happens as the numbers go this way?" I asked.

"They get bigger," was the communal response. As I slowly continued moving my hand, I said, "Bigger, bigger, bigger . . ." The children joined in. ". . . until I'm at the end!" My hand was now at the end of the line.

"That's the biggest, twenty is," said Armando.

"What if I start at twenty and go the other way?" I asked. I slowly moved my hand from right to left, and the children joined in, saying, "Smaller, smaller, smaller . . ." and I finished with, "Until we're at zero, nothing at all. In this guessing game," I continued, "I'm going to choose a secret number, and you are going to try to guess my number."

I showed the children two triangles with tape on the back, one large triangle with the words *Too Big* and a small triangle labeled *Too Small*. I explained that I would tape the triangles above the numbers as we played. "If your guess is too big, we'll tape the big triangle above it. But if your guess is too small, we'll tape the small triangle above it. That might help you remember the clues."

"I have a secret number," I said, and I wrote the number *16* on an index card, holding it so the children couldn't see. I folded it over so the number would remain hidden. "See if you can guess my number."

"Six," guessed Robert.

I paused. I wanted the children to think about what Robert had said. "Can you find six on the number line?" I asked, giving the children a chance to connect the number word to this new representational tool. Several children's eyes seemed to move right to 6. Becky pointed with her finger, counting from one. "Six!" she said, smiling.

"Six is too little," I said, and I taped the small triangle above the numeral 6.

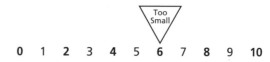

							Too Small			
0	1	2	3	4	5	6	7	8	9	10

11	**12**	13	**14**	15	**16**	17	**18**	19	**20**

"What do you know so far?" I asked.

"It's not one or two," said Victoria.

"How do you know that?" I asked her.

"Well, if six is too little, then one is really little, and it can't be one," she explained.

"It's not four," said Alicia.

"Why do you think that?" I asked her.

"Four isn't so much as six," she said.

"I see," I said, restating her words in standard mathematical language. "Four is less than six. Now," I continued, "think about what a good guess would be."

Omar spoke up. "Eleven."

I paused to let the children look at the number line and see where 11 would be.

"Eleven is too little," I said.

"Ooh!" exclaimed several children. I moved the small triangle and placed it above the 11. "I put the little triangle above eleven to show that eleven is too small," I said, helping to clarify what this triangle symbolized.

"Now what do you know?" I asked. "Think about that, and then decide what a good next guess would be."

"Eight," offered Becky. "Hmmm," I said. "Eleven was too small, and eight is also too small." I moved the small triangle so that it pointed to the 8. "What do you know so far? Think about what your next guess might be. I'd like you to talk to your math buddy about what a good guess would be."

I waited while the children whispered among themselves.

"Oh, I know, I know," said Victoria, her hand waving in the air.

"I know!" said Cristina. "Seventeen."

"Seventeen's too big," I said, taping the large triangle above the 17. "Take a look at the number line," I suggested. "It has some information to tell us. Look at what number is too little, and what number is too big. See if your math buddy can agree on a good number to guess." I waited once again for the children to talk. Having math buddies talk together allows more children to engage in thinking, and to use mathematical language.

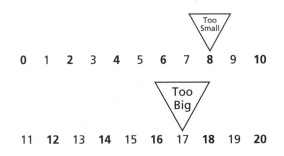

It was Robert's turn. "Is it fourteen?" he asked.

"Why did you guess fourteen?"

"It's bigger than eleven," he answered, and I continued his idea saying, ". . . and it's smaller than . . ."

"Sixteen!" Robert smiled.

"That's the secret number!" I answered, showing the children the number I had written at the beginning of the game.

"Let's do that again!" said Becky.

I wrote a new secret number on a card and turned it over.

"Seven," guessed Nina.

"Seven is too small," I answered, moving the small triangle above the 7. "Think for a moment about what you know now." I paused. I wanted to help the children incorporate the clues into their own logical thought process.

"Could the secret number be two?" I inquired.

Alfredo nodded. "It could be two."

Robert shook his head. "I don't think it's two, 'cause the seven is little and the two is more little."

"So," I said, "Robert remembers that seven was too small. He knows that two is even smaller than seven. So Robert thinks the secret number can't be two." As I spoke, I pointed to the numbers on the number line.

"Ooh, I know what it is!" Victoria's hand waved in the air. "Seventeen."

"Hmm," I replied. "Seventeen is too big." I taped the large triangle above the 17. "So what do you know now?" I asked. "Could the number be twenty?"

Some children nodded and others shook their heads "no." It's to be expected that children are at different stages of understanding. As we played I accepted all guesses but had children articulate their reasoning. Over time this would encourage children to move to new levels of understanding.

Robert guessed ten. "Ten is too little," I said, and I moved the small triangle to 10.

Some of the children said, "Ooh!" with their eyes widening.

Navin guessed thirteen. "Thirteen's too little," I said, moving the small triangle to 13. The tension was clearly building in the room. "Fifteen," guessed Carina.

"Fifteen's too little," I answered. Many children drew in their breath as they looked at the number line. "Ooh!" they said.

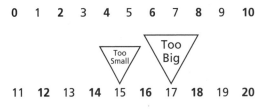

"You gave us the clue!" said Robert. "Now we know!"

"It's gotta be sixteen again," said Alicia. "This is too little and this is too big." She pointed at the numbers 15 and 17.

"What's too little?" I asked.

"Fifteen," they answered.

"And what number is too big?" I asked.

"Seventeen," they answered.

"So you know it has to be . . ."

"Sixteen!" they cried. I unfolded the paper and showed the children that number.

Children Choose the Secret Number

"Now let's play a new way," I suggested. "This time one of *you* will choose the secret number and move the triangles." I called on Alicia. She came up, wrote her number on an index card and turned it over.

Robert guessed first. "Three!"

"Too small," Alicia said softly. She picked up the small triangle. "What do I do?" she asked me.

"You put the too-small triangle over the too-small guesses," I said.

"What'd you say?" Alicia asked Robert. He told her his guess and Alicia placed the small triangle over the 3.

Next Becky guessed twenty. "Too big," reported Alicia, and she moved the large triangle above 20.

"What is the number?" asked Juanita.

"I can't tell you!" Alicia responded, smiling.

Gerardo guessed ten.

"It's too big," Alicia said. She moved the large triangle above the 10.

"Oooh!" said Heriberto, "Thirteen!"

"Too big," said Alicia. And she moved the large triangle above the 13.

"That's right," I commented. "Ten is too big and thirteen is too big. Do you think fifteen is too big?"

"Yes," said Robert, "and fourteen and twenty."

"It's two," guessed Laura, even though we already knew that three was too small.

"Too small," said Alicia. She moved the small triangle above the 2.

"I'll go with eight," said Juanita.

"Too big," answered Alicia, moving the large triangle above it.

Next, Cristina guessed six. When Alicia moved the small triangle above the 6, hands shot up into the air. "I know!" filled the room.

"You're very excited," I replied. "You know something for sure. What is it?"

"It's seven!" the children said. Laura explained this time. "It can't be eight and it can't be six so it's seven." Number relationships were clearer to her

when the numbers were closer together. Carina had another way to articulate it. "The eight is too big and I know that the six is too little and it has to be seven." "These ones are all too big," Gerardo explained, pointing to all the numbers larger than eight. "And all these are too little," added Nina, pointing to the numbers less than six.

Alicia turned over the card with her secret number and there it was . . . 7!

Becky went next. Her secret number was 20. I told her that I would help her with the triangles if she needed me to.

"Ten," guessed Juanita.

"Ten is . . . too big or too small?" I asked Becky.

"A too-big number?" she responded.

"Find twenty with your eyes," I whispered to her, "and then look at ten. It's over by the little numbers. So ten is too little."

"Too little," Becky announced, placing the small triangle above the 10.

As we played I continued to help Becky think through what it took to place the triangles correctly: how the guess related to her secret number and which triangle needed to be moved. In this way she had a chance to develop number relationships, as well as the mathematical language of comparison.

"Twenty!" Carina finally guessed.

Becky turned the card over, her eyes shining. "You got it!" she said triumphantly.

It was time to stop for the day. I planned to use this short game at the beginning of the math period for the next week or so. I also planned to play it with a small group of children, being sure to group children who used number relationships with children who did this less consistently. When less-experienced children hear the thinking of other children, they have opportunities to develop similar understandings about number relationships.

Linking Assessment and Instruction

You may wish to make the following observations:

- Did the children recognize that the smaller numbers are to the left of the number line and the larger numbers are to the right?
- Did they make use of previous clues as they made guesses? Did they do this consistently? Children may make a guess that makes sense one time, and then make an unnecessary guess another time. These children are still developing a sense of number relationships, and perhaps how the number line represents these relationships.

- What kind of mathematical language did you hear the children use? Did they use the terms *more*, *less*, *bigger*, *smaller*, as well as the language of logic? If they used other words, how did they describe these concepts? Could the children articulate that given certain information, some numbers were no longer possible?

- When a child decided on the secret number, did he or she have the number sense to tell whether the guesses were larger or smaller than his or her number? Did the child move the triangles to correctly illustrate that number relationship, or did he or she need your help?

CHAPTER 8

What Do You See?

OVERVIEW

In this lesson children are encouraged to find the smaller numbers that are part of larger numbers. They look at a card with a number of dots and describe the groups of smaller numbers that they see within the arrangement; the teacher writes the addition equation that describes it. In a different variation of this activity, the children use counters to duplicate the arrangement that they saw. Then the children discuss the groups of dots they saw within the arrangement.

MATERIALS

- "What Do You See?" cards, enlarged to $8\frac{1}{2}$ by 11 inches, 1 set (see Blackline Masters)
- counters, 10 per student
- copy paper, 1 per student for Lesson 2

TIME

Lesson 1

- fifteen-minute whole-class routine

Lesson 2

- thirty-minute small-group lesson

Teaching Directions

Lesson 1
Whole Group

1. Show a "What Do You See?" card to the class for about three seconds. Then quickly hide the card.

2. Do this several times so the students figure out how many dots there are and any smaller groupings that they see there.

3. Leave the card in view. Ask the students to explain how many dots they saw and how the smaller groupings helped them remember the image. For example, a student may say, "I saw eight dots, three and three and two." Point out where those smaller groups are on the dot card.

4. On the board, label what the student saw in the form of an equation: $1 + 3 + 4 = 8$ or $8 = 3 + 3 + 2$. (See page 41 for further elaboration.) As you write each numeral, show the group of dots that it represents, making a clear connection between the dots and the numerals.

5. Have other students share what they saw. Each time, record what the student saw by writing an equation on the board. Encourage students to see each arrangement in various ways, to help them decompose numbers flexibly.

Lesson 2
Small Group

1. Show a "What Do You See?" card to the group for about five seconds.

2. Ask the students to place the counters on their workspaces (a piece of copy paper) to duplicate the arrangement that they saw.

3. Show the card again to the students for about five seconds. Tell them that they can revise their arrangements, if desired.

4. Once again show the card to the students for five seconds and let them revise their arrangements.

5. Now leave the card visible to the students so they can further revise their arrangements. For students having difficulty, let them put the card on their workspace and instruct them to place the cubes on top of the dots on the card.

6. Ask the students what images or groupings helped them remember the arrangement of dots. As the students talk about the smaller groups of dots that they saw, write the corresponding addition equation, helping children make a connection between the groups of dots and each number in the equation.

Teaching Notes

This engaging activity promotes the habit of looking inside larger numbers for smaller groups of numbers. Building this kind of flexibility with numbers allows children to later develop powerful computation strategies based on number sense. Continually asking children to look for different ways creates the classroom norm that encourages children to look for different combinations of numbers that work best for them.

I encourage children to do this kind of thinking often during the school day. If we read a story together and we come to a page with pictures of many things, such as ladybugs or animals or leaves, we count them, and then make a game out of seeing the smaller groups that are "hiding" within the larger group. Children develop the habit of automatically decomposing numbers in the same way that, after they work with patterns, they begin to see patterns everywhere.

This activity, as with most, can be done at a variety of levels. Teachers can begin by just talking about the numbers alone, they can describe them by using the language of equations ("Oh, you see four plus four plus two and that equals eight."), or the equations can be written by the teacher or student. Teachers determine what will be most effective for their students.

Some teachers are surprised by how I occasionally write the total number first in an equation, such as in $8 = 4 + 2 + 2$. It's important for children to see equations in a variety of forms, so that they learn that the equals sign means "is the same as." Many children come to believe the equals sign can only function like the enter key on a computer, and indicates that an operation is to be performed. This incorrect notion is partly responsible for the confusion that older students encounter in algebra classes. We can support correct understandings by varying how we write equations, and by even writing equations such as $4 + 3 = 2 + 5$.

Lesson 1: Whole Group

The children sat around me on the rug, looking expectantly at the cards that I held in my lap. I explained that I was going to show them a card with dots. They were to watch closely and tell me how many dots they saw, and the smaller groups that they saw inside.

I warned the children that I wouldn't give them much time to look. I knew that limiting their time to look would move them away from counting individual dots and toward remembering chunks or smaller groups of dots. I told the children, "Don't call out the number, just think it. Ready, set, go!"

I gave the children a few seconds to look, and then hid the card. Then I wanted to give the children a second look. "Maybe you're not sure what the number is," I said. "Would you like to see it again?" I showed the children the dots for three more seconds, turned it over, and then showed them the dots for three more seconds. I paused, then showed the card one more time.

"So how many dots were there?" I asked, this time leaving the card visible. Most answered, "Eight!"

"Wait," I protested teasingly. "I never gave you enough time to count each dot. So how did you know how many there were?"

"It was four and four," Alicia said.

"I see," I answered. "You saw four and four. Was it this four and this four?" I used my hand to group one set of four and then the other.

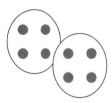

"Wow!" said Carina. "That's neat!" I thought to myself, it *was* neat to suddenly see something that we hadn't before. It reminded me of optical illusions that at first we don't see at all but suddenly become obvious.

On the board I wrote the equation $8 = 4 + 4$. "Alicia said that there were eight dots on the whole card." I pointed to the 8 in the equation. "Then she showed us how she knew. She saw this group of four," I said, covering dots so that the first group of four was visible. I pointed to the first 4 in the equation to help the children connect the number with the group. "Then she saw the other group of four," I continued, pointing to the other group of four dots and the other 4 in the equation.

"Did anyone see the eight dots in a different way?" I asked.

Heriberto raised his hand. "I saw four and two and two."

"Was this how you saw the eight dots? Four and two and two?" and I used my hands to show the groupings I thought he meant. "That's it," Heriberto agreed.

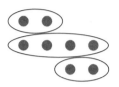

"Ooh!" laughed Lorena. "I didn't even see that."

"This is how we can show what Heriberto saw," I said, writing *8 = 4 + 2 + 2.* Then I again showed how each group of dots corresponded to each number in the equation. In an activity like this, children benefit from frequent opportunities to see the connection between numbers and what they represent.

"Did anybody see the eight dots in a different way?" I asked. More hands went up.

"I did," said Alejandrina. "It's like Heriberto's but I saw the two and two and then the four."

"Oh, neat," I said. "I hadn't thought of that. You saw the same groups but a different order: two and two and four. Can you see what she did? You can change the order of the groups and it will still be eight." I wrote *8 = 2 + 2 + 4* and again pointed to each part to connect the numbers to the dots they represented. Then I paused. "Did anyone see the dots in a different way?" I asked.

"I saw three and three and three," said Robert.

"Did you see this three and this three?" I asked, grouping the three on the top and the three on the bottom.

He nodded. "And then I saw the three in the middle."

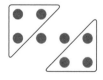

"You already counted that dot, so you have only a group of two dots left," I explained. I showed him the remaining two dots. "So you saw three and three and two." I again wrote the equation and connected each number to the group of dots that it represented.

We continued this way, as long as the children's interest held, using various cards.

Lesson 2: Small Group

I sat with a group of five children gathered around a table. A tub of cubes was in the center of the table and each child had a blank piece of paper.

"Remember when I showed you a picture of dots for just a short while?" I asked them. "We're going to do the same thing today, but this time you'll use your counters on a piece of blank paper to make the same arrangement."

I placed a card in front of me on the table, facedown. "Remember, you need to arrange the counters in the same way that they're on the card," I stated.

"Ready, set, go!" I held the card up for five seconds:

"Now," I said, "make the arrangement that you think you saw the best that you can. I'll give you another look in a moment."

I watched as Gerardo found five counters and arranged them in the same manner as was on the card. Omar was having a harder time. He had gotten three counters and had simply put them down on the paper, unsure of how they were to go. Juanita had gotten five counters and had placed them all in a square shape. And Heriberto had gotten five counters and had made them into a large V-shape:

Cristina wasn't sure how to start. "Watch again," I told the group. "Look for small groups of dots inside the larger arrangement. They will help you remember how it looks. Let's try again." This time I held the card up a few seconds longer.

Gerardo nodded, checking his arrangement, satisfied that it matched the card. Omar put his three counters in a diagonal shape and got out two more, which he laid on his recording sheet. Juanita moved one counter into the center of her square, completing the design. Heriberto whispered, "Three," and modified his arrangement:

Cristina had taken six counters and placed them in a diagonal line on her paper. I left the card visible so the children could change their arrangements by looking and checking and looking and checking. The children eventually all duplicated the arrangement. Cristina was still having difficulty, so I gave the card to her. She built right on the dots, using one-to-one matching.

Then we discussed what helped the children remember the arrangement. "I saw three and two, and that makes five," said Heriberto. "The three is in a V and there's two at the bottom."

"This is one way to describe what you saw: three plus two equals five." I wrote the equation on the board and showed how each number matched each group of dots. This time I ended with the total, because it matched Gerardo's words.

"It's like the dice," said Gerardo. "That's how I knew what to do."

"What part reminds you of the dice?" I asked him.

"Well, I see the four on the outside and one in the inside," Gerardo answered. I was surprised; I thought he recognized the entire arrangement for five. Instead he was recognizing separate parts: the four and the one.

"We can write what Gerardo sees in this way," I said, writing *4 + 1 = 5*. I again showed the dots that matched each numeral in the equation.

Cristina had an important contribution. "There's that one in the middle and then four!" She excitedly pointed to the dots in each corner, very proud of herself. I remembered how interested she'd been when we played the game with the whole class. "That's right!" said Juanita. "It's got a square in it." I wrote the equation that matched what they saw: *1 + 4 = 5*.

I took out a new card to investigate:

After the first view, Cristina said, "I see it! *Three*." She put three counters in a column and placed three more beside them:

Omar made an arrangement similar to Cristina's, as did Gerardo. And Heriberto's first arrangement had only the four central circles:

Juanita put two groups of two on her paper, and a single dot below:

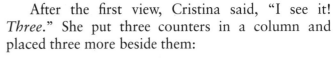

As the children had more chances to see the card, their arrangements more closely resembled the card, and eventually they all matched. When we discussed what the children saw, Cristina, Omar, and Gerardo agreed that it looked like three and three. But then Gerardo said, "It can be three and three this way," and he showed me groupings different from those that Cristina and Omar saw:

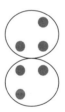

"Yeah, I see that now," Omar said with a smile. "I like this game."

"How would we write what you saw in a number sentence?" I asked.

"It's three plus three," said Omar. I wrote the equation and again showed the sets of three dots on the card, to make an explicit connection between the numerals and the dots.

"But I see something different," interjected Juanita. "Look! It's two and two and one and one. See?" And she showed us her groups of counters:

"How would you write what Juanita sees?" I asked the children.

"I think it's two plus two plus one plus one," said Cristina. I wrote the equation, pleased with Cristina's use of standard mathematical language.

Linking Assessment and Instruction

You may wish to make the following observations:

Lesson 1

- Did the children recognize smaller groups of dots that are inside larger dot arrangements? Did they quickly recognize familiar dot patterns, such as those that appear on dice? Did the children find numbers that repeat within the arrangement? Did they use symmetry to help them remember parts?
- Did the children exhibit flexibility by visually decomposing the dots in many different ways? Were they confident and did they enjoy this process?

Children with these traits are developing important habits of mind.

- What mathematical language did you hear the children use? Did they describe the dots in terms of individual dots? Or did the children use the language of equations, such as "one plus two plus five equals eight"? Did they speak of where the dots were with spatial language such as top, bottom, rows or lines or diagonals?

Lesson 2

- Did the children have good visual memory, and quickly duplicate arrangements? This is an indication of good number sense.
- Did the children revise their duplicate arrangements, and consistently get closer to the original design? Or did the children need to build directly on top of the card? These children are still developing the ability to see a number in terms of its parts.

Snap It!

CHAPTER 9

OVERVIEW

These activities develop children's understanding of how numbers can be decomposed. In Lesson 1, a small-group activity, the teacher determines what the target number is (for example, seven), and each child makes a cube train using the number of cubes. When directed to, all the children snap their cube trains into two parts, hiding each part behind their backs. They take turns showing first one part and then the other to the group, and the other children observe and comment on the various number combinations (for example, five and two).

In Lesson 2, a more challenging activity, the children are given the target number and again build a cube train using that number of cubes. They take turns snapping their trains in two, showing one of the pieces but keeping the other hidden. The other children count the cubes in the visible piece, and predict how many cubes the hidden piece has.

Lesson 3 is a whole-class activity that involves the children in determining the possible ways that a specific-size cube train can be snapped. This is an important investigation into part–whole relationships.

MATERIALS

Lessons 1 and 2

■ Unifix cubes, 10 per student

Lesson 3

■ trains of 10 cubes, 1 per student
■ butcher paper
■ 2 different-colored markers

TIME

Lessons 1 and 2

● twenty-minute small-group activity

Lesson 3

● one class period

Teaching Directions

Lesson 1
Snap It, Show It

1. Ask a small group of students to each make a cube train using a specific number of cubes.

2. Say, "One, two, three . . . Snap!" and have the students break their cube trains into two pieces.

3. Have each student take a turn showing first one train piece and then the other. The children name the number of cubes in each part—for example, "Five and two."

4. Using these same trains, have the students continue playing, snapping their trains in different ways.

5. Do the same with a different-sized cube train.

Lesson 2
Snap It, Hide It

1. Ask the students to make a cube train using a target number of cubes.

2. Explain that they will take turns snapping their cube trains as the other students say, "One, two, three . . . Snap!" The student who snaps the train will then place one part on the table and hide

the other part behind his or her back. Using the number of cubes on the table as a clue, the other students will then guess how long the missing part is. After they've made their guess, the student who snapped the train will show the hidden part, so that the others can see if their guess was right.

Extension: Write, or ask the students to write, the equation that describes how the cube train was broken, such as 5 + 2 = 7.

Lesson 3
Snap It Different Ways

1. Ask the students to make a cube train using the target number of cubes.

2. Have the students investigate and record all the different ways that the cube train could be snapped in two.

3. Ask them to record their thinking on paper. Explain to them that they can use numbers, words, and/or pictures to show their findings.

4. As a whole group, discuss students' findings. As they share, on butcher paper write equations that match their cube configurations, as well as a representation of how the cube configurations looked. Use different colors to represent the two different parts. For example, if the student investigated the number five and snapped his or her train into a two-cube piece and a three-cube piece, you would write *2 + 3 = 5*, and draw a figure like this:

Teaching Notes

This activity focuses children on the part–whole relationship of numbers. When decomposing numbers, children have to consider the whole number (such as 6), and then they have to consider two other parts (such as 2 and 4), which are inside it. This is cognitively more challenging than simply comparing two numbers. Lesson 1 allows children who are just beginning, to see both the parts. Lesson 2 allows children who more easily decompose numbers to figure out the part that is missing. And Lesson 3 challenges children to investigate different ways that a number can be decomposed, with the eventual goal of finding all the possible ways. These different versions make it possible to meet the needs of a range of first graders.

Decomposing numbers eventually allows children to move away from counting strategies for computation, and toward developing more complex strategies based upon number sense. This new understanding develops first as children think about smaller numbers. Children later will use these same strategies with larger numbers.

Sometimes teachers feel pressure to abandon work with smaller numbers and instead move to larger numbers. Doing so often results in children depending on counting as their sole strategy.

When doing an individual assessment of children's number sense, I often do Lesson 2 with them. I have the child make a train of five. Then I play *Snap It, Hide It* with the child several times, snapping the train in several different ways. If the child quickly can tell me how many cubes are hiding, each time without counting, I note that five is a number that the child knows well. If the child has trouble with five, I try four and then three. If a child is successful with five, I try the numbers six through ten. (I stop when the child has difficulty.) This quick assessment gives me a good picture of the child's knowledge of number decomposition.

Lesson 1: Snap It, Show It

Cristina, Gerardo, Laura, and Joaquin joined me at a table. I knew that decomposing numbers was difficult for these children. I wanted them to have a chance to see the smaller numbers that were inside the numbers three through six. While I often group children so that there is a mixture of experience levels, today I wanted these children to have a chance to explore numbers that were appropriate for them.

"We're going to play a game called *Snap It, Show It*," I said. "I'd like you to each get four cubes and connect them together." I watched the children do this easily, and made a train for myself.

I continued. "Now I'd like you all to hide your train of four behind your back. Then we'll all say 'One, two, three, snap!' When we say 'Snap!' you break your train into two pieces. Ready?"

We all said, "One, two, three, snap!" and all broke our trains.

"Now we show what we did," I continued. I held out my hands.

"My trains are one and three."

Cristina showed her trains. "Mines is two and two," she said.

Joaquin had the same thing. "Two and two makes four," he told us.

Laura showed us her trains. "There's a two and another two," she said.

"And what did we start with?" I asked the group, turning their attention to the original whole. "Four," they said.

Gerardo held out his trains. "I got a three and a one," he said. "That makes four."

We continued in this same way with the numbers six, five, and three, always talking about the original number that we had snapped, and the two parts that resulted.

Lesson 2: Snap It, Hide It

I sat at a table with four children. The others were engaged in math workshop activities and were working independently. Today I had gathered together Nina, Jennifer, Armando, and Navin.

"We're going to play a game that lets us think about the number five and the smaller numbers that are inside that larger number," I explained to them. "I'd like everyone to make a train of five and put it on the table in front of you."

When all the children had done this, I continued. "I'm going to take my train and snap it into two pieces. I'll hide one of them and you'll see if you can figure out how many I have hidden in back of me. Ready?" I asked. I paused, building up their curiosity. "One, two, three . . . Snap!"

I quickly broke my train in two pieces and hid one of them behind my back. I laid the piece that was two cubes long on the table. "You can see two cubes," I said. "Can you tell how many cubes are hiding?" I watched the children to see how they would respond.

Earlier I had predicted that Nina might find this difficult, and that Navin would find it relatively easy. I planned to start the group out together, so that Nina could observe other children's strategies for identifying an unknown addend. And I wanted Navin to articulate his strategies as well. After all four children played for awhile, I would probably invite Navin

and Armando to find many different ways to snap a number.

"It's three!" said Navin instantly.

"I'd like you to just think your answer and put your thumb up to show me you know," I said. "That will let everyone have some time to figure it out. Now," I continued, "what do the rest of you think? How many cubes are behind my back?" Soon all four thumbs were up.

"Three," the children all chorused.

"How do you know it's three?" I asked Armando. "I just know," he answered. And indeed, Armando probably did just know the answer. Eventually I wanted him to internalize all the combinations for numbers up to twelve. In the meantime I wanted to make sure that he, and all the children, had a strategy for finding out, or for verifying a prediction for the missing part.

"If you didn't know, what could you do?" I asked him.

"Well," Armando said, "there's this two and I see it, and it's three, four, five on the other." He showed us with his fingers.

"I see," I said. "You can count on. There's two in front and you know the other ones would count three, four, five." I used my fingers to count on. "That tells me there must be three more hiding."

I invited Jennifer to take her train of five and snap it into two pieces. "One, two, three . . . snap!" we all said together.

Jennifer hid one part and showed us the rest—a single cube.

"So how many is she hiding?" I asked the group. "Everyone think about the number of cubes that you think she is hiding."

Navin and Armando agreed that there were four, and Nina wasn't sure. "One?" she asked.

Jennifer brought out the other piece of her train, which was four cubes long. We counted it together.

"Armando," I asked, "how did you know that four cubes were hiding? You couldn't see them but you knew anyway. It almost seems like magic. How did you know?" I wanted him to articulate his strategy.

"Well, you can know and then you know," Armando began. "But if you don't know you can see the one and you ask what goes with one to make five. And you see the one and then go two, three, four, five." He used his fingers to count on.

"So," I said, "it's like you see the one and you have pretend cubes there." I pointed to the single cube and then laid four fingers on the table next to it.

I counted the cube as one, and then my four fingers: "Two, three, four, five. There's four missing cubes." Counting on is actually a complex strategy, which Nina had not yet fully constructed.

"Let's choose a new number," I suggested. I had them make trains for six and I snapped mine together also. "One, two, three . . . Snap!" we all chanted. I showed them the piece that was four cubes long. "How many are hiding behind my back?" I asked.

Now there were three unsure faces, with Navin smiling triumphantly with his thumb up. After a moment I called on him. Navin said, "There are two."

"How do you know?" I asked.

"I just know," Navin answered.

I wanted to push for a strategy that all the children could use. "Can you use the train that's in front of you if you don't know?" I asked. I held the four that I had snapped next to Nina's six. "Can this help you in any way?"

"Oh, I see," said Armando. "It's four," he said pointing at my piece of four, "then five, six," he said, pointing at the extra two cubes in Nina's train of six. We held my piece next to Nina's whole train.

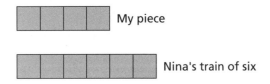

My piece

Nina's train of six

"Five, six," Jennifer said, counting the extra cubes in Nina's train. I think it is fine to occasionally offer strategies to children. The important thing is to not require them to use the strategies. Children should only use strategies that make sense to them.

I had the children take turns snapping their trains of six for us to guess. Armando was getting better at figuring it out, and Jennifer was coming along. But how to think about the missing part was hard for Nina. We did a few trains for seven, so I could make sure that Armando and Navin had a way to think about the numbers. Then I set the boys free to work on any size train up to ten. Jennifer and Nina and I continued playing with six. Jennifer was getting good at figuring out what number was missing.

After playing a few rounds, Nina said, "I see it. Here's the three, and you need three more!" Nina put the pieces back together and laid them next to Jennifer's train of six. She was beginning to understand

the part–whole relationship of numbers. I knew that Nina needed much more practice with these smaller numbers to reinforce this very important idea. But I was pleased that it was beginning to make sense to her.

After a bit I noticed that Navin and Armando had taken to making long, long trains and had apparently abandoned the task that I had set for them. I concluded that I needed to up the ante for them.

I asked Navin and Armando play *Snap It!* with ten cubes while I observed. Navin just knew the combinations, and Armando efficiently used his strategy of using the visible train to visualize the missing piece. He could even do it without looking at the visible train and looking up at the ceiling, as if the train were floating up there!

I suggested the boys play a new version, *Snap It Different Ways*. "See if you can find all the different ways that it's possible to snap eight cubes," I suggested. "Every time you find one, record it so you can show as many different ways as possible."

Lesson 3: Snap It Different Ways

I reminded the class about how to play *Snap It, Hide It*. I made a train of seven, snapped it, hid my four-cube train and showed my three train. "What am I hiding?" I asked. "It's a three," chorused many children.

"So, four is in the front and three in the back. Is there any other way I could snap my seven?" I asked. Brittney had an idea. "Two in the front and five you can't see," she suggested. I snapped the train to illustrate her idea. "How could you show this on paper?" I asked.

Robert raised his hand. "I think you should draw the cubes," he said. "Like a hand with three cubes and four next to it," he said. "Drawing is one possibility," I agreed. "What else could we do?" I didn't actually draw what Robert suggested because I didn't want to make a model that the children would copy. I wanted them to represent in a way that made sense to them.

Victoria had an idea. "You can make the numbers," she said. "So you could write a three and a four," I agreed. "What else could you do?"

"It's three plus four," offered Navin. "But you don't need a period." I think that Navin was referring to the term "number sentence" that I often used in the place of the term "equation." "Yes, you could write a number sentence or equation," I agreed.

"After you find one way to snap the train," I continued, "you need to find a different way to snap that same train. Show that way on paper. Then snap your train in a new way. Find as many different ways as you can to snap your train."

I showed the children the bucket of trains of ten. "We'll be investigating ten, so each of you will take a blank paper and a train of ten. You each can snap and write, but be sure to share what you discover with your math buddy."

Most children got settled, and began snapping and hiding their trains of ten. Not so for Omar and Alicia. "You can't draw the line," Alicia insisted, looking at Omar's paper. "That's not how you write it." "Yes, I can so," countered Omar. I moved closer to see what the problem was. Omar had written *2/8* on the paper. "Hmm," I said, "Omar wrote that to show how he snapped it into a two and an eight. I think Omar is writing it in a way that makes sense to him. On your paper, Alicia, you can show the snap however it makes sense to you."

Lorena was at my elbow. "How do you make a nine?" she asked. "Can I get a number line?" "Of course," I said. "They're supposed to be in your pencil box at all times. There's an extra one on the math shelf."

I watched Brittney and Nina at work. Or rather, Brittney was writing on Nina's paper while Nina watched. "See, you can break it," said Brittney in her best teacher voice. "See, you can count it, it will help you: one, two, three. I took away how much? One, two, three, four, five, six, seven." Brittney then set down the cubes and wrote *3 + 7 = 10* on Nina's paper. I noticed that all of Nina's work was in Brittney's neat handwriting. "I'm glad you're helping each other," I said, "but make sure that you each do your own writing."

Armando had snapped his train and had four in front of him. "We already did that," said Robert, pointing to the 6 + 4 on his paper. "It's not the same," said Armando. "Yes it is," said Robert. "Four and six. One, two, three, four. One, two, three, four, five, six."

"But we did six in the front and four in the back," said Armando. "It's not the same." The boys were having a mathematical discussion about commutativity, a big idea in addition. I decided to bring up the question "Is four and six the same as six and four?" during discussion time.

Many children had recorded duplicate combinations, which was all right with me. I would reinforce the idea of different ways during the group discussion. And they would have a chance to revisit the investigation over and over with various target numbers. Navin and Victoria had a long list of numbers on both sides of their paper. "What does this number mean?" I asked, pointing to an 8 on the left. "It goes with the two," Navin said, pointing to the 2 on the right. "How can you show that they go together?" I asked. Navin used his finger to draw an imaginary connecting line. "Yes, a line would help," I agreed.

I surveyed the room as a whole. The children were enthusiastically snapping and recording, and even Alicia and Omar were cooperating. I saw that there was a variety of ways that the children were recording, which was consistent with my expectation. They all think in various ways, so it makes sense that they would record their thinking in different ways.

Discussing Lesson 3

"Who had a partner that helped them learn?" I asked, wanting to provide positive examples for the few children who'd had difficulty working together.

"I did," said Alicia. "Omar helped me." I was surprised, but glad to hear this. "How did Omar help you?" I asked. "He told me how much am I hiding."

"So Omar helped you find out how long the missing train was," I reiterated. "That must have made it easier for you to do the investigation."

Victoria shared next. "Navin got a pencil for me when I didn't find one in the basket."

"So partners help each other by getting the things you need," I said. "Did anyone else have a partner do this?" I wanted to involve more children in the conversation, and have others reflect on what they did to be helpful to their partners.

After another child shared, I moved on to the mathematics. I held up a train of ten. "What's one way you snapped your train?" I asked.

"Five and five," answered Armando.

"Five plus five equals ten." I wrote the equation on butcher paper and drew the train, explaining that I was using the red marker for the piece in front and blue for the piece that was hiding.

The children shared other combinations. The board looked like this:

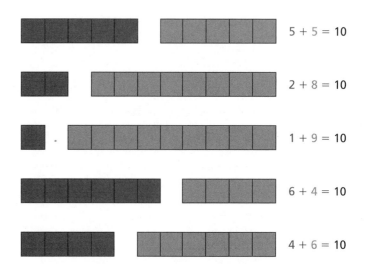

"Are these the same?" I asked, pointing to the last two arrangements. "I'd like you all to think about this."

"Well, they have the same numbers," offered Victoria after a few moments. "Six, four, four, six."

"Yeah, it's four and six," said Heriberto, "but it's not the same thing. See, you have four on the table and six in back and then six on the table and four in back."

Juanita had another way to think about the question. "It could be the same but it's not, because it's not the same thing. You can have four in front of you or you can have six in front but it's not the same. It's like opposites."

"What are opposites?" I asked.

"Hot, cold," Heriberto said.

"Yeah, and up and down too," said Omar.

"Why could we call these combinations opposites?" I asked the children.

"It's like it's the other way," Lorena explained to us.

"I wonder if other combinations have opposites," I asked. "Like one plus nine, does it have an opposite?"

"Nine plus one," Lorena said promptly.

"I wonder if we have all the ways to make ten," I said.

"There's no nine plus one," said Carina.

"Tomorrow you can continue looking, to see if you can find any new ways to make ten," I said. I wondered if more children would use "opposites" or commutativity to find other combinations.

The children needed more time to grapple with this question. Eventually I planned to have a discussion where we would build the different ways with the cubes. The pattern of the possible combinations would become evident (see next column).

The children might encounter this pattern for themselves. But for now they needed to continue investigating.

Linking Assessment and Instruction

You may wish to make the following observations:

Lesson 1

- Did any children get quickly bored with this activity? They need more challenge and are ready to do one of the other versions of this activity.
- What language did the children use to explain that smaller numbers are inside larger numbers? When they described their trains, did they talk about the number that they started with, as well as each of the parts?

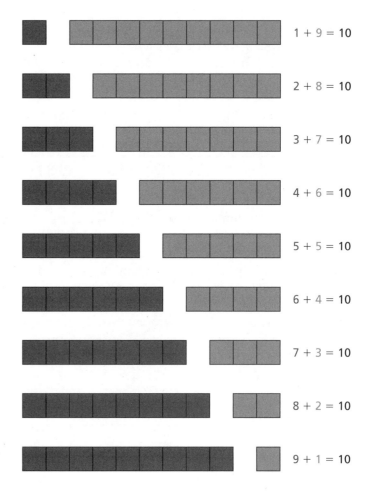

$$1 + 9 = 10$$
$$2 + 8 = 10$$
$$3 + 7 = 10$$
$$4 + 6 = 10$$
$$5 + 5 = 10$$
$$6 + 4 = 10$$
$$7 + 3 = 10$$
$$8 + 2 = 10$$
$$9 + 1 = 10$$

Lesson 2

- Did the children have strategies for figuring out a hidden piece? For example, did they count on from the train they could see? Did they try to visualize the missing piece? Or did they need a more concrete method, such as holding the visible piece next to a complete train to find the difference?
- Did any children just know the missing number with ease? Watch to see at what number the children begin having difficulty. Many first graders will be able to do this with four and five, but may have difficulty instantly knowing what addend is missing from larger numbers.

Lesson 3

- Some children may try to find more than one way, or even all the possible ways. But others may not be particularly interested. Some children may independently look for an orderly way to find all the possible combinations, but many won't be concerned with this. Note which children instinctively look for patterns.

- How did the children figure out the different ways that the trains can be snapped? Did they find combinations randomly? Did they find one combination and then adjust it systematically to find another?

- Did the children use "opposites" such as 3 + 7 and 7 + 3 to find other combinations? (This is the commutative property of addition.)

- How did the children represent the different ways to snap a number? Did they draw pictures of cubes? Did they use color to differentiate the combinations? Did they write words or numbers or equations?

Mouse Count

In Mouse Count, *by Ellen Stoll Walsh, a hungry snake finds ten mice on the grass and puts them into a jar, one at a time. The last mouse cleverly sends the snake on a fruitless hunt to find an even bigger mouse to eat, and the other mice tip the jar over and escape. In this activity, children investigate the different ways that the ten mice could be arranged when some are in the jar and some are on the grass.*

MATERIALS

- *Mouse Count*, by Ellen Stoll Walsh (New York: Harcourt Brace & Company, 1991)
- 8-by-11-inch green paper, 1 sheet per student
- clear plastic cups, 1 per student
- Unifix cubes, 10 per student

TIME

- two class periods

Teaching Directions

Day 1

1. Read the story to the class. Enjoy the language and encourage the students to predict what will happen next.

2. Explain that as you reread the story, you want them to act it out using props. Give each student a piece of green paper, a clear plastic cup, and ten cubes.

3. Ask the students to pretend that the plastic cup is the jar, the green paper is the grass, and the cubes

are the mice. Begin the story with all ten "mice" on the "grass." Each time that a page shows a new arrangement, explain to the students that they should put that number of cubes in the plastic cup (the "jar"). For each arrangement, talk about what just happened, how many "mice" are now in the "jar," and how many remain on the "grass."

Day 2

1. Read the story again to the class. Ask the students to find different ways that the ten mice could be arranged, with some in the jar and some on the grass. Explain to them that they can use anything in the room to help them figure it out. (Have the plastic cups and cubes available, but do not insist that the children use them. Some children may find drawing or other models more effective.) Instruct them to record their findings on a blank piece of paper. Explain that they may record using words, numbers, and pictures.

2. If a student finds one way, ask him or her to try to find another way that the mice could be arranged. If students find many possible arrangements, invite them to try and find all the possible arrangements.

3. Have a class discussion about what the students discovered. Ask a few students to share how they represented the mice on their paper. Make sure the examples show a variety of representations, such as simple pictures, tallies, shapes, words, numbers, or equations.

4. Have the students share the number of arrangements that they found. Make a class chart showing these arrangements. Using a blue marker, draw something to represent the jar and underneath it, list the number of mice that were in the jar. Using

a green marker, draw a representation of the grass and beneath, list the number of mice on the grass. Add a plus sign and an equals sign at the appropriate spots to form an equation representing the various arrangements of mice. Read each equation with the students, clearly connecting the equations with how the mice looked at different times. For example, the chart might look like this:

4	+ 6 = 10
5	+ 5 = 10
2	+ 8 = 10

5. Ask the students to share how they found new arrangements. For example, they might talk about "opposites" (three in the jar and seven in the grass, seven in the jar and three in the grass—the commutative property of addition). They also may have systematically moved one cube at a time to find new arrangements. If appropriate, you may want to discuss the pattern revealed by this approach.

$$1 + 9$$
$$2 + 8$$
$$3 + 7$$
$$4 + 6$$
$$5 + 5$$
$$6 + 4$$
$$7 + 3$$
$$8 + 2$$
$$9 + 1$$

Teaching Notes

This investigation is an example of a *Ways to Make* problem. In this case children find ways to make ten by combining two smaller numbers (for example, $2 + 8$, $3 + 7$, and so on). I offer children many *Ways to Make* problems in first grade, varying the total number and the context. For example, I sometimes vary the number by having children investigate the *Mouse Count* problem for six mice or twelve mice. I vary the context by having the children investigate how seven balloons could look if some were red and some were green, or by having them find out what could be inside a marble box if there are nine marbles, some black and some red.

These kinds of explorations give children a chance to decompose numbers. To do this, children have to think of three numbers: the whole number and the two numbers that are parts of the whole. This can be cognitively difficult for children at first, as they must hold three different numbers in their minds at the same time, while they consider the relationships of those numbers. Less-experienced children may expect to find only a single answer, some children may find a few ways, and more-experienced children may be able to find all the possible ways, perhaps using patterns in the number combinations.

When we retell the story, I have the children act it out, using a plastic cup for the jar and cubes to represent the mice. I use the words *let's pretend* with the children, helping them use their imaginations to model a problem mathematically. Some children solve the problem using this model, but other children move to different models, such as drawing. The children are free to represent their findings on paper in any way, which allows them to make sense of the process of representation. Finally, the discussion involves the children in making a chart to organize their findings, reformulating their information into standard equations.

Discussions should be short and focused. I usually plan how to focus the discussion before I gather the children. I find that I structure discussions according to what I know about the children's number understandings and strategies that I've observed them using during the work time. (See "Linking Assessment and Instruction.")

This lesson often leads to a discussion on "opposites" (such as $3 + 7 = 10$ and $7 + 3 = 10$, the commutative property), as is presented here. Another discussion might revolve around how children used number relationships to find new number configurations. For example, a child might have five mice in the jar and five on the grass, and then move one mouse from the jar to the grass to have four and six. Still another discussion might revolve around the consecutive pattern of combinations: $1 + 9$, $2 + 8$, $3 + 7$, and so on, which helps identify every possible combination.

The Lesson

Day 1

Reading the Story and Acting It Out   Since the class has children dominant in both English and Spanish, I read the book's Spanish version, *Cuenta Ratones*. I gave a quick overview of the story in English. "You'll see a big snake and some little mice. I bet you can guess what the problem is going to be in this story." Robert suggested that the mice would get eaten up. "It could happen," I agreed. "We'll read the story and find out whether they escape." The pictures are self-explanatory, and I planned to read the mathematical parts in both languages.

We looked at the cover and began our discussion in Spanish. "Look at the snake!" Victoria said. "It keeps going!" I opened the cover so that the children could see the serpentine body continuing to the back.

"It's got a pattern!" Heriberto noted. We "read the pattern" together: "Blue, green, blue, yellow, blue, green, blue, yellow."

Cristina commented, "The mice are scared. The snake's going to eat them."

"No, they'll get away," Alicia said.

After we read the first page I asked, "So how many mice are there?" We counted ten on both pages.

"But there's four there," noted Armando, pointing to the left page.

"Hmm, there are four on this page, but ten altogether," I said. "How many mice must be on the other page?" I paused to give the children time to think.

Sereslinda's brow was furrowed in thought. A moment later I called on Navin. "It's six," he said. "Four and six makes ten and there's ten mice."

Omar held up ten fingers and put down four. "Six mice," he announced. Sure enough, we counted six mice on the other page. "Four mice on one page and six mice on the other makes ten," I said, emphasizing the parts and how they relate to the whole.

We continued reading the story. When the mice began to nap, Heriberto piped up, "Oh, no, there's gonna be trouble!" The children loved the repetition of "little, warm and tasty," and chimed in as I read those parts. As the snake wrapped its body tightly around the jar full of shivering mice, Heriberto said, "They're scared!"

"You'd be too," responded Brittney.

When we finished reading the story, I said, "Now we're going to read the story again. But this time we're going to act it out. This will be the jar," I continued, showing the children a clear plastic cup, "and this will be the grass," I said, pointing to the green construction paper. Then I held up ten Unifix cubes. "Let's pretend that these cubes are the mice. Can you imagine their tails and their ears and their little feet?" I wanted it to be clear to the children that the cubes stood for the mice. The concept of representation is important in mathematics, but such abstractions can be difficult for young children.

I passed out trains of ten cubes to each child, as well as a green piece of paper, and a clear plastic cup. Many children broke off a cube and began pretending it was a mouse. "Where's my cheese?" squeaked Alicia playfully.

I reread the story aloud. When we got to the part where the snake puts three mice in the jar, I had the children put three cubes in their plastic cups. Each time we put more mice in the "jars" I focused the children on what they would be investigating, by asking, "Now how many mice are in the jar?" and "How many mice are on the grass?" As I finished reading the story, we all continued modeling it with the cubes.

As we read about the mice escaping, the children took cubes out of their cups one at a time. "Can we do it again?" asked Victoria. We did. Knowing the story well would help the children solve the problem the next day. Again we used the cubes and cups to act out the story. And again, for each arrangement, I verbalized how many mice were in the jar and how many were on the grass.

Day 2

Introducing the Problem   I began the math period by reading the story aloud one more time. Then I said, "I have a question for you to investigate. I'd like you to find as many different ways as you can that the ten mice can be arranged. Some mice are in the jar and some mice are on the grass," I continued. "I'd like you to find out different ways those ten mice could be."

I opened the book to the page showing three mice in the jar. I said, "For example, on this page there are three mice in the jar and seven on the grass. How else could the mice be, with some in the jar and some on the grass?"

I paused. Navin was counting on his fingers. Brittney whispered, "Nine and one." They clearly had a sense of the question, and the others seemed comfortable with what I was asking. We had done several other *Ways to Make* problems before.

"Once you have one way," I continued, "find another way. Then maybe you can find another way. See how many different ways those ten mice can be in the jar or on the grass."

I showed the children the materials that would be available to each pair of them: a clear plastic cup and ten cubes. "You can use any of these if you like," I said. "You'll work with your math buddy. You can each have a plastic cup and ten cubes, and you'll each need your own paper to record on. But be sure to talk to each other and help each other as you work."

I invited the math buddies, two at a time, to gather their materials and sit down. Before the first pairs of children sat down, I asked them to explain their task to the group, so I could be sure that they knew what to do.

When all the children were seated, I moved from table to table, talking with children and making observations. I watched Amanda make two groups of tallies. She counted one, two, three, then left a space and made more tallies, counting "four, five, six, seven, eight, nine, ten." She wrote *3 + 7 = 10* on top of her paper. She seemed to have a good sense of part–whole relationships. Carlos, however, seemed confused. I suggested that he use cubes and a plastic cup to show how Amanda's number sentence looked. Carlos brightened up. He put three cubes on the table. Then he counted the cubes in the cup and then recounted the three on the table. Amanda helped him as he wrote *3 + 7 = 10*.

Heriberto was writing on his paper, ignoring both his partner, Carina, and the cubes. He seemed to find his drawing more "concrete" than a cube, which looks nothing like a mouse. I watched Heriberto draw ten mice in a line. He crossed out two mice. "Those is in the grass," he assured me, pointing at the remaining mice. "Now the snake comes," Heriberto explained, "and it snaps up another mouse." He crossed out another mouse in the line. His picture was reflecting the continuing story but I could no longer see the first combination, 2 + 8. "Now the snake gets another mouse, Snap!" he said, crossing out another of his figures. Heriberto continued on this way for some moments.

"You know," I finally intervened, "I'm getting mixed up. You found some different ways the mice could look. Right now your paper shows me four in the jar and six on the grass. But I want to also remember the other ways that you found, like when you said there were two mice in the jar and eight in the grass. What can you do to show that?" Heriberto drew a 2 under the jar. "And how many mice were on the grass when there were two in the jar?" I asked. Heriberto reached for the cubes and put two in the plastic cup and counted the eight remaining mice on the grass. He wrote *8*.

Next Heriberto again crossed out the next mouse on his paper. Then he drew another mouse in the cup and wrote *3* beneath the 2. Heriberto counted the remaining cubes on the grass and wrote *7* beneath the 8. Then Heriberto continued crossing out other mice on his paper. He had found a way to represent each event. And he was using a pattern to help find different number combinations. (See Figure 10–1.)

FIGURE 10–1 Heriberto found a way to represent eight combinations. He used number patterns to find different ways the mice could be arranged.

I moved to Navin and Cristina, children with very different mathematical backgrounds. They were using plastic cups and cubes. Cristina showed me the two squares she had made next to an eight. "What does that mean?" I asked her.

"I forgot," she said. But Navin could explain. "That's two in the jar and eight on the grass," he said. I had Cristina show me how this looked with the cubes and the cup.

Navin told me, "I wrote this." He read his number sentence in Spanish: "*Seis más cuatro es igual a diez*" (Six plus four equals ten.). "Hmm," I wondered aloud, "do you have six mice in the jar or six mice on the grass?"

"It's six on the grass," Navin answered. He drew a wiggly line under the 6 and a jar shape around the 4. During these individualized discussions I can encourage children to think in ways appropriate to their own levels of understandings.

Robert and Armando had drawn lovely representations of the story. Robert had included a snake very similar to the snake in the book. He had drawn a jar with ten circles in it and a line to stand for the ground. Robert enjoys drawing and he seemed very pleased with his representation, but I wanted to encourage him to answer the question.

"How many mice are in the jar?" I asked. Armando leaned over Robert's paper and counted the ten circles.

"What can you put so that we can remember how many mice there are?" I asked, encouraging him to

FIGURE 10–2   Armando and Robert drew an elaborate picture to represent two ways to arrange the mice.

FIGURE 10–3   Armando and Robert began to represent combinations in a simpler way: with numbers.

use the symbols that he knows. Armando carefully wrote a *10*.

"What about the grass?" I asked. "How many mice are there?"

"It's zero," Robert answered, and he wrote *0* next to the 10. Then they carefully drew nine mice on the grass and one mouse in the jar. (See Figure 10–2.)

"Are there any other ways to put your ten mice?" I asked. They nodded.

"It might take a long, long time to draw such a fancy picture for each way," I said, encouraging the boys to simplify their representations. "What can you put on the paper that won't take so much time?"

"Numbers are good," Robert answered. He put three cubes on the paper. Armando put a handful of cubes in the cup. He counted all the cubes and got eight. Then Armando looked at the cubes that remained in his hand. He put them in the cup, again counted all the cubes, and this time got ten. Robert picked up his pencil and represented the combination with numbers. (See Figure 10–3.)

Alejandrina was busy writing. She had represented the different arrangements of mice in several ways: squares, tallies, circles, Xs, numbers, and equations. Then she wrote: *I yosd all the nombrs can you do a nombr santins upto ten __+__=___* (see Figure 10–4).

"What do you mean that you used all the numbers?" I asked her.

"I have all the ways," she answered. "I did the one, the two, three, four, five, six, seven, eight, nine, and the ten. There's no other way."

She had used all the numbers one through ten but had neglected the "opposites," such as three plus seven and seven plus three. "I see that you used all the numbers," I said, "but you may want to check with your math buddy to see if you have all the ways, before you decide for sure."

"Look," said Alicia. "It's the same."

"What's the same?" I asked.

"It's a seven and a three and a seven and a three," she said. Alicia picked up her pencil and made a *3* and a *7* beneath the original 7 and 3. She drew crossing lines as she said, "Seven, three, three, seven." (See Figure 10–5.)

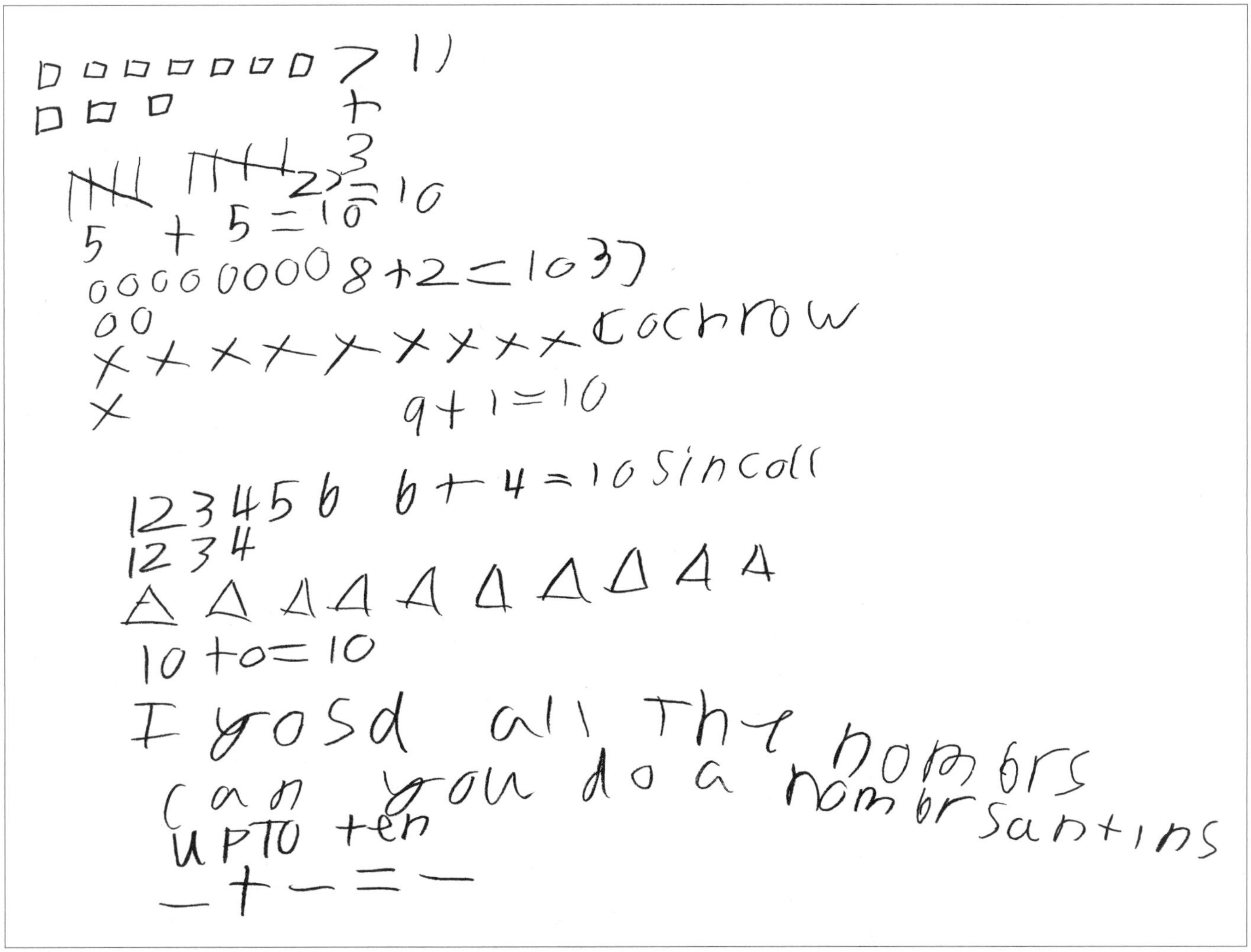

FIGURE 10–4 Alejandrina represented in a variety of ways. She used each number once but didn't find "opposites" such as 2 + 8 and 8 + 2.

"Wow!" I said, "The numbers *are* the same!" I shared her enthusiasm for this discovery. Then I tried to further her thinking. I asked, "Does that mean that the mice are in the same places?"

Nina shook her head. "It's the jar and the grass."

I wasn't sure what she meant, so I tried again. "Is the picture for seven and three the same as the picture for three and seven?" I asked, pointing at the pairs of numbers.

"No," Alicia answered, "they're not." The girls seemed to be grappling with the commutative property of addition. I decided to bring this idea out during discussion time.

Sereslinda had been working quietly. I asked her to explain her paper to me. On the first side she had drawn an elaborate picture, complete with mice, snake, rock, and blades of grass. On the back she showed a new way with simplified mice. From there Sereslinda had moved to an elaborate systematic method. She had labeled one column *Jore (Jar)* and another *Grass*. The numbers in each section matched up to show each possible combination. (See Figure 10–6.)

Miguel and Alfredo were engaged in seeing if they had written each possible equation. "I have six and four and you have four and six," Miguel said. "They're the same."

"Are they the same?" I asked. "Let's use the cubes to see." I put four cubes in the cup and six on the grass. "Alfredo had four mice in the cup and six in the grass," I said. "And you have six mice in the cup and four in the grass." I poured out two cubes. "Is that the same?"

"Nope," said Miguel, "but the numbers are." He was right. The boys continued comparing equations to see if they had all the different ways. "I have eight and two but not the opposite," said Miguel.

FIGURE 10–5 **Alicia and Nina discovered the commutative property of addition.**

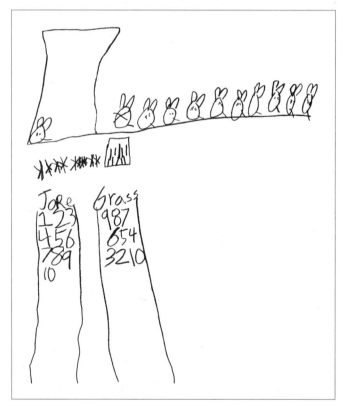

FIGURE 10–6 **Sereslinda found all the possible combinations of ten.**

Discussion I watched a colleague, Luis Carbonell, discuss this lesson with his first-grade students. He had the children sit in pairs on the rug. "Please put your paper on the rug in front of you so that you both can see it," he said.

As the children watched, Luis drew a chart on the white board with colored pens. He talked out loud as he made the chart, helping the children see what each part stood for. "This is the jar," Luis said as he drew a blue rectangle. "And this is the grass." Luis drew a green zigzag line. "I'm going to draw lines between them so we don't get them mixed up. His chart looked like this:

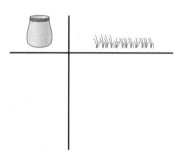

"Now," Luis continued, "you can tell me what you discovered about how the ten mice can be arranged, and I'll write what you tell me."

Reynaldo raise his hand. "There could be one in the jar." Luis wrote a *1* with the blue marker below the blue jar. "Then how many mice would be on the grass?" he prompted. "Nine," answered Reynaldo, and Luis wrote a green *9* below the grass. "So," continued Luis, "There is one mouse on the jar and nine mice on the grass and there are ten altogether." As Luis spoke he pointed to the corresponding numeral. With a black marker he added a plus sign, an equals sign, and the numeral 10. The chart now looked like this:

"Raise your hand if you found the same thing," said Luis, and several hands went up in the air.

"Did anyone get anything else?" Luis asked the group.

"I got two mice in my jar," said Elisa. Luis wrote a blue 2 in the jar column. "So how many mice did you have on the grass?" asked Luis.

"I forgot," Elisa answered with a smile.

"Ask your partner," Luis suggested, and Patricia then answered, "Five."

"Did anyone else get two and five?" asked Luis. He paused.

"Two and five is seven," responded Pablo. "There's ten mice in the story."

"So if there are two mice in the jar, how many would be on the grass?" Luis asked. Some children checked their papers, others began using their fingers.

"It's eight," said Eduardo, holding up his fingers. "See, I put two down, and five and three are left. That makes five . . . six, seven, eight."

"Interesting," said Luis. "Can you all see what Eduardo is saying? Try it yourself; hold up ten fingers to stand for the ten mice." He paused while the children did that. "Then Eduardo put down two fingers for the mice that are in the jar. And look at what's left: three on one hand and five on the other. Eduardo says three and five make eight." Luis emphasized Eduardo's use of five as an anchor point for thinking about eight, so that the other children might use that same strategy. Luis added $2 + 8 = 10$ to the chart, color-coding and explaining what the numbers stood for as he wrote. This verbal connection between symbols and what they represent must happen continually in first-grade classrooms, and Luis takes advantage of every opportunity to do this.

"Did anyone else get two and eight?" asked Luis. Hands went up. "Did anyone have a different one?" he continued.

Joaquin raised his hand. "We got four plus seven. No, that's not right," he corrected himself, then consulted with his partner, Andres. "It's four mice in the jar and six out on the grass," Joaquin said.

"Did anyone else get four and six?" Luis asked. Several hands went up. Fernando said proudly, "I got that!" Other children used their fingers to check four and six. Luis added this combination to the chart. "Did anyone get a new way?"

Mauricio's hand went up. "We've got six in the jar and four in the grass." Luis continued adding the combinations and talking about what the symbols stood for. A few times children repeated a combination that was already listed. Luis pointed to it on the chart and said, "Yes, we have that one," and he read the number sentence to the children. As the list grew I was struck by how the children were engaged in the mouse story. The equations truly were stories to the children, pictures of possible ways the snake could have arranged the mice. At the same time I heard a lot of mathematical language: *plus, altogether, that makes, too many, equals,* and so on.

Patricia offered three in the jar and ten on the grass, so Luis made the corresponding number of sticks next to the pictures of the jar and grass. When the children counted and got too many, Patricia said, "Uh oh, we've got extra mice."

Luis then turned the children's attention to an important property of addition—the commutative property. He looked at the chart. "Do any of these ways look almost the same?" Most of the children noticed the 6 and 4 and the 4 and 6, which were close together. "What is almost the same?" He asked. Marisa said, "They're both a six and a four." Andres had another way to explain the similarity. "They've both got the same numbers."

"So," Luis continued, "the numbers are the same. Do they tell the same story? If you drew a picture of each one, would it look the same?" He paused a moment. "Right now close your eyes and make a picture in your head of six mice in the jar and four in the grass." He paused. "Good. Now erase that picture and make a picture of four mice in the jar and six in the grass. Did your pictures look the same?"

"Well, no," Martha responded. "'Cause the jar's not the same. First it's got six mice and then it changes to four mice. They move over to the grass."

Joaquin explained his thinking this way: "The numbers are the same but the mice are in different places." This was a nice introduction to the commutative property of addition. Luis had the children find other combinations that went together. He underlined them in red. In this way the children discovered that they were missing 0 and 10. "We had ten mice in the jar and none in the grass, but we don't have the other way," David explained.

"If you want to find all the different number combinations, maybe looking for opposites will help you," Luis said, articulating a strategy that the children might find helpful in other situations.

Linking Assessment and Instruction

You may wish to make the following observations:

- Did the children have a way to model, solve, and represent the problem independently? Did they need support? If children need a lot of support, this may indicate that the number they are decomposing is too large.
- How did the children find different arrangements?

  - Did they randomly put cubes in the cup and on the grass, and count to make sure there were ten? If there were not ten, did they use number relationships to adjust one quantity?
  - Did they put some cubes in the cup and count up to find out how many should be on the grass?

- Did the children make one arrangement and then systematically move a cube at a time to find other arrangements? These children are using what they know to figure out what they don't know, an important habit of mind for developing number sense.
- Did they use number relationships to find new arrangements? (For example, if a child tried four and five, and found that there were not enough, did he or she know to add me to a group?)
- Did the children use "opposites" such as 3 + 7 and 7 + 3 to find other combinations? This is the commutative property of addition.

- Did the children know by heart any combinations of numbers that make ten?

- Did the children look for and find more than one solution? How many different solutions did they find? Did they use the pattern of consecutive numbers to find all the different arrangements? This indicates good number sense.
- How did the children represent the different arrangements? Did they draw pictures or use shapes or tally marks? Did they write words or numbers and/or equations?

Shake and Spill

CHAPTER 11

OVERVIEW

In this lesson children explore the small numbers that are inside larger numbers—number decomposition. Using a target number of two-color counters, they drop the counters on their workspace and record the combinations of red and yellow that result, by coloring circles on a worksheet, and writing the corresponding number sentence. The children explore how different numbers are decomposed, by doing this same activity with different numbers of counters.

As an extension activity, the children see which number combinations come up the most often. They shake and spill the counters only four times, recording on one-half of a recording sheet. The children use their record sheets to make and interpret a class graph.

MATERIALS

- the target number of two-color counters—5, 6, 7, or 8—1 set per student
- red and yellow crayons, 1 of each per student
- *Shake and Spill* Recording Sheet for target number, at least 1 per student (see Blackline Masters)
- piece of butcher paper, about 4 feet long
- 1 red and 1 yellow marker
- 9 small pieces of paper or index cards, about 3 by 5 inches

TIME

- two class periods

Teaching Directions

Lesson 1

1. Show the students how to cup the counters in their hands, and then "shake and spill" them onto their workspace. Show how they can record the combinations of red and yellow by coloring the corresponding circles on their recording sheets and writing the number sentences in the space below the circles. Make sure that the students understand that each section of the recording sheet matches one time they spill the counters. Do several examples.

2. Ask the students to shake and spill their counters, and record their results on their record sheet.

3. As the students work, note when they discover "opposites" (such as two reds and three yellows, and two yellows and three reds—the commutative property of addition). Listen for other discoveries, such as "We keep getting the same answer!" (These children are still developing conservation of number—the arrangement looks different, so they think the total number must change as well.)

4. When the students finish, gather them to share what they discovered.

Lesson 2

1. Show the students six counters. Explain that today, they will do an experiment and spill the counters just one time. Have the students predict which combination the class will spill most often. Have them shake, spill their counters one time and color the circles, and write the number sentence on their sheet.

2. Gather on the rug for a class discussion and to make a class graph. Discuss what combination came up the most in the class.

3. Talk about all the possible combinations. Put the target number of counters out (for example, six) so that they show all red. Use red and yellow markers to write a label on a 3-inch-by-5-inch piece of paper: *6 + 0 = 6*. Turn another counter over and write the next possible combination on another piece of paper: *5 + 1 = 6*. Continue turning over one counter at a time and making labels until you have recorded all the combinations. Tape the labels on the left side of the paper to make a graph, spacing the labels to allow the recording sheets to fit. The graph labels should look like this if six is the number you're working on:

$$6 + 0 = 6$$
$$5 + 1 = 6$$
$$4 + 2 = 6$$
$$3 + 3 = 6$$
$$2 + 4 = 6$$
$$1 + 5 = 6$$
$$0 + 6 = 6$$

4. Discuss the patterns that the students see in the label numbers.

5. Have the students post their recording sheets on the graph. Have the students who got the first combination tape their recording sheet on the top line. When that line is complete, count the papers and predict whether the next line will have more or less. Do the same until all the students' papers are posted and the graph is complete.

6. Discuss what the students notice about which combinations came up the most and the least. Have them describe the shape of the data. Write the children's statements on the graph.

7. Discuss why they think the graph turned out this way. Predict whether the graph would look about the same if the students repeated the experience tomorrow.

8. Continue the investigation other days to check the children's predictions. You can do the activity with the same number as well as with the numbers five, seven, and eight.

Teaching Notes

In this activity, children enjoy seeing the new configuration that comes up every time they shake and spill. They wonder why the number sentence ends with the same number each time (something that is obvious to adults but not to all first graders). The children wonder how the class graph will look this time, and whether the new number of counters will change how the class graph looks. Over time it dawns on some of the first graders that some combinations are simply difficult to get, such as all yellow or all red. The stage is set for the children to learn about probability in their later years of school. Meanwhile, the children have gotten a great deal of practice with number combinations.

I like to have the children post their *Shake and Spill* Recording Sheets on a large piece of butcher paper so they can later compare its appearance to the same graph done with different numbers, or the same number done a different day. I sometimes find it difficult to predict how large a sheet of butcher paper I will need, so I keep a smaller sheet of butcher paper ready to add to the larger sheet if necessary. (It's fun for the children to guess whether there's enough space, and to be surprised if there's not, as I often am!) However sometimes I don't use any butcher paper at all, and simply post directly on the board.

The Lesson

Lesson 1

We began this lesson, as we so often do, gathered on the rug. I showed the children a two-color counter. "What do you notice about it?" I asked.

"It has red and yellow," said Juanita.

"It's half and half," added Omar. "Half red and half yellow."

"It looks like a tire," said Gerardo. He was referring to the round hole in the middle of the counters we were using.

"Today we're going to work with the number six, so I need six counters," I said. We counted the five that were in my hand. "How many more do I need?" I asked. "I have five counters but I need six. Hold up your fingers to show how many more I need." I scanned the group. In a few moments most of the children were showing one finger. I picked up one more counter and we checked to see that there were six in all.

"When you get your six counters, you're going to shake them and spill them right on your paper," I said. "But I'd like you to explain about how you're going to spill the counters." I wanted to make sure that the children spilled the counters carefully.

"Not so big," said Cristina. She remembered from when we played *Spill and Compare*.

"Pretend that your hands are little and drop them soft like this," explained Carlos, showing us his cupped hands.

"They *could* fall on the floor," observed Carina.

"That's true," I said. "But you'll be careful to spill the counters on your paper so you don't lose any counters. Be sure to spread yourselves out," I said. "Some of you might want to sit on the rug to shake and spill."

"Are we going to work with partners?" Robert asked.

"Not today," I said. "You'll each have your own counters, but of course you can always help each other."

"After you shake and then spill your counters," I continued, "you need to record what happened on your recording sheet." I held one up to show the children. "This section is for one time you shake and spill," I said, masking off one section of the recording sheet, "and this part is for the next time you shake and spill. How many times are you going to shake and spill altogether?" I asked. The children counted the sections and answered eight.

"You'll record by coloring the number of reds and yellows that you spilled," I continued. "And then I'd like you to write the number sentence that describes what happened. If you spill three red and three yellow, you'll write three plus three—"

"Equals six," interjected Nina. I wrote this number sentence on the board. "The first three is for the red counters and the other three is for the yellow counters," I explained, making explicit the connection between the equation and the counters. I continued. "So if there are two red and four yellow you'll write . . ."

"Two plus four equals six," said Omar.

I spilled a few times and had them practice how they would record the number sentence.

I had Heriberto explain again what the task was, and then the children got up two at a time to get a recording sheet and six two-color counters. Then off they went to do the activity.

A quiet hum filled the room. I circulated as the children worked. I saw Alicia spilling one counter at a time. "Do you think it might go faster if you spill them all at once?" I asked her. She nodded and did so.

Robert's first equation showed $3 + 2 = 5$, even though he had colored in four reds and two yellows. "Show me how you got your number sentence," I said. Robert counted four reds, and when he saw the 3 he had made, he erased it and carefully wrote a 4. Robert then counted the yellows and looked at his 2. "It's right," he told me.

Omar called to me from the next table. "Mrs. Confer, I got the same thing again. It's three red and three yellows!"

I saw that he had colored in three red and three yellow in two other sections. "Why did that surprise you?" I asked. The concept of probability would not be introduced to these children until a later grade, and I was curious to hear his early perspective.

"Well," Omar answered, "I kept on rolling and rolling and I got the *same one* again."

Clearly, Omar's expectation was to get different combinations.

Armando looked up at me. "Look, I got the opposite," he said.

"What do you mean?" I asked him.

"It was two red and four yellow, and now it's four red and two yellow. Four and two, two and four," he explained. Armando was encountering the commutative property of addition.

Robert had disregarded the separate sections of the paper and was coloring in circles arbitrarily. I redirected him to the task by drawing a dark line around one section at a time as he worked. Robert was also having trouble recording the number sentences. I helped him with a few, and then he continued on his own. Sometimes I modify the activity and let specific children skip the equation part, but I felt that Robert could do it.

I watched Alicia work. "One, two, three, four red . . . two yellow!" she said. She didn't have to count the yellow circles.

"I got all yellow!" said Armando excitedly. A few other children rushed over to see. The result was noteworthy to the children, because Armando was the first to throw this outcome. They were building an early foundation for later thinking on probability, as they came to see that throwing a set all of one color was less likely than throwing a mixed set.

Many of the children counted all the reds and then all the yellows, finally counting all the counters to write the total. "This is really weird," Carlos told me excitedly. "It's six and six and six and six!" He was surprised that the total was always six.

"What does the six mean?" I asked.

"It's all the time six," he said, pointing to the counters. "It keeps being six!" Since the numbers of reds and yellows were changing, Carlos clearly thought that the total should change as well. He was still developing conservation of this small number.

Amanda looked over at him, unimpressed with this finding. "I *already knew* it was going to be six, because we had six of those things." Conservation was clearly obvious to Amanda.

I asked Luis to read the number sentences that he had written. "They all end in six," I said. "What do you think the next one will end with?"

"I dunno," he said. Luis counted all the circles he had colored and said, "Six." "I know," he added suddenly, "'cause there are six of these." He pointed at the counters. But then Luis went on to the next section. He shook the counters, spilled them, counted the reds, wrote the number, counted the yellows, wrote the number, and then counted the total. "Seven," he said, and wrote $2 + 4 = 7$. He seemed pleased with this sum.

"How do you know it's seven?" I asked.

He counted them again. "I was right, it's six!" Luis said. His ability to conserve this small number was fragile indeed.

A Discussion   The children gathered around me for a short discussion, their papers on the rug in front of them.

"So what did you discover?" I asked them.

"It was six and six and six," said Robert.

"You got an answer of six a lot?" I asked him. "Why did six come up so much?"

"It's always six," Heriberto said.

"It can't be anything else," Alfredo added.

"How many counters did we start off with?" I asked.

"Six," the children answered.

We counted them to check. "Then you shook them and spilled them," I said. "How many counters are there in all now?"

"Six?" Luis said tentatively.

"Let's check," I said. We counted them and found six. "Let's shake and spill again. Now how many are there in all?" I said. We did this a few more times and each time counted six.

It was clear that some of the children were still struggling with the concept of conservation of number. We would continue to revisit the activity and discuss this very important concept. It's important to remember that children's construction of new understandings occurs over time.

Day 2

Making a Class Graph   We sat in a circle on the rug. I reminded the children what we had done with the six counters the day before. "What different combinations did we get?" I said, laying out six two-color counters on the rug in front of me.

"I got all yellow one time," Omar said proudly.

I showed this with the counters and wrote $6 + 0 = 6$ on a 3-by-5-inch piece of paper. "Omar got six yellows and no reds," I said. "What else did you get?" I asked the class.

"Two yellow and four red," Alicia said. I wrote that on a separate piece of paper, also color coding the numbers.

"I know how we can make sure that we get them all," I said. "Let's make all of our counters red and just turn over one at a time."

We did that, turning over one more yellow each time. Soon I had seven pieces of paper in front of me. "These can be the labels for our graph," I explained.

"It goes zero, one, two, three, four, five, six," said Laura. "And six, five, four, three, two, one, zero," added Fabian. "It's a pattern."

"Right," I said. "And yesterday many of you noticed that your answers were all six."

"I got five one time," said Nina.

"Let's look at all the cards we just made to show how the counters could look," I said. "Do any of them end in five?"

Nina shook her head. "But let me do the counters," she said.

I let Nina try to make five with the six counters. "It's only six today," she said, "but yesterday I got five." Nina's thinking, like that of all children, is governed by past experiences. With more experiences of number conservation, over time her thinking will develop.

I looked at the labels we had made. "Which of these did you get the most of yesterday?" I asked.

"Three and three," said Alicia.

"Did that happen to anyone else?" I asked.

"Two reds and four yellows for me," said Omar.

"How about the rest of you?" I asked.

"I got three and three a lot," Juanita told us.

"Today I'd like you to shake and spill one more time. Record just like you did yesterday," I said, "by coloring in the circles and writing the number sentence that describes what happened. When you finish, come sit on the rug so we can see which came up the most for the whole class. Which do you *think* will come up the most?" I asked. "It's just a guess and can't be wrong," I reminded them.

"It could be three and three or five and one. I don't know," said Heriberto. He seemed to be voicing the opinion of the group. They just weren't sure.

Off the children went to do one more shake and spill, and I taped the labels to the left side of the graph.

It wasn't long before the children were gathered on the rug, their recordings in hand. "Let's find out what we got the most," I said. "Everyone look at your paper." I pointed to the top label. "Who has six red and zero yellows?" Three children stood up and we taped their sheets in the top row. We counted the sheets. I asked the children, "If there is one sheet in this line, do you think the next line will have more than one?" The children made different guesses.

Then we read the second label, *5 reds and 1 yellow*; two children came up and we taped their sheets in that line.

As the children posted their papers, I periodically had them take a moment to look at the graph. "Which line has the most?" I'd ask. "Which has the least?"

Discussing the Graph   When the graph was complete, we stepped back to look at it. "Look!" I said. "Isn't our graph amazing?"

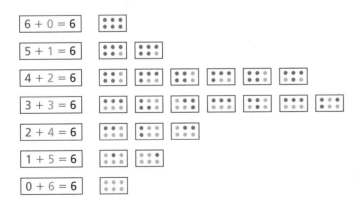

"Are you surprised about what the graph looks like?" I asked.

"All the threes have a lot," explained Richard as other children excitedly raised their hands, anxious to share what they saw. I write children's statements

on the graph because I want the children to know that a graph has a story to tell, and that the children's mathematical thinking can be written down.

"Does anyone else have an observation?" I asked.

"The fours almost reach the threes," Laura told us.

"What do you mean by the fours?" I asked her.

"It's the four red and two yellow," she explained. "It's almost the three and three." I wrote *The 4 red and 2 yellow almost reach the 3 and 3.*

"All the threes reached all the way to the end!" said Omar excitedly. I wrote his words.

"What about the top and bottom of the paper?" I asked. "What does it tell us?"

Alicia spoke up. "All the yellows have a little bit."

"A little, like the reds," added Nina.

I wrote these ideas down.

I then turned their attention to the shape of the data. The shape of a graph can be informative. It can tell a story that we can interpret and understand. "What does the shape look like?" I asked.

"It's like two tall buildings," Heriberto said. "Like in New York." It did look like a city skyline.

"It looks like an elevator going up with the circles," Fabian said. I wrote these observations down.

"Anything else?" I asked.

"It's a hotel with little round windows," said Alicia.

"Or a flag," added Carina. I added these ideas to the summary statements.

"You've explained in many ways that the graph is long in the middle and has only a few all-reds or all-yellows. Why do you think it's that way?" I asked.

The children looked at me blankly until finally Amanda raised her hand. "We just kept getting three and three."

"Four reds came up a lot," added Omar. "I threw them and I got it."

I tried to ask the question in a different way. "Do you think if we did the same thing tomorrow, that the graph would still have a lot in the middle and only a few all-reds and all-yellows?"

Amanda spoke up again. "It won't be the same," she said. "We're doing it again and it's not gonna be the same."

"It won't be exactly the same, but do you think it'll look kind of like this? Or do you think you'll get a whole lot of all-reds and a whole lot of all-yellows?" They were beginning to develop expectations of which color configurations were common and which were less common, and I wanted to reinforce this thinking even though they were some years away from learning about probability. I wanted them to see that this activity would always yield a graph of a similar, if not exact, shape.

"I don't know," said Carlos. "Let's try it!" And we did repeat the investigation again and again. We tried six counters several times, and then we explored five and seven and eight. The children got some good number practice, and at the same time they were developing an early understanding of probability.

Amanda summed up her findings by saying, "It's really hard to get all reds or all yellows. But you can get the ones in the middle a lot." When Amanda studies probability when she's older, she will find a way to explain why this happens.

Linking Assessment and Instruction

You may wish to make the following observations:

- Did the children have to count each red and yellow dot? Did they instantly recognize quantities?
- Once the children counted one of the colors, could they predict what the other color would be?
- Could the children easily record the equations to match the counters?
- Were the children surprised to consistently have the same answer for the number sentences? Or did they expect that to happen?
- What language did the children use to describe the graph? Over time, did the children continue to be surprised to get all reds or all yellows? Did they come to expect that the graph would have a bell-shaped curve?

Bead Boards

SIX BIRDS

OVERVIEW

This lesson introduces children to the characteristics of bead boards and conventions for using them. The children begin by discussing how to use bead boards and then explore them in different ways.

Then the children use the boards to figure out all the different ways that six birds can be arranged on two branches, with some birds on an upper branch and some on a lower branch.

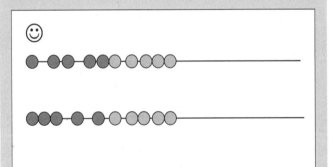

MATERIALS

- bead boards, 1 per child (see "Teaching Notes")
- For each bead board:
    - 18 inches of $\frac{1}{8}$-inch elastic
    - 10-inch-long piece of $3\frac{1}{2}$-inch vinyl blind (purchase the lightest, least-expensive kind)
    - 10 pony beads of one color
    - 10 pony beads of a contrasting color
    - 1 permanent marker

TIME

- one class period

Teaching Directions

1. Pass out the bead boards and have the students help decide on the norms for how they will be used. For example, no pulling on the elastic or "playing the guitar."

2. Point out the happy face and explain that it indicates the proper way to hold the bead board.

3. Explain that the numbers they'll build will be on the side with the happy face. Show them how to carefully slide the beads. Give them a chance to explore the boards for themselves.

4. Ask the children to explain what they notice about the beads on the boards. Discuss the fact that there are twenty beads, that there are ten in each row, and that the colors are in groups of five.

5. Help the children become better acquainted with the organization of the bead board by having them build special numbers with it (for example how old they are, how many sisters they have, how many pancakes they eat for breakfast). Or have the children sing a favorite counting song or retell a counting story using the bead board to represent the changing numbers.

6. Introduce the story. Tell them that one winter morning you peeked out your frosty window and saw two tree branches with six birds on them. Explain that the birds on each branch were cold and huddled closely together. Some of the birds were on the top branch, some were on the bottom. Explain to the students that you want them to pretend that the beads are the birds and the elastic is the branches, and that you will be building arrangements and talking about several ways the birds could be arranged.

7. Introduce the investigation: There are six birds. Some are on the top branch and some are on the bottom branch. How many could be on each branch? What different ways can six birds be arranged? After the children find one arrangement, ask them to record it on paper with words, numbers, or pictures. Then have them look for another arrangement.

8. As the students work, observe how they find different combinations of six and how they represent their work.

9. During discussion time, invite the students to share what they discovered. On the chalkboard write number sentences showing all the different arrangements that they found. Write the combinations vertically, the upper number representing the birds on the top branch and the lower number representing the birds on the bottom branch. (Include 6 and 0 if the children decide that it fits the story.)

$$
\begin{array}{ccccccc}
0 & 1 & 2 & 3 & 4 & 5 & 6 \\
+6 & +5 & +4 & +3 & +2 & +1 & +0
\end{array}
$$

10. Ask the students to discuss the pattern that they see in the numbers and why it is there. Discuss how a pattern can help us know whether we have all the possible combinations.

Teaching Notes

The bead board promotes thinking in specific ways. The organization of beads into fives and tens helps children use these numbers as landmarks as they build numbers. Furthermore, "compensation," or adding a quantity of beads to one number and subtracting the same amount of beads from the other number, is a strategy that is likely to emerge. With cubes, children often take some from one area and then put those same beads in the other area. When using the bead board, children actually have to add beads and then subtract different beads to maintain the same quantity.

Bead boards are a useful tool that are simple and inexpensive to make. Materials cost about $1.50 each, if you purchase the longest vertical blinds in packs of ten at a home-improvement store. Pony beads are generally available in small or large quantities at craft or fabric stores. And although packages of elastic can be purchased at many craft stores, I often find that it's less expensive when purchased by the yard at fabric stores.

It takes about ten minutes to assemble a bead board once you have the materials gathered and the elastic and vertical blinds cut to length.

Instructions for making the bead boards are as follows:

Using an eight-penny nail and a hammer, tap four holes in the vinyl, 1 inch apart vertically and 8 inches apart horizontally. (Optional: Drill holes with an $\frac{1}{8}$-inch drill bit.)

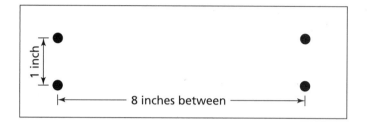

Twist the nail in the holes to enlarge the holes as much as possible.

Holding the vinyl piece so that the convex side is facing you, thread the two ends of the elastic through the back right holes, so that the elastic dangles out in equal lengths over the convex side. String five beads of one color and five of the other on the top and bottom elastic lengths.

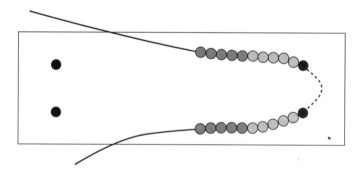

Thread the elastic ends through the left-hand holes to the back of the vinyl. Tie the ends of the elastic tightly. Trim the ends to $\frac{1}{2}$ inch. (You may want to press the holes against the table to flatten any vinyl edges that feel sharp.)

With a permanent marker, draw a happy face on the top left corner of the board. Ensure that the beads on all of the boards are strung in the same order.

The Lesson

A group of children surrounded me on the rug. I held a stack of bead boards. "I'd like you all to know one thing about the bead boards," I said. "They're a very special tool that we are going to use during math time. They're very precious and you'll need to treat them with care. What will it look like when we are using the bead boards carefully?"

"We won't bang them or hurt them," said Alejandrina.

"Or throw them," added Omar.

"Those are good ideas," I agreed. "And even though they have stretchy elastic, you'll never pretend you're playing the guitar or be rough with them. What words describe how you'll work with the bead boards?" I asked.

"Gentle," answered Navin.

"Be careful," Luis added.

I handed each child a bead board, doing so with almost exaggerated care. I watched as the children's body language reflected my instructions. I find that when I communicate how precious our math tools are, whether cubes or counters or anything else, and when I show special care for the tools myself, the children respond likewise.

"We're going to use these to help us think about numbers," I said. "The beads slide back and forth on the elastic." I showed them what I meant. "Take some time now to try them out and see what you notice about them." I know how important it is for children to have the opportunity to freely explore new materials. They need to try out new items for themselves before they can be expected to focus on what I ask of them.

Once the children had had sufficient time to explore the items, I said, "I'd like you to tell me all the things you notice about the bead boards."

"Some beads are red and some beads are blue," Sereslinda offered.

"There's one, two, three, four, five, six, seven, eight, nine, ten on the top," said Heriberto, moving each bead as he counted.

"And there's ten on the bottom too," added Gerardo.

"Ten and ten is twenty," said Navin.

"Do you notice anything else?" I asked. I wanted to bring the students' attention to the groups of five.

"There's a happy face," said Sereslinda.

"I'm glad you noticed that," I said, "because that tells you how to hold the bead board. Make sure that the happy face is right side up, so that the eyes are on top and the smile is at the bottom." A few children readjusted their bead boards. Gerardo turned his upside down and then right side up, to see the difference.

"What else do you notice?" I inquired.

"There's one, two, three, four, five red beads," said Alejandrina.

"Let's check," I said, wanting all the children to understand that the beads were grouped in fives. The children counted these beads independently.

"And there's five blue, and five red, and five blue," added Navin.

"Is that so?" I said. "Let's all check." Again, I focused the students' attention on this important attribute of the bead board.

I moved on to introduce other conventions of the tool. I slid all the beads to the right, away from the happy face. Then I covered all the beads with my hand. "Right now the bead board shows zero. And now it shows one," I said, sliding a red bead into view. "Now it shows two." I slid another bead over. "You show how many by sliding beads over to the happy face." I gave the children a moment to try this for themselves.

"Let's sing a song," I said, wanting to give the children a chance to consolidate this idea of building numbers by sliding the beads to the left side. I began to sing, "One little, two little, three little pizzas, four little, five little six little pizzas, seven little, eight little, nine little pizzas, ten little pizza pies." The children joined in and as we sang we slid beads one by one to the side with the happy face.

"Now we're going to eat our pizzas," I said, and I sang, "Ten little, nine little, eight little pizzas," and so on, moving the beads one at a time to the other side. When we finished, Alejandrina said, "Let's sing 'La Bamba.'"

"Let's do that at circle time today," I answered. "Right now, I'm going to tell you a story."

"You know it's January and it's very cold these days," I began. "I got up on a cold and cloudy morning. I was shivering and quivering. I got out of bed and peeked out of the window. Do you know what I saw?" The children's eyes were on me. They like when I tell made-up stories. "I saw a tree outside and on a branch were six birds, shivering and quivering. Can you show me those six cold birds on the top part of your board?" I asked.

The children slid six red beads over to the left side on the top elastic. Some of their beads were separated by a space, and I wanted them to be close together, so I reinforced this through the story. "The birds were so cold that they were huddled closely together to keep warm. Push your beads together to show this." I wanted the children to decompose numbers into just two parts today.

"Then I peeked out my window again, shivering and quivering," I continued, "and I saw *another* branch underneath. And there were *still* six birds, shivering and quivering. But some birds were on the top branch and some birds were on the bottom branch. What do you think I saw?" I asked.

I waited while the children arranged their beads. "Remember," I reminded them, "build on the side with the happy face." I paused. "Who wants to show us how those six birds might have looked?"

"I've got three birds on the top and three on the bottom," said Gerardo. Doubles seem to come easily to Gerardo, as to many of the children.

"Mine's four on the top and two on the bottom," said Navin. "But I can take two off the top and bring two over on the bottom and it's still six." Navin was demonstrating his understanding of compensation, keeping the total constant by taking off one amount from one place and adding it to the other.

Alejandrina built on Navin's idea. "I've got two on top and four down on the bottom. I can change it to two down and four up."

Sereslinda tried out the same idea. "I think it's four on top and one on the bottom. I could do it one on top and four on the bottom."

"Does that make six birds?" I asked.

"Oops, I mean five and one," she said, correcting herself.

"It can be like this," said Navin, showing me two beads, a space, two beads, a space, and two more beads and a space.

"These birds are cold and are all huddled together," I said, wanting to maintain the convention of how we would be using the bead boards.

Navin slid two pairs of beads together on the left, removed a pair of beads from the top, and added a pair of beads to the bottom.

I moved on to the activity. "Today I'd like you to find all the different ways that you can to have those six cold birds be on two branches. I'd like you to show on paper what you find out using pictures or numbers or however you can. When you find a way, show it with pictures or numbers," I said. "Then see if you can find another way, and record that. Find as many ways as you can that the six birds can be arranged."

The children got to work. Some selected red and blue crayons, matching the red and blue beads, but none used the different crayon colors to stand for the different bead colors.

Navin began by placing his beads so that two were on top and four were on the bottom. He then drew two lines on his paper and used circles to represent that number of beads.

Alejandrina kept all six of her beads on the top of her board. "It's six birds," she told herself. She drew

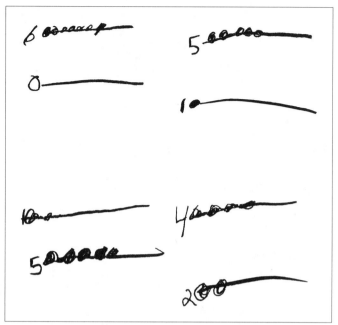

FIGURE 12–1 Alejandrina made five and one and then turned it into one and five by removing four beads from the top and adding four beads to the bottom.

two lines and made seven blue circles on the top line. "One, two, three, four, five, six, seven, cross out the seven," she said. "It's six. I messed up. I could make a six and zero." Alejandrina often thinks out loud as she works. (See Figure 12–1.)

Alejandrina returned to her board and removed one bead from the top and added one to the bottom. "Five birds on the top. That's one on the bottom," she said. Alejandrina again used her blue crayon to draw two lines. Then she drew five circles on the top and one circle on the bottom. "Five plus one makes six," she said.

Alejandrina then demonstrated her understanding of the commutative property of addition. "So it can also be one and five." She drew the corresponding circles without using her bead board.

"What made you think of that?" I asked her.

"I just knew," she answered.

"Can you build that on your bead board?" I asked. I wanted to watch her demonstrate her thinking on the board. "Take four off and put four on," she said, using the strategy of compensation to adjust her board.

Luis and Alicia put three beads on top and three beads on the bottom of their boards. Luis wrote *3 + 3*. Then he took one bead off the bottom and added one to the top. "It's four and two," he announced.

Alicia carefully drew two branches with three birds on the top and three on the bottom. Then she

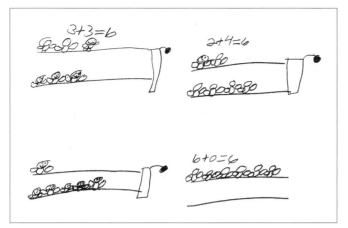

FIGURE 12–2 Alicia made a combination and then slid off each bead before making another combination.

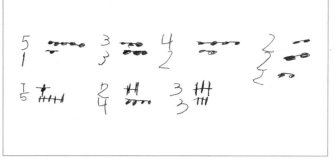

FIGURE 12–3 Nina found six combinations and then changed the story to have three branches.

wrote the equation *3 + 3 = 6*. I watched Alicia slide all the beads away before building her new combination of two birds on the top and four on the bottom. "Four and two," she told me.

"Yes," I agreed. "That makes six altogether." (See Figure 12–2.)

Jennifer was working randomly, trying different numbers of beads and then counting them to see if there were six. I watched as she counted seven beads. "You need six beads," I said. "Is that more or less than seven?"

"It's not so many," answered Jennifer.

"Then how can you change the beads?" I asked her.

"Take some away?" she answered uncertainly. But she persisted in her random counting. She found six and made six dots on one line. I let her do what made sense to her.

Navin showed me his paper. "They're not the same," he told me.

"What's not the same?" I asked.

"They're five and one right there, and one and five right there."

I wanted him to move to more precise language. "What is the same?" I asked.

"The numbers: one and five," Navin answered.

"What's different?" I asked.

"They're in different places," Navin answered. He was demonstrating understanding of the commutative property of addition.

Alejandrina called out to me. "Oh, Mrs. Confer! I made another way. Two and four, and four and two."

"How did you find that out?" I asked.

"They're just a different way," Alejandrina explained. "The two could be up or down."

Next to Alejandrina, Sereslinda was looking at her picture of beads, which didn't match the numbers she had written. "That's not right," Alejandrina informed her.

"Oh!" Sereslinda laughed. "One more!" She added another dot. "I wish I could make one and take it home," Sereslinda said wistfully.

"Maybe our families could make them during family math night," I suggested.

I watched Nina find six different combinations. Then she just used the top line and made three groups of two. "Three branches," she said to herself. (See Figure 12–3.)

A Discussion

When the children had seemed to run out of ideas, I asked for their attention. "I'd like to find out what you discovered," I said. Hands shot into the air confidently.

"There's three birds on the top and three on the bottom," said Javier. "Three plus three makes six." So in the center of the chalkboard I wrote:

$$\begin{array}{r} 3 \\ +3 \\ \hline 6 \end{array}$$

I then showed this on my bead board.

I intended to write the children's ideas in consecutive order so we could later talk about patterns.

"Who found out something else?" I asked. Again hands waved. I was pleased that the bead board was proving a helpful tool for the children.

"See, there could be two birds on the top and then that makes four on the bottom, because you took one off the top and you have to put one more on the bottom," explained Navin. I had watched several children search for combinations randomly. I wondered if Navin's explanations made sense to them.

Jennifer had an idea. "You could have one on the top and five on the bottom," she said, showing this configuration on the board. I wrote this combination in front of the previous one. I wanted to end up with the equations in a sequence. As the children shared new combinations I showed them on my bead board and then wrote the equation. Eventually the sequence showed:

$$\begin{array}{ccccc} 1 & 2 & 3 & 4 & 5 \\ +5 & +4 & +3 & +2 & +1 \\ \hline 6 & 6 & 6 & 6 & 6 \end{array}$$

I drew the children's attention to the chalkboard. "What do you notice?" I asked. The children's hands shot up immediately.

"It goes one, two, three, four, five," said Jennifer.

"And it's the other way on the bottom. You start over there and go one, two, three, four, five," said Gerardo, pointing the opposite way.

"It's all sixes on the bottom," said Alejandrina.

"Why is that?" I asked.

"'Cause all the birds are six," she told us.

Gerardo came up to the chalkboard. He touched the numbers at the beginning and end of the equation line. "See, one, one," he said, pointing to the 1s in 1 + 5 and 5 + 1. "And five, five, and two, two, and four, four, and three and three are together," he said, pointing to these numbers as he went along.

"Let's look at this pattern together and talk about why it's there," I said. "The top numbers are getting bigger and the bottom numbers are getting smaller. Why does that happen?" There were no suggestions. So I said, "Let's build the combinations on our bead board."

I held up my bead board and made the combination as I spoke. "Let's build one bird on the top and five on the bottom." The children did likewise. "Now," I continued, "What's next?" I pointed to the next combination. "Two on the top and four on the bottom."

I watched as the children manipulated the beads to reflect this combination. Most added one bead to the top and took one off the bottom. Jennifer cleared all the beads from the first arrangement and then added two beads to the top and slid four on the bottom. My bead board still showed one and five. "What should I do?" I asked, prompting the students to articulate a strategy. "You just put one more on the top and take one away at the bottom," Sereslinda said. Other children nodded their assent.

"Now, what's next?" I asked, pointing to the next combination. Again most children added a bead to the top and removed one from the bottom. But Jennifer, and this time Gerardo, too, had slid all their beads off and then built three and three. I again asked the group to explain what they did, and I again showed the compensation strategy with my bead board.

We continued this way until we had made the entire series. Jennifer was still taking all the beads off each time, which was fine. I wanted all the children to do what made sense them.

I returned to the consecutive pattern that the children had noticed. "Why do the top numbers get bigger and the bottom numbers get smaller?" I asked.

"Because you always put one more on the top and you always take one away from the bottom," Sereslinda explained.

"It goes one, two, three, four, five," said Alicia.

"But why?" I asked.

"When you put a new one on top you get it from the other one," she said. "It's still six." It would be interesting to see whether the children would use this consecutive pattern as a tool in similar investigations with other numbers.

Linking Assessment and Instruction

You may wish to make the following observations:

- How did the children make combinations of six? Did they make random arrangements and count to see whether there were six in all? Did they take off the first arrangement before building a new arrangement?
- Did children adjust an arrangement to make a new arrangement? For example, did they take off a quantity from the top and add that same quantity to the bottom? This indicates good understanding of number relationships. Other children remove all the beads before building a new arrangement.
- How did the children represent the arrangement? Did they draw the beads? Did they draw birds? Or did they use numbers and/or equations?
- Did children independently talk about relationships and patterns in the different arrangements? This habit of mind will encourage the children to develop new understandings about numbers and our number system.

Roll and Add

CHAPTER 13

OVERVIEW

This activity helps children develop strategies for addition. A die is rolled four times to identify four numbers. The teacher uses those four numbers to write an addition number sentence. The children figure out the answer and share how they solved the equation. The teacher records their thinking, also in the form of equations. Later this turns into a game that partners play independently.

MATERIALS

- dice with 1 to 6 dots (a large foam die works best in a whole group setting, but any 1–6 dot die can be used), 1 per group of players
- sets of 24 counters, available for any children who might need them
- small dot die, 1 for each student or pair of students

TIME

Lesson 1

- fifteen-minute classroom routine

Lesson 2

- one class period

Teaching Directions

Lesson 1
Whole Group

1. Gather the students in a circle on the rug. Have four students each roll the die one time. Write each number as it is rolled in the form of an addition equation, leaving the total blank. For example, if the students roll 4, 3, 4, and 2, write $4 + 3 + 4 + 2 = $.

2. Ask students to add the numbers, mentally if they can, or by using the cubes if necessary.

3. Ask the students to share how they solved the problem. As the students share, record their thinking on the board by writing equations. Name the strategies that each child used, such as counting all, counting on, using doubles, making fives, and so on.

   For example, with the numbers rolled in the above instance, a student might add the 4s first, then add the 3 by counting on, and then mentally add the 2. To record this, you might write:

$$4 + 3 + 4 + 2$$
$$8 \ldots 9, 10, 11$$
$$11 + 2 = 13$$

4. Repeat Steps 1–3 to build and solve several problems.

Lesson 2
Playing Independently

1. Invite the students to play *Roll and Add* individually or with a partner.

2. Give each student or pair of students a small dot die. Provide each student with a blank sheet of paper on which to record his or her equations.

Teaching Notes

In this activity, children develop strategies for adding strings of numbers. Children use various addition strategies to make computation easier. Through class discussions, all children are exposed to these ideas. Over time these strategies spread throughout the group, as children try them out, make sense of them, and finally adopt them as efficient ways to add numbers.

Some strategies that first-grade children use are counting all, counting on, finding doubles, using doubles, and making tens. For example, to solve 5 + 6 students might:

- Count all. These children will count five fingers by ones from one, "One, two, three, four, five," and then put up six fingers, and continue counting, "Six, seven, eight, nine, ten, eleven."
- Count on from five. These children remember that they have five and count on their fingers, saying, "Six, seven, eight, nine, ten, eleven."
- Find doubles. These children will add the doubles first rather than add the numbers in sequence.
- Use doubles. These children might say, "I know that I have five and inside the six is another five. Five and five makes ten, and one more is eleven." They might use doubles in another way by saying, "I know that six plus six is twelve, but this is six plus five, so one less is eleven."
- Make tens. These children might say, "Inside the five is a one and a four. I can add the four to the six, and that's ten. One more is eleven."

When the children share a strategy, I record it by writing a number sentence. I try to use different recording methods so that the children see there are many different ways to record. For example, if a child thinks about 9 + 7 as 10 + 6, I might simply write 9 + 7 = 10 + 6. Or I might show all the steps in the child's thinking by writing:

$$9 + 7$$
$$\diagdown\diagup$$
$$1 \quad 6 \qquad 9 + 1 = 10$$
$$10 + 6 = 16$$

In the same way that I want children to constantly make sense of mathematics, I also want them to make sense of ways to record mathematical thinking.

I introduce the whole-group version of the game first. I do this early in the year, often beginning by rolling the die three times, rather than four. The activity becomes a short routine game that we play during morning circle time throughout the year. After children are well acquainted with this activity, they play the game in partners. They take turns rolling the die. Both children record the equation, and they each record how they solved the problem.

Lesson 1: Whole Group

I showed the children the large fuzzy die that had hung from my adult son's rearview mirror. "We're going to use this to think about easy ways to add four numbers," I told them. I familiarized them with the die by rolling it and having them call out the numbers they saw on its face.

Then I held up the side of the die with six dots. "How did you know this was six?" I asked. I wanted to remind the children that they know that smaller numbers are inside larger numbers. This concept is basic to building number strategies. "It's three and three," Carina said. "I see four and two," added Becky. We did the same thing with the side showing five dots.

Then I introduced the activity. "We're going to roll the die four times and write down the numbers that we get. We're going to add up those four numbers to see how many dots we rolled altogether."

Miguel rolled the die first. "No, roll it like this," intervened Alfredo, showing him how to shake the die first. "No, I like how I did it," said Miguel. "I've been playing this game for, like, two years." Miguel rolled a 6. "I'm six years old!" he crowed.

I wrote a 6 on the board.

Juanita went next and rolled a 3. "My brother's going to be three," she said.

I find it fascinating how young children consistently make connections to their lives. I wrote a 3 on the board. After other children rolled two more 3s, we had the following equation:

$$6 + 3 + 3 + 3 = \underline{}$$

"What I'd like you to do is think in your head about how many dots we rolled altogether. When you know, I want you to put your thumb up like this, so that I know that you have an idea. If you can do it in your head, fine," I said. "The cubes are here if you need them." I placed zip-top bags containing sets of cubes near the children.

Jennifer, Carlos, and Alfredo used the cubes to solve the problem; several used their fingers to count on; and many added the numbers mentally. When most of the children had signaled that they were finished, I called on Lorena.

"It was fifteen," she said. "I figured it out."

"How did you figure it out?" I inquired.

"I know," said Alfredo, "it's easy. She copied me."

"You'll all get a chance to share how you thought about the problem," I said. "Right now Lorena's going to talk. See if you can understand what she did."

"I made six and then with six, I made twelve, and . . . then it's fifteen," Lorena said.

"Let's see if we can write what Lorena did in numbers," I said. "There are many ways to show her thinking; this is one way." I wrote and spoke at the same time. "Lorena knows that three and three makes six. I can draw lines to show that she combined three and three. I'll write *six* under that." I did this, and then continued. "Next Lorena saw the other six and put them together; that's what these two lines mean. Six and six makes twelve, so I'll write a *twelve* under the lines." I had drawn this:

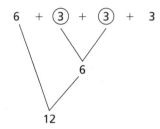

"But Lorena knew that she still needed to add that last three," I continued. "What did you do to find out what twelve and three are?" I asked her. Lorena shrugged. I tried again. "How did you know that twelve and three are fifteen?"

"I counted on my fingers," Lorena said.

"How did you count?" I persisted. "What numbers did you say?"

She finally was able to answer my question. "I went twelve, then I knew thirteen, fourteen, fifteen." I repeated her words, then articulated her strategy to the group. "This is one way to show that you counted on using your fingers":

12 . . . 13 14 15

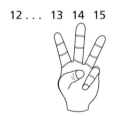

I continued. "I know that some of you did it in a different way, because we all think differently. Who has another way to share?" I wanted the children to see a variety of strategies.

Alfredo spoke up. "It's six and three and three and three."

"That's true," I said. "How did you put those numbers together?"

"It's six and then three more," he answered.

"What does that make?" I asked.

"Can I use the cubes?" Alfredo asked.

"Of course," I said. Not all of the children could do this activity without using manipulatives. We made a train of six and three trains of three. Alfredo counted all six cubes and then the three cubes and got nine. "And then I put three more and that makes one, two, three, four, five, six, seven, eight, nine, ten, eleven, twelve, thirteen, fourteen, fifteen," he said.

"I wonder how we could write this," I said to the children. "Draw the cubes," Alicia suggested, so I drew the following:

| 1 | 2 | 3 | 4 | 5 | 6 | | 7 | 8 | 9 | | 10 | 11 | 12 | | 13 | 14 | 15 |

"Did anyone do it a different way?" I asked. Miguel wanted to share. "I did three plus three and it's six." I drew two lines to connect the threes and wrote a 6 under it:

$$6 + 3 + 3 + 3$$
$$6$$

"Then I put three more and that makes nine," Miguel continued.

"How did you know six and three makes nine?" I asked.

"Seven, eight, nine," he said, counting on with his fingers. I wrote those numbers in a line. "I put commas between the numbers so it doesn't look like one giant number," I commented. "Then what did you do?" I continued.

"Then I put the six and nine together, and ten, eleven, twelve, thirteen, fourteen, fifteen," he said, counting on using his fingers.

"I'm going to write all the numbers you said, and I'm putting commas between each number," I told the group. I had illustrated Miguel's thinking this way:

$$6 + 3 + 3 + 3$$
$$6 + 3 = 9$$
$$6: 7, 8, 9$$
$$9 + 6 = 15$$
$$9: 10, 11, 12, 13, 14, 15$$

"I don't get it," said Alfredo.

"Miguel counted on," I explained. "He knew there were nine already, so he didn't need to count them again. Some people think one way is easier, some people think another way is easier. What's important is that everyone finds a way that makes sense to them. What if you wanted to count by ones?" I continued.

Alfredo put up six fingers and we counted them.

"And now we can add three more," I said.

Alfredo put up three more fingers and we kept counting: "Seven, eight, nine . . ." We continued this way until we got to fifteen, and I said, "One way to write it is like this":

1, 2, 3, 4, 5, 6, 7, 8, 9, 10, 11, 12, 13, 14, 15

"The commas help you know that it's not just one large number," I reminded them.

"We have time to hear one more way to think about this problem," I said.

Sereslinda had an idea. "I put three and another three. That makes six."

I connected the 3s and wrote 6 underneath. To name her strategy for the children, I commented, "You did the doubles first, three and three."

"Then I put the six with the three," Sereslinda continued.

"What did you get?" I asked.

She counted on her fingers. "It makes nine."

"Hey, that's my way," Miguel said. I was glad that he had made a connection between his strategy and Sereslinda's.

"So now you have nine and six," I said to Sereslinda. "How many is that?"

"That's eleven," she answered. "No, no." She corrected herself. "It's fifteen." She counted on from nine to fifteen.

Sereslinda's thinking looked like this:

$$6 + 3 + 3 + 3$$
$$9 \qquad 6$$
$$3 + 3 = 6$$
$$6 + 3 = 9$$
$$9: 10, 11, 12, 13, 14, 15$$

The children had seen several strategies, and that was enough for now. We would play this game over and over during the year. Over time the children would be introduced to and try out new strategies and ways of representing their thinking.

Lesson 2: Playing Independently

Eight children sat in a circle around me during math workshop; I had gathered together this particular group to focus on strategies for combining numbers.

"In a minute you're going to play *Roll and Add* as a partner game, and you'll represent your thinking on paper by yourselves. But let's play a few times together first, so we remember how to play. Let's take turns rolling the die," I said, showing the children the regular small dot die with dots for 1 through 6. Four children took turns rolling the die, and I recorded their numbers as an equation on the board:

$$2 + 4 + 4 + 5 = \underline{}$$

"Take a moment to think about it," I said. "You can use cubes, or your fingers, or just do it in your head. When you think you know the answer, put your thumb up quietly so the others can keep thinking."

After they'd had sufficient time to solve the problem I asked, "Who has an idea that they'd like to share?"

Carina said, "It's fifteen." Other children nodded.

"It's fourteen," said Juanita.

I wrote both of these numbers on the board. "Who'd like to share how they got their answer?" I asked.

"I will," said Alejandrina. She put her index fingers on the two 4s. "It's four and four and you get eight. Those are seven," she said, moving her fingers to the 2 and the 5.

"You know what four and four is," I said, drawing lines to connect those numbers, and writing 8. "And you also know what five and two is," I said, also connecting those two numbers.

$$2 + 4 + 4 + 5$$
$$8$$
$$7$$

Alejandrina continued, explaining, "I think that seven plus seven is fourteen. So eight plus seven has to be fifteen."

"How did you figure out eight plus seven?" I asked. "I'm not sure I followed your thinking."

I wanted the other children to hear Alejandrina's numeric reasoning, which used doubles.

"Well," said Alejandrina, "it's one more than fourteen. It's seven plus seven and then you add one more."

I restated Alejandrina's reasoning for the group as I recorded her thinking in equation form. "You want to know what eight plus seven is," I said, writing:

$$8 + 7 =$$

"You know that seven plus seven equals fourteen." And I wrote:

$$7 + 7 = 14$$

"But you have eight plus seven, so it has to be one more than fourteen," I said, writing:

$$14 + 1 = 15$$

"Can anyone else explain what Alejandrina did?" I asked.

Navin spoke up. "She had to put on an extra."

"I used one way to write how Alejandrina thought about the problem. But she might write her thinking a little differently. And that's OK—there are many ways to represent someone's thinking. Did anyone think about this problem in a different way?"

Victoria had an idea. "Five and four is nine. And four plus two is six. I forget nine and six," she said.

"Take a moment to think while I write what you told us," I said. I wrote:

$$2 + 4 + 4 + 5$$

"Now," I said, "what did you do with the six and the nine?"

"I did the nine first," she answered, "and I counted nine . . . ten, eleven, twelve, thirteen, fourteen, fifteen."

Victoria had not moved beyond counting on. In time she would begin using other strategies. She was aware of them, but she didn't yet trust her own ability to adopt them.

"You counted on from the nine," I said. "You could have counted on from six. Is it faster to count on from the bigger number?" I asked.

Victoria nodded. I wrote:

$$9: 10, 11, 12, 13, 14, 15$$

"Did anybody do it a different way?" I asked again.

"It's fifteen," Juanita said, correcting her first idea. "I can see the six and nine and then I can give one to the nine to make ten. And ten and five makes fifteen. I just know that."

"Let's think about what you said," I told Juanita. "Did you start like Victoria did?" Juanita nodded and I copied how Victoria began:

$$2 + 4 + 4 + 5$$

Juanita continued. "There's a one inside the six and I gave it to the nine. That makes ten." Although many children in the class liked to look for tens in a sequence of numbers, few could break a number apart to make a number that would complete a ten. This was a big step for Juanita.

"Did you split the six into five and one?" I asked her. Juanita nodded. I wrote:

$$6 \quad + \quad 9$$
$$5 + 1$$
$$1 + 9 = 10$$
$$10 + 5 = 15$$

"You wanted to make a ten, and you know that nine plus one makes ten. So you got a one from the six and gave it to the nine. It's a lot easier to add when you can make a ten," I concluded.

"Now I'd like you to play *Roll and Add* with a partner," I said. "Let's have Carina with Alejandrina, Navin with Juanita, Amanda with Robert, and Victoria and Heriberto." These children were already seated next to each other. "I'd like you to take turns rolling the die until you have four numbers to add. Then each of you writes the problem and figures it out in your own way. When you're both done, look at what your partner did and see if you can understand that person's thinking. Then play a few more times." I left the table to check on the other children engaged in math workshop. In a few minutes, I returned to the children playing *Roll and Add*.

Alejandrina had written two 2s and two 4s on her paper without any addition signs. Although this was not standard representation, I chose not to intervene, as my goal was to have the children represent problems in ways that made sense to them. Over time we'd move toward conventional representations. "I hope it's not another five!" Alejandrina said, referring to the numbers we had rolled together as a group.

Carina wrote the equation using the plus sign and grouped the 4s and the 2s. She wrote *8* under the 4s and *4* under the 2s. "That's weird; eight and four," Carina said. "Four and four is eight."

Alejandrina had also combined the doubles but seemed to be having trouble with the equation she had written: $8 + 4 = $. Her brow was furrowed.

"What are you thinking?" I asked her.

"Let me think," she said; she wasn't ready to talk. After Alejandrina stared at the numbers a minute, she carefully wrote a *12*. "It's twelve," she announced.

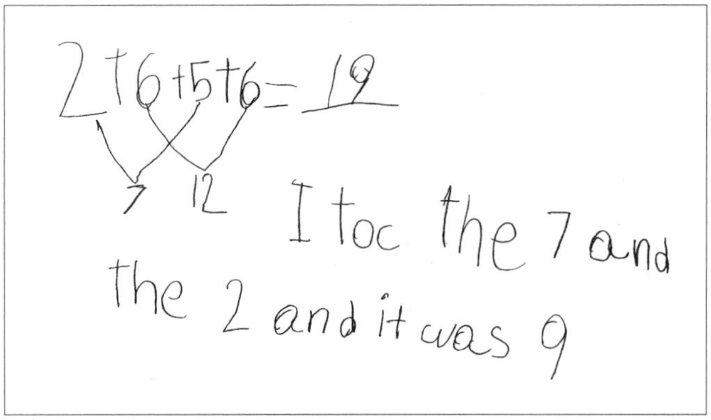

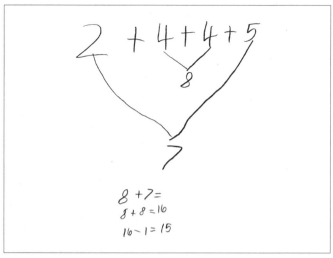

FIGURE 13–1   To add 7 + 12, Heriberto first decomposed the 12 into 10 + 2. Then he gave the 2 to the 7. Heriberto knew that 10 + 9 is 19.

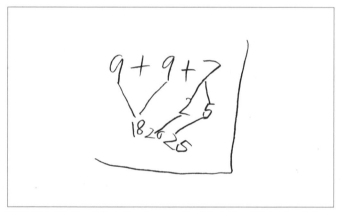

FIGURE 13–2   Since Amanda knew that 8 + 8 is 16, she realized that 8 + 7 had to be 15.

"How did you figure out that eight and four are twelve?" I asked.

Alejandrina shrugged. "The numbers are in my head," she said.

"Can I hear the numbers in your head that helped you figure it out?" I asked.

Alejandrina tapped her head with an index finger, saying, "Eight . . . nine, ten, eleven, twelve."

Carina nodded. "It's twelve. I counted too. It looks like a necklace." Carina pointed to the lines she had made to show how she had combined the doubles.

Victoria and Heriberto had rolled 2, 6, 5, 6. "Six and six is twelve!" said Heriberto. "Then I get the ten from the twelve." He recorded his thinking on paper (see Figure 13–1).

I checked in with Amanda and Robert, who had just rolled 2, 4, 4, 5. Robert, as he often did, had combined the doubles first. Amanda did the same, but how she proceeded was different. "I didn't know eight plus seven," she explained. "But eight and eight is sixteen, so it has to be fifteen." (See Figure 13–2.) She wrote:

$$8 + 7 =$$
$$8 + 8 = 16$$
$$16 - 1 = 15$$

Navin wanted my attention. "This is too easy," he told me.

Navin and Juanita had rolled 1 + 1 + 2 + 1 and 4 + 4 + 3 + 1.

"It's two, three, five," said Juanita, pointing at the first problem. She had easily counted on.

Navin said, "And we got eight, then it's eleven and twelve. Can't we do anything else?"

FIGURE 13–3   After Navin saw that 9 + 9 = 18, he took 2 from the 7 to make 18 + 2 = 20. He easily added 20 + 5 = 25.

I showed them a die with numerals 4 through 9. "Try this," I said. "You might want to roll it three times though, at least at first." The game would be much more challenging with the new die.

They rolled 9, 9, 7. "I know what nine plus nine is, it's eighteen," said Juanita. "Then, eighteen . . . nineteen, twenty, twenty-one, twenty-two, twenty-three, twenty-four, twenty-five." Juanita counted on with her fingers.

Navin was hunched over his paper, deep in thought. He had drawn what appeared to be a jumble of numbers and lines. "How were you thinking?" I asked him.

Navin hesitated, as if to trace his thinking back to the beginning. "I knew nine and nine is eighteen," he said. "And I wanted twenty, so I took two from the seven—eighteen, nineteen, twenty. Then I thought how much was left from the seven and that was five. That's twenty-five."

I looked again at Navin's paper (see Figure 13–3).

"I see," I told him. "You split the seven apart so you could give two to the eighteen and make it twenty. That left five, and you added it to twenty and you got twenty-five." Inviting Navin to use larger numbers changed what he'd thought was a "boring" game into an intriguing problem. He continued to find the activity challenging for the rest of the period.

Extension

To increase the level of difficulty, use a numeral die with the numerals 4 through 9. (You can cover a regular die with blank stick-on labels and write numerals on them, or you can write numerals on a blank wooden die.) The larger numbers encourage children to develop different strategies.

Linking Assessment and Instruction

You may wish to make the following observations:

- Did the children count by ones from the first number? This shows that children's sense of small numbers is still fragile.
- Did the children count on from a larger number? The ability to count on shows number-sense development.
- Did the children combine doubles first? This is one of the first strategies that children adopt.
- Did the children use their knowledge of doubles to solve problems they didn't know?
- Did the children combine numbers to make "friendly numbers" such as five or ten?

CHAPTER 14

Over in the Grasslands

OVERVIEW

Anna Wilson's Over in the Grasslands *reworks a favorite story,* Over in the Meadow, *in a different context, the grasslands of Africa. Children hear about new animals, such as the wildebeest, and think about the familiar pattern of "plus one"— the mother animal and increasing numbers of babies. They then investigate the question: How many feet and tails are there in the lion family? The children use words, numbers, and pictures to explain their thinking.*

MATERIALS

- *Over in the Grasslands*, by Anna Wilson (Boston: Little, Brown, 2000.)
- counters, enough for the children who need to use them
- butcher paper
- markers

TIME

- one class period

Teaching Directions

1. Read the story to the students. Highlight the un- usual kinds of animals, the rhythm of the lan- guage, the familiar pattern, and the illustrations. Frequently bring the students' attention to the number of babies in the families, and the "plus one"—the mothers.

2. Make a chart showing "Number of babies," "Number of moms," and "Number of animals in the family." Fill it in for each family and discuss the patterns that the students see:

Number of babies	Number of mothers	Number of animals in the family
1	1	2
2	1	3
3	1	4
4	1	5
5	1	6
6	1	7
7	1	8
8	1	9
9	1	10
10	1	11

3. Present the problem that the students are to solve: How many feet and tails are in the entire lion family? Ask the students whether they think there are a hundred, or two, and discuss why these can't be the answer. Have partners repeat the question to each other so all students understand the task. Explain that they can use anything in the room to help them figure out the problem. Tell them that they should use words, numbers, and pictures to show their thinking on their paper. Inform them that they will work with a partner but that each will have his or her own paper on which to record.

4. When the students are finished, gather them for a discussion. Discuss the specific things their part- ners did that helped them learn. Then discuss their work by having them share the different ways they represented feet and tails, as well as dif- ferent ways that they combined the numbers.

Teaching Notes

This familiar story pattern invites children to think about the "plus one" number pattern. The number of babies increases by one each time, and each family has one more member than the number of babies. This awareness usually emerges naturally, but I bring it up myself if it does not.

Presenting a problem for children to solve is something of an art. I don't want to model for the children because they often try to copy me rather than do it in a way that makes sense to them. At the same time I do want them to understand what is being asked of them. This is why I spend a lot of time making sure that they understand the problem. We talk about a similar or smaller problem (such as numbers of eyes). I have the children restate the new problem to their math buddy. And I often have the first several children who take a seat explain to the group what they are going to do. If children have questions at their tables, I encourage them to ask their partners or tablemates before they ask me.

Although I make cubes available to students, I find that most children prefer to draw their own less-abstract representations.

In first grade, children are becoming accustomed to explaining their thinking in words, numbers, and pictures. So after the children solve the problem, I frequently have a group discussion about how they represented the problem. Over time I want the children to have a "toolbox" of ways to represent a mathematics problem, as well as strategies for managing the numbers.

The Lesson

The children sat next to their math buddies on the rug. I showed them the book's cover and read the title. "We live in the desert," I said. "What kinds of animals do we have in the Sonoran Desert?" The children had been studying their environment, and readily listed roadrunners, coyotes, quails, javelinas, and jackrabbits. "There's bobcats too," said Alicia, "but not so many. My *tío* had one at his ranch."

"What is a 'grassland'?" I wondered aloud, "And what kinds of animals might we find there?"

"Lions?" said Heriberto, pointing to the cover.

"They're in Africa," said Armando, "like tigers and pythons. They've got big teeth and eat people."

"Lions, tigers, pythons . . . we'll see if they're in this story and what other animals there are," I said.

As I read the first pages of the book, the children became engaged in the rhythm of the language and the beauty of the illustrations.

Suddenly Alicia interrupted us. "Hey, I know this book!" She jumped up and ran to the classroom library. "It's like this one!" She held up *Way Out in the Desert.* I took the book from her. "You're right," I said. "We'll look at it after we finish reading this book."

We continued reading until we got to the page with the lions. "Mrs. Confer!" said Alfredo excitedly. "It's four and five, and three and four was on the other page."

"Oh, you mean there are four babies and five animals in the family," I said. "How many more animals are in the family than babies?"

"One more," said Cristina. "It's the mom."

"And Alfredo noticed that the page before had three babies and four in the family. He sees an important pattern. What do you think will happen on the next page?"

As we continued reading we checked Alfredo's idea by counting the animals in each family and comparing it to the larger written numeral that stood for the number of babies. "It's always one more in the family," said Cristina.

I made a chart on the board that listed "Number of babies," "Number of mothers," and "Number of animals in the family." "This might make it easier to see the patterns that you were talking about," I said. As we reread the book, a different child filled in the chart for each animal family. The chart looked like this:

Number of babies	Number of mothers	Number of animals in the family
1	1	2
2	1	3
3	1	4
4	1	5
5	1	6
6	1	7
7	1	8
8	1	9
9	1	10
10	1	11

"What do you notice about the chart?" I asked.

"It goes one, two, three, four, five, six," said Alfredo, pointing to the first column.

"What goes that way?" I asked, pushing for specific language.

"The babies," he said. "It's always more by one."

We read those numbers aloud. "They do get bigger by one," I agreed, at the same time modeling standard mathematical language. "What else do you notice?" I asked.

"It's one, one, one, one, one, one," said Sereslinda.

"I saw that," Alicia piped up.

"Why is there a one for every family?" I asked.

"There's always one mom," said Laura.

"The family's one more than the babies," Gerardo said. "Two plus one is three and three plus one equals four."

I wrote the equation on the side of the chart. "Where does this number sentence happen in the story?" I asked, pointing to $2 + 1 = 3$. I wanted to help the children see how equations simply describe something that we see.

Gerardo sighed with exaggerated patience. "You see," he said, "two baby hippos and one mom makes three. And three babies and one mom is three plus one equals four. That's how it goes."

I wanted to make sure that I returned to Alicia's comment from the beginning of our talk. "Alicia said that this book is like *Way Out in the Desert*. What do you think she noticed?" I asked, holding the other book up.

"It's like the babies and the moms," said Carina. "It has the same pattern."

"But there's no javelina in this one," countered Juanita.

"They're the same," repeated Alicia.

"Let's do a book comparison study tomorrow during reader's workshop," I said. "We can compare the books and see how they're the same and how they're different. Alicia noticed something very important. Right now," I continued, "I'd like you to solve a problem. Remember this lion family?" I showed the picture on the book's cover. We counted the eyes in the family. "Now I'd like you to find out how many feet and tails are in the family altogether," I said.

I continued. "You can use anything in the room to help you. I'll put cubes on the table to use if you want. But you need to use words, numbers, and pictures on your paper to show how you thought about how many feet and tails are in the lion family. Now I'd like you each to explain the question to your math buddy," I said. I paused as most children turned to each other to talk. When children are on the rug I like to use this technique to keep them talking and actively engaged. Cristina and Brittney just sat there. I reminded them to explain to each other what the problem was about.

After a bit I got the children's attention again. "Who can tell us the problem you're going to solve?" I asked.

"It's the lions," said Cristina. "How many."

"How many what?" I asked.

"How many feet they have," she said.

"Feet and tails," added Carina.

"That's right," I said. "How many feet and tails there are altogether in the lion family. What do you need to put on your paper?"

The children answered "words," "numbers," and "pictures."

I had Amanda and Carlos again explain the question before they went to sit down. As they sat down I congratulated them for quietly finding a place to sit, getting pencils, and writing their names and the title of the book. In this way I labeled my expectations for all the children.

The Children at Work

A quiet buzz filled the room as the children talked at their tables, getting started on the problem. But soon Robert was at my side. "What do we do, draw a lion?" he asked.

"Did you ask your partner your question?" I inquired. "She doesn't know," Robert answered.

"Then you need to check with your tablemates before checking with me. See if you can figure out what to do." Robert returned to his seat. Part of my job is to help children know and use the resources that they have to solve problems for themselves. It's easier in the short run to simply answer children's questions, but in the long run this extra effort pays off in children's independence.

I watched Alicia, who was busy writing a string of 4s. "How old are you?" she asked me. I remembered that I had told them it was my birthday. "I'm older than forty and younger than fifty," I said. "We can play *Guess My Age* after lunch, just like we play *Guess My Number*. What do the fours on your paper stand for?" I inquired.

Alicia thought for a moment. "Wait," she said, her brow furrowed. It's interesting to me how fragile young children's ability to represent can be. Alicia had just been writing 4s, which I assumed stood for each lion's feet. Now she was having trouble retrieving what the 4s meant. I waited, giving her time to think.

"What problem are you trying to solve?" I asked.

"How many the lions have, feet and tails," Alicia told me.

"Would it help to draw a picture?" I asked her.

Alicia drew a lion, emphasizing the feet and tails, and then counted the feet. "One, two, three, four. Oh, I know." And Alicia wrote two more 4s. Then she tapped the four feet on her lion five times, counting the feet and tails for each lion. As she did so, Alicia counted from one to twenty. She wrote = *20* at the end of her equation.

I checked in with Robert, who seemed to be on a path, and then I looked in on Cristina. I was pleased with her positive attitude toward math these days, and her ability to count had grown dramatically. Cristina had written the book's title, her name, and a series of numbers, and she had drawn a lion with teeth. "How's it going, Cristina?" I asked her. She shrugged. "Would you like to think about two lions?" I asked her. "How many feet and tails are on two lions?"

Cristina smiled and drew another lion. She knew just what to do with this smaller problem. I watched as Cristina carefully counted and then recounted the feet and tails. "It's ten," she said, and reached for the number line and found the 10 to copy. "When you finish, you can think about how many feet and tails on three lions," I suggested. I was very pleased with the growth that Cristina had made. (See Figure 14–1.)

Amanda and Carlos had finished the problem quickly. "Would you like a challenge?" I asked them. They nodded.

"I'd like you to think about the wildebeests," I said.

"The what?" asked Carlos.

"The funny-looking piglike creatures," I answered. "There were six babies and the mom. How many feet and tails do *they* have altogether?"

"Whoa-hoh!" said Carlos. He likes a challenge.

Alfredo had written *1 2 3 4 5 6 7 8* on his paper. He was staring at these numbers, confused. "Are you mixed up, Alfredo?" I asked him. He nodded. "What does the one two three four stand for?" I inquired.

"It's the baby feet," he said.

"You did a smart thing," I said. "You showed each foot by making a number. Can I offer you a suggestion?" I asked.

Alfredo nodded.

"Maybe it would help to draw something that shows they go together for one baby," I said. I had often seen other children use this device as a way to organize their work. Alfredo picked up his pencil and drew a shaky line around the first four numbers.

Armando was involved in drawing an intricate picture of lions. One stood high on a cliff and another swung from a vine. "It's the Lion King," he told me, as he bent to count the feet and tails by ones. (See Figure 14–2.)

I looked at another table and saw Navin helping Lorena count in Spanish. A few children had finished. I asked them to do some independent reading until I could look at their papers.

I returned to Alfredo, who had written the numbers *1* through *16*, although several numbers had reversals. He had circled groups of four numbers for each baby and had sketched a small lion inside each circle. My

FIGURE 14–1 Christina successfully counted ten feet and tails on two lions.

FIGURE 14–2 Armando counted twenty-five feet and tails on his intricate lions.

FIGURE 14–3 Alfredo found it helpful to circle the numbers that stood for each lion's feet.

suggestion had made sense to him. Alfredo also had drawn a larger mother lion. He seemed unsure how to proceed numbering the feet. "Is it twenty-one?" he asked me.

"Why don't you read the numbers that you already wrote and see where you are?" I suggested.

Alfredo read his numbers from one and got to sixteen. "It's seventeen, eighteen, nineteen, twenty," he said, and wrote those numbers. Alfredo wrote *fet 20* at the top of his paper.

"What are you going to do now?" I asked Alfredo.

"The tails," he answered. (See Figure 14–3.)

I moved on to check on Alicia. She had written a series of equations that, although correct, seemed to have nothing to do with the problem. "You said number sentences," she told me. I could see that the equations were not a helpful tool for her right now. I focused her back on the meaning of the problem. "Let's see what you can do to solve the problem," I said. "You drew a lion."

"It's the mommy," Alicia informed me.

"Would it help to see what Erin did to solve the problem?" I suggested. Alicia looked at Erin's paper, and when I looked over later I saw Alicia drawing more lions.

Carlos and Amanda returned with their papers. "The pig thing has thirty-six feet," said Carlos.

"No, it's thirty-five," countered Amanda.

Amanda counted the legs and tails on her paper: "Twenty-eight, twenty-nine, ninety, ninety-one."

"It's twenty-nine, thirty," Carlos told her.

Amanda counted again. "I got thirty-five," she said.

"You have two different answers, thirty-five and thirty-six," I said. "Can they both be right?" While Amanda's answer, thirty-five, was correct, I could see that her paper contained nine animals with four legs each. There were actually seven animals in the family. To get the correct answer, she must have miscounted.

I invited the two children to talk to each other to see if they could find where their thinking was different. After I moved away, I heard them at their table: "It's thirty-five!"

"No, thirty-six!"

"Thirty-five!"

"Thirty-six!"

This wasn't going to get them anywhere.

"Maybe it would help to tell each other why you think your answer is right," I suggested. Amanda showed Carlos her nine circles, each with four feet. She counted and this time got thirty-six.

"See, I'm right!" said Carlos. Actually Carlos wasn't. I intervened.

"Are your nine circles for nine babies?" I asked Amanda. There were actually six babies and one mom in the wildebeest family.

"Oh," said Amanda, realizing that there were actually seven animals in the family. She erased the extra animals and recounted the feet and tails. "It's thirty-five," she said again.

Carlos looked at his paper. "I go with her," he said quickly. "I got five feet. It's thirty-five." Carlos discovered his error: he had drawn five feet on the mother wildebeest.

It was almost time to stop when I noticed that Navin had a long number sentence on his paper and a picture but no words.

"What did you do to get the twenty-five?" I asked him.

"First I wrote a four a bunch of times and then some ones," Navin said.

"What do the fours mean?" I asked him.

"It's the feet," he explained. "And the one makes a tail." (See Figure 14–4.)

"It would help the reader understand better if you put what you just told me on your paper," I said.

Discussing the Children's Work

The children were seated next to their math buddies on the rug. I had their papers on my lap. I began the discussion by commenting on how the children had worked together.

"I saw a lot of children helping their partners learn today," I told them. "That was quite a birthday

FIGURE 14–4 Navin explained, "I first did the numbers."

present. I'm happy that you're really growing in your ability to help each other. Who had a partner who helped them?" I continued, "And what did that partner do?"

"Carina helped me find a pencil," said Armando.

Robert raised his hand. "Cristina told me what to do," he said. "You weren't sure what the problem was and she told you," I said. "She really did help you."

Jessica raised her hand. "Valeria helped me count."

"I didn't know how to make a lion," said Brianna. "Anthony showed me."

"You really helped each other learn today," I said. "Now let's look at the math. As I walked around I saw many different ways of representing the lions' feet and tails. That was wonderful, because I know that we're all different people and we think in different ways. I'm going to show you some different representations that I saw. Please let me know if any of you do *not* want me to show your paper." Children can be shy about having their artwork shown, but not this time. On the contrary, "Show mine, show mine!" was what I heard.

I held up Alicia's paper and said, "Alicia made this for the lions' feet and tails." Then I transferred her sketches onto the board:

Feet

"Did anyone else do something similar?"

Several children raised their hands.

We looked at Lorena's paper and I sketched the tallies that she had used for feet and tails. "It looks like tallies were fast and easy to do," I said. Lorena nodded. "Did anyone show the feet and tails in a similar way?" I asked.

"Mine's like that," said Heriberto.

Then I wrote a *4* and a *1*. "How does this show the feet and a tail?" I asked. There was a pause. A few hands went up, but still I waited. "Can the four and one show the problem you worked on?" I asked again, giving more children time to think. More hands went up. I called on Armando. "It's the feet. There's four on the lion. And one tail," he added.

"Can you see that?" I asked the group.

"One of us wrote a long number sentence for all the feet and tails in the lion family," I said. I wrote Navin's equation:

$$4 + 4 + 4 + 4 + 4 + 1 + 1 + 1 + 1 + 1 =$$

"What does this have to do with the question you worked on?" I asked. "Turn to your math buddy and see if each of you think this equation describes the lion family's feet and tails." Since my goal was for more children to be able to represent stories with equations, I wanted the children to talk about this example.

Still, only five or so hands went up when I asked the whole group the same question. I could tell that I needed to give the children more experiences writing equations for number stories. For the moment I asked the children, "What does the four stand for?"

"It's lion feet, like the baby. He's got four feet," said Juanita. I pointed to a lion on the book's cover.

"What is this four for?" I asked.

"That's another lion's feet," said Cristina.

I pointed to the second baby lion on the book's cover. "And this four?" I asked. I continued connecting the fours to the individual lions.

Then I got to the one. "What does this stand for?" I paused, wanting more children to engage with this idea. Slowly more hands went up.

"It's the baby's tail," said Carina, "and so is the other ones, they're all the tails."

I moved on to the process of combining the numbers. "I'd like you all to think about how many there are altogether," I said. I waited. Some hands went up right away, other children pointed at the numbers and counted. Still others used their fingers, counting four fingers over and over again.

FIGURE 14–5 Jonathan drew arrows to show that each 5 stood for one lion's tail and feet.

I called on Miguel. "It's twenty-five, 'cause that's the answer I got," he said.

Heriberto said, "You can count it," so we did, counting all the numbers from one. I wrote *25* at the end of the equation.

Then I showed the children Jonathan's paper and the equation he wrote: $5 + 5 + 5 + 5 + 5 = 25$ (see Figure 14–5). "How does this equation match the story?" I asked.

"Five is the lion," said Alejandrina.

"How does the five match the lion?" I persisted.

"It's the feet and the tails," she answered. We counted by fives together and got to the same answer: twenty-five. "I wonder if we can find the fives in Navin's number sentence," I said, pointing to his equation.

"Four and one!" said Amanda.

"There's another four and one!" chimed in Cristina.

I drew lines to connect the pairs of 4s and 1s so the children could see where the 5s were:

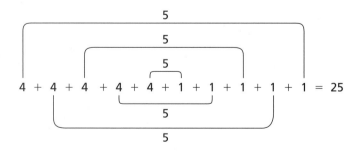

"It's five, ten, fifteen, twenty, twenty-five!" said Alicia.

"That was fast," I commented. "Sometimes making fives can help us work faster."

"Well, you did a lot of math thinking," I concluded, gathering up their papers.

"My brain is tired," Heriberto agreed.

I smiled. Mine was too. "I'm going to post all the ways you represented the feet and tails, and we'll put it on the wall. That way you might use a new idea next time."

Linking Assessment and Instruction

You may wish to make the following observations:

- How did the children represent the problem?

  - Did they use cubes or pictures or tallies or numbers or equations?
  - Did they represent in an efficient way or did they illustrate in great detail?
  - Could they keep track of what they were representing and recall what each symbol represented?

- How did the children manage the numbers?

  - Did they count correctly by ones? This is a strategy that many first graders will use.
  - Did any children count on?
  - Did they create groups of five to find the total, as Jonathan did? He used this friendly number to make the computation easier.

- Did the children have a way to solve the problem immediately or did they need support? Heriberto began using a numbering strategy, but then needed support in using it. The next time he uses this strategy, he may do it independently.

- Did the children work confidently? Did they persist when they encountered difficulties? Did they work cooperatively?

Bead Boards

SECRET NUMBERS

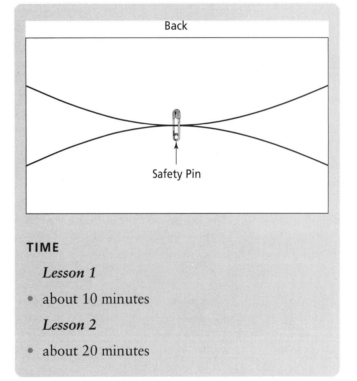

Back

Safety Pin

OVERVIEW

This short routine encourages children to identify and use the fives and tens that make up other numbers. The teacher makes a secret number on a bead board and shows the arrangement briefly. The children can either simply say the number and how they remembered it (Lesson 1), or they can build it on their own board and talk about the landmark numbers that helped them remember it (Lesson 2). In Lesson 2, the teacher records the child's thinking by writing numbers and equations.

MATERIALS

- bead boards, 1 per child (For materials and directions for making bead boards, see Chapter 12.)
- optional: large bead board (Use red and blue beads or Unifix cubes strung on $\frac{1}{4}$-inch elastic, wrapped in two lines around a large cookie sheet; see below.)

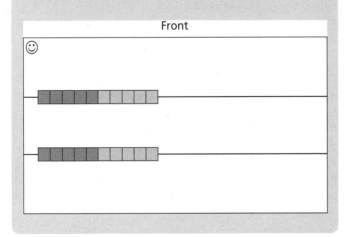

Front

☺

TIME

Lesson 1

- about 10 minutes

Lesson 2

- about 20 minutes

Teaching Directions

Lesson 1

1. Gather the students, either the whole class or a small group. Have them tell you what they know about the bead boards, to remind them how the beads are chunked into groups of five and ten.

2. Make a secret number on the side of your bead board that has a happy face, keeping the beads hidden from the children.

3. Show the arrangement on your bead board to the students for only a few seconds. Ask the students

to tell you what number you built on the side with the happy face.

4. Do this again to give the students a quick second look. If necessary, do it a third time, so that all the children know what the number is.

5. Leave the bead board visible. Ask the students to tell you how they knew what number it was. As each student explains, help describe his or her strategy. Celebrate all strategies, but note that those such as counting on and using chunks of five or ten can be faster than counting each bead.

Lesson 2

1. Provide each student with a bead board. Review the rules for how the bead boards are to be used. If the students have not had time to freely explore the boards, provide them with this time. Have them tell you what they know about the bead colors, to remind them of the chunks or groups of five and ten beads.

2. Make a secret number on your bead board and keep it hidden from the students.

3. Reveal the beads to the students for only a few seconds. Ask the students to build the number arrangement on their own boards. Do this several times, with the students editing their arrangements each time, until they look like yours.

4. Leave the beads visible to discuss how the students remembered the beads. As they describe what they saw, record their thinking in numbers and operations. For example, if a student counts all six beads from one, write *1, 2, 3, 4, 5, 6*. If a student saw five red and one blue bead, write *5 + 1 = 6*. Label the landmarks that they used (such as five or ten or twenty). Also make clear the strategies that they used, such as "counting on from five" or "subtracting from twenty."

Teaching Notes

The bead board is a model that promotes decomposition of numbers into the chunks of fives and tens that are inside other numbers. The children are also more likely to see how a number relates to five, because each row of beads has five of one color and five of another. They also see how numbers relate to the

landmark numbers ten and twenty, since the beads are in two rows of ten.

For example, when a child sees "six," it is visually decomposed into five red beads and one blue bead, or $5 + 1$. Another child might focus only on the top row of beads, and notice that there are four blue beads that are not part of the arrangement. That child sees $10 - 4 = 6$. Still another child might focus on all two rows of beads, and see that four beads on the top, and all ten beads on the bottom, are not part of the arrangement. That child sees $20 - 14 = 6$.

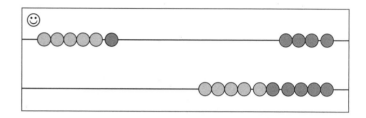

Bead boards provide a visual model for strategies. Over time the bead board becomes a mental model that children can use for computation.

Lesson 1 often serves as a bridge to young children to help them move from counting all to counting on. Counting on is more likely to occur because there is a predictable organization of fives and tens that children learn to trust in, which they are encouraged to use when not given time to count each bead. Lesson 2 is especially useful for delving into the different ways that children chunk numbers, and which number relationships they find useful. It also allows the teacher to model ways that this kind of thinking can be recorded.

Before children can use these kinds of strategies, they need to have freely explored the bead board and to know how the beads are organized into fives and tens. Be sure to provide them with this opportunity so that they are familiar with its organization.

Some children will continue to think only in terms of individual beads, and will continue to count by ones. This is natural in first grade. It's important for children to always do what makes sense to them. Accept and value these responses as well.

I use bead boards to promote a specific kind of thinking: using chunks and landmark numbers. Since this is a new challenge for the children, I do the recording for them. Over time the children will learn to use numbers and equations in a way that makes sense to them, and then they will do the recording for themselves.

I often use this activity for ten minutes at the beginning of the math period, before the children break into groups for math workshop time. It's also a valuable way to use those short amounts of time that are left before a scheduled activity such as lunchtime.

Lesson 1

A small group of children sat around me. I had earlier observed that Erin and Robert generally used the strategy of counting all from one, and rarely counted on. I had purposely put them in a group with children who often counted on, to encourage them to use new strategies.

I showed the children my large-sized bead board made of Unifix cubes strung on a large cookie sheet. "What do you remember about the bead board?" I asked them. They had used the bead board several times before and I wanted to make sure that they remembered the special way that the beads were arranged.

"There's five and five and five and five," said Robert. We counted to check.

"And ten at the top and ten at the bottom," said Erin. Again, we counted to check.

"It makes twenty. Twenty beads. Ten and ten is twenty," explained Omar.

"I'm going to make a secret number on my bead board," I told the children. "But I'm only going to let you look at it for a moment. See if you can figure out how many beads there are on the side with the happy face."

I turned my large bead board toward me and secretly moved some beads to the left. "Ready, set, go!" I said, showing them the bead board for just a few seconds, making it hard for the children to count each individual bead. I kept the beads on the other side covered with a hand.

"Ooh, that one's six!" said Robert.

"Six," echoed Erin.

"I'll give you one more chance to check. Ready, set, go!" I said. I again gave the children only a few seconds to figure out how many beads there were.

"I know, I know!" said the children excitedly. "It's six!"

"How did you figure that out so fast?" I asked. Erin was waving her hand earnestly. "Erin, you didn't have time to count but you knew the number right away. How did you know there were six?"

"The five and the one," she said. "Five, six."

I was pleased that Erin had counted on. Always before she had counted from one, touching each

numeral that number of times, even though I *knew* she had the number sense to use other strategies.

I revealed the board so that we could all examine the arrangement of five red beads and one blue bead. "See if you still think it's six," I said.

"One blue bead," said Sereslinda. "And I know there are five red beads," she continued. "One plus five is six."

This was precisely the kind of discussion that I was hoping for—the children were clearly using strategies such as counting on from five. But I wanted all the children to be included, so I articulated Sereslinda's thinking in a different way. "Sereslinda, you said that there are five red beads. Let's check."

We counted the five red beads out loud. "You knew that there were five red beads," I said. "The red beads were all there and you didn't have to count them. All you had to do was count on from five. The blue bead made 'six.'"

"Me too," said Victoria. "It's just five, six."

I wanted to encourage the children to keep thinking about these chunking strategies, so I did another secret number. "I'm going to show it to you really quick," I warned them. "Ready, set, go!"

"Eight!" the excited voices chorused.

"You didn't have *time* to count them!" I teased. "How did you know there were eight?"

"Because we saw them," said Robert.

"But how did you know?" I asked him.

He giggled. "There's five red beads and three blue beads," he said. "Six, seven, eight"—he counted on his fingers. Now Robert was counting on! Another milestone.

"Let's check," I said, showing them the beads. "You knew there were five red beads and you didn't need to count them. All you did was count the extras: six, seven, eight." I pointed to these groups as I spoke.

"And two blues are on the other side so they don't count," explained Sereslinda. "Ten take away two is eight."

"Oh," I said. "Sereslinda saw the two beads that we didn't use. She knows there's ten in all and if we didn't use two, there must be eight." We counted the beads from one to make sure.

"You guys are brilliant," I said, laughing. "So now I'm going to give you a really hard one. Here's my secret number. Ready, set, go!"

"Twelve!" the children called out.

I looked at them in mock disbelief. "I'm positively, absolutely, undoubtedly sure you didn't have time to count each bead. So how could you tell how many beads there are?"

"There's ten on the top and then I saw two on the bottom," Erin told me. "Eleven, twelve."

"Five red and five blue on the top is ten," said Omar. "Ten . . . eleven, twelve."

We checked the board, counting all the beads from one. "We were right!" Victoria said proudly.

"I'm going to make you a really, *really* hard one," I said. "Ready, set, go!"

"Oh!" Omar said, "Let's see it again."

I showed it again.

"Thirteen!" said Erin.

"Fourteen!" said Robert.

I let them peek once more.

"There's ten on the top and four on the bottom!" cried Robert. "Ten, then eleven, twelve, thirteen, fourteen!"

"And there's one red that isn't over, so four are, and with the ten, it's fourteen," added Omar.

What a wonderful few minutes we spent! I finally saw Erin and Robert consistently counting on from five and ten. I knew that this was a beginning step, and that they would still need to consolidate this new understanding until it became a useful tool for them in other contexts. But it was beginning to happen! I planned to frequently play this quick game with all the children.

Lesson 2

A small group of children was gathered around me, bead boards in hand. This time I had a board that was the same size as the children's. We quickly reviewed what they remembered about how the bead boards are organized, and how to use them carefully.

"I'm going to show you a secret number," I said. "Watch carefully, because I'm only going to show it to you for a short time. I'd like you to build the same number in the exact same way on your board. Make sure that you have your happy face pointing the right way," I added. Armando and Gerardo turned their boards around.

I secretly moved nine beads to the left, an arrangement that would appear as five red beads and four blue beads:

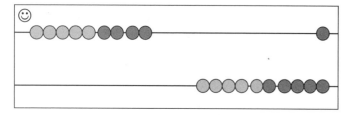

"Ready, set, go!" I said, and turned my board to face the children. After a brief two seconds, I hid it from view again. The children looked down to build the number that they thought they saw—everyone except Gerardo, who was looking at the ceiling. "What are you doing?" I inquired quietly.

"I can see the colors up there," Gerardo answered. He seemed to be visualizing the bead arrangement. "Now I've got it," he said, and he leaned over to adjust his board.

"I'll give you a chance to see the secret number again so you can edit your arrangements," I said. I did this a few times and then left my bead board visible so we could discuss what the children had seen.

"What number did I make?" I asked. The children all agreed that it was nine. "How did you remember it?" I continued.

Armando counted by ones to nine. He said "five" in a louder voice. Jennifer nodded her head. "That's what I did," she said. I wrote the numbers on the board. I underlined the 5: *1, 2, 3, 4, 5, 6, 7, 8, 9.*

"Why did you say five louder?" I asked.

"Because it's these," Armando said, showing us the group of five red beads on his bead board.

"So it's important to know that all five red beads are in the arrangement," I said, trying to articulate the importance of the chunk of five.

"Did anyone see the nine in a different way?" I asked.

"It's five reds and four blues," answered Amanda. "That makes nine, 'cause five plus four equals nine."

I wrote: $5 + 4 = 9$.

I pointed to where each number was on the board, to help the children make a connection between the number sentence and the bead arrangement it described. "You saw a chunk of five without counting. You knew that if all the red beads were there it had to be five. How did you know there were four blue beads?" I asked.

"It's one less," said Amanda, "so it has to be four." This was a slightly different way of seeing the number, I realized. "You can write what you just said like this," I said.

I wrote: $5 + (5 - 1) = 9$.

"The first five is the set of five beads," I continued. "The five minus one shows that you knew that there could have been five more blue beads, but we were missing one of them. There are nine beads altogether." Again, I helped the children make a connection between the number sentence and the bead arrangement.

"Who saw the nine in a different way?" I asked.

"I did," answered Alicia. "It's a five, I knew that, then I went six, seven, eight, nine."

"How did you know there were five red beads?" I asked her.

"It's all of them," Alicia answered. "That makes five. I counted the rest."

I wrote 5: 6, 7, 8, 9 on the board and said, "Alicia knew there were five—she didn't need to count them. We call this 'counting on from five.'" I wanted the children to have the language to describe this strategy.

Heriberto had an idea. "You can just know that there's one that you don't got, so it's ten take away one, so it's nine."

I wrote: $10 - 1 = 9$.

We played again, and this time I built fourteen, by sliding over all ten on the top and four on the bottom. I gave the children three short peeks at the arrangement, and they built what they had seen. Then I revealed my board so we could discuss how they had seen the number.

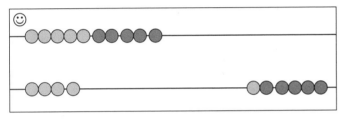

They explained what they saw in similar ways.

"It's all the top beads 'cause I see five and five and that's ten. And four more makes eleven, twelve, thirteen, fourteen," said Heriberto.

I wrote:

$$5 + 5 = 10$$
$$11, 12, 13, 14$$

"Heriberto saw two chunks of five and knew that was ten," I explained, helping the children make a connection between the number sentence and the bead arrangement. "And then he counted on from ten until he got to fourteen," I continued. I wanted to provide the children with the language to describe strategies.

"Did anyone think about the arrangement in a different way?" I asked. Jennifer counted from one all the way to fourteen.

"That's true," I said, and I wrote that number sequence on the board. It's important to accept "counting all" as a valid strategy. Some children are simply at that stage, and they need to solve problems in a way that makes sense to them.

I asked, "Did anyone think about it in another way?"

Amanda nodded. "It has to be ten on the top because they're all there, five and five. And you don't have another five on the bottom line, it's missing one so it's four. Ten and four makes fourteen."

I wrote this:

$$5 + 5 = 10$$
$$5 - 1 = 4$$
$$10 + 4 = 14$$

I had Amanda explain her thinking again. As she talked about each step, I pointed to that equation and showed where it happened on the bead calculator. She was using the landmark of five in a different way, which I wanted all the children to see.

"Did anyone see my fourteen beads in another way?" I asked.

"I did," answered Heriberto. "The bottom is missing a five and a one. Twenty take away six is fourteen."

"How did you know the bottom was missing a five and a one?" I asked.

"Well, there's no blue beads, so that's five. And there's only four red so you're missing a red one." I wondered how I could write that equation. Sometimes children's thinking is so different from mine that I have trouble recording it. So I had Heriberto explain his thinking a step at a time, and I tried to record each step.

"There's a ten, with a four, and a five and a one," he said.

I wrote: $10 + 4 + 5 + 1$.

"There's six missing," he said, and I crossed out $5 + 1$:

$$10 = 4 + \cancel{5 + 1}$$

"Twenty take away six is fourteen," he continued.

"Where did you get the twenty?" I asked.

"There's twenty beads on the whole thing," he explained. "And six are showing on the other side, so they aren't in the number."

I wrote: $20 - 6 = 14$.

Young children are capable of complex thinking, and it can be hard to understand and record what they say. I find that if I pay close attention to each part of what a child says, and if I turn each part into an equation that describes it, I can usually represent a child's thoughts. It's amazing how often children's thinking is extremely complex, and represents sophisticated mathematical understandings.

Over time, as children see ways that other children chunk numbers and use number relationships, they develop more flexible ways to see numbers. And, with the bead board, they become especially adept at using the landmarks that are important in our base ten system: five, ten, and twenty.

Linking Assessment and Instruction

You may wish to make the following observations:

- Did the children count all the beads or did they count on?

- From what smaller numbers did they count on? Did they count on from five? From ten?

- Did children use landmark numbers such as five, ten, and twenty, and subtract beads that were not in the arrangement? Heriberto saw the number fourteen by realizing that there were twenty beads altogether, and six were missing.

- Did the children seem to understand how the equations represented their way of seeing the beads?

Bead Boards

STORY PROBLEMS

OVERVIEW

In this lesson children use bead boards to solve word problems and develop new strategies for computation. The teacher tells number stories that require children to add two numbers that are less than ten, such as seven plus eight, or six plus nine. The children use the bead board to represent the problem and then share how they figured the problem out. The teacher connects each child's thinking to the symbols by writing the equations that mirror the strategy.

MATERIALS

- bead boards, 1 per student (For materials and directions for making bead boards, see Chapter 12.)
- optional: large bead board (see "Materials" section in Chapter 15)

TIME

- one class period

Teaching Directions

1. Review with the students the rules for how the bead boards are to be used.

2. Tell the students a number story that will require them to combine two numbers that are less than ten.

   Below are some sample contexts, but any two groups of things can work:

   - Birds on upper and lower branches. *I looked out the classroom window and saw some birds on two branches. Nine birds were on the upper branch and seven birds were on the lower branch. How many birds there were altogether?*
   - Books on two shelves. *My daughter has two shelves where she puts her favorite books. Amanda has eight books on the upper shelf and seven books on the lower shelf. How many books does she have?*
   - Stuffed animals on the top and bottom bunk beds. *My nieces have bunk beds and a collection of stuffed animals. Last weekend Ashley had six stuffed bears on the top bunk and Courtney had nine stuffed animals on the bottom bunk. How many stuffed animals did they have in all?*
   - Cookies on two different plates. *My plate has six cookies and Omar's plate also has six cookies. How many cookies do we have altogether?*
   - Tables with pencils on them. *My table has eight pencils on it, and the other table has five pencils. How many pencils are on both tables?*

3. Ask the students to use their bead board to figure out the answer, then have them share their thinking. Each time that a student shares, use a bead board to model his or her thinking. (If you are working with a large group, you may want to use a large bead board to model students' thinking.)

4. On the board, write an equation that represents each student's thinking. Label the strategy, for example "count all" or "count on" or "made a ten" or "used doubles." Over time students will adopt this same language to describe their own strategies.

5. Optional: Have the children represent their own thinking in numbers and equations.

Teaching Notes

The bead board is a model that promotes thinking in specific ways. Children are more likely to see a number as composed of five and some leftovers, because each row of ten beads has five of one color and five of another. Secondly, children are likely to find the tens when adding numbers, because they often visually combine the two fives that are the same color. Furthermore "compensation," or adding a quantity of beads to one number and subtracting the same amount of beads from the other number, is a strategy that may emerge.

Bead boards also serve as a bridge, moving young children from counting by ones to using strategies for addition and subtraction. They provide a visual model for strategies with small numbers that over time become mental models that children can use with larger numbers.

When one child shares a strategy, my first goal is to help other children try to understand that child's thinking. I do this by restating what the child did, having other children explain the child's thinking, and by using my large bead board to illustrate that child's thinking. Then I represent the thinking using equations. Over time the children learn to connect the thinking with the numeric representations. And eventually children begin to use numbers and operations to represent their own thinking.

One of the hardest things about teaching can be encouraging children to try more-efficient strategies without imposing such strategies on them. After all, it's important that children always do what makes sense to them. And a less-efficient strategy may actually be an important discovery for a less-experienced child at his or her point of development.

This is why children need to hear different strategies and ways of thinking about number, and they need to be reminded to solve the problem in a way that makes sense to them. In group discussions, I have children share different ways of thinking. I also try to observe children closely, to know when they are ready to be nudged along to new and different ways of thinking about number problems.

The Lesson

On this day, I had half the class working with me during mathematics time. They were seated on the rug. I had a large bead board made of Unifix cubes strung on elastic and wrapped around a large cookie sheet. On the chalkboard I planned to write equations to represent the strategies that different children used.

The children were accustomed to working with bead boards so I very quickly reviewed the norms for how this tool was to be used. "Think about how we have used bead boards so that they'll last a long, long time. Who can remind us of one thing we do?"

Laura raised her hand. "You don't pull on the strings or play them like a guitar."

"You hold the plastic part," Gerardo added.

"And move the beads carefully," said Alfredo.

"Can we make one to take home?" asked Juanita hopefully. She had been asking for a long time. I decided right then to have a parent-child workshop so the children could have one at home to use.

"Let's plan a date to invite our parents or other family members to school," I said. "Can you put that on the class meeting agenda?" Juanita nodded, pleased.

I then addressed the whole group. "Today we're going to use the bead board to solve problems. Make sure you're holding your bead board so the face has the eyes on top and the smile on the bottom," I reminded them. "Then I'll tell you a story."

"My nieces Ashley and Courtney sleep in bunk beds," I began. "Do you know what bunk beds are?" I asked.

Nina raised her hand. "There's one bed on the top and another bed under it," she explained. "My cousins have those."

"That's right," I said. "Ashley and Courtney also have stuffed animals, which they keep on their beds. See if you can figure out how many stuffed animals they had on their beds one day. Ashley had nine stuffed animals on the top bunk and Courtney had seven stuffed animals on the bottom bunk. How many stuffed animals did they have on both the beds?"

"Is it for real?" asked Alicia.

"It's true about my nieces and their bunk beds," I said, "and they love stuffed animals. But I made up the numbers. How many stuffed animals are there if there are nine on the top and seven on the bottom?" I took this opportunity to repeat the story because I wanted to make sure that everyone understood the scenario.

As the children bent their heads over their boards to model the problem, I again repeated the story. I checked Alfredo's bead board. "It's nine on the top," I reminded him. Alfredo slid off the extra bead. Many children counted the beads one at a time. I noticed Carina made the nine by sliding over the five and then four. Several children partitioned off the one from the top ten, and slid the nine over at once.

The children were ready to share. I began by building the problem on my large bead board. "Some of you made nine by leaving one on the end because you know that there are ten on a line and nine is one less," I said. "And some of you made the seven by moving over a five and two more."

Then I moved on to how the children had solved the problem. "How did you decide how many animals there were altogether?" I asked.

Alejandrina raised her hand. "I saw that the nine was almost ten so I put an extra one on the top and took one off the bottom. Then I counted on, ten, eleven, twelve, thirteen, fourteen, fifteen, sixteen."

I found it interesting that she had used compensation to make a friendly number, ten, but then counted on by ones instead of using the ten-plus combination that I had thought would have been easier for her. I merely nodded and used the large bead board to show the class what Alejandrina had done. Then I wrote on the chalkboard:

Alejandrina

$$9 + 7 = 10 + 6$$
$$10: 11, 12, 13, 14, 15, 16$$

"Can anyone explain what Alejandrina did first?" I asked. I wanted other children to explain the strategy of compensation.

"She put one on the top and took one off the bottom," said Alicia. "I did that too."

"Why did she do that?" I asked.

"It's easy," Alicia said.

"So nine and seven is the same as ten and six," I said. "Then Alejandrina counted on from ten by ones," I continued. It's important for children to hear, and later use, mathematical language for strategies. "Did anyone else use Alejandrina's strategy?" I asked. A few hands went up in the air.

"Who solved the problem a different way?" I asked. Hands waved. I called on Nina.

"I counted," she said, and then counted from one to sixteen. I wrote Nina's name and those numbers and said, "You counted all the beads." It is important and appropriate for Nina to use this beginning strategy. As she sees other children use other strategies, as her number sense develops, and as she comes to trust other strategies, she will adopt more efficient ways.

"Nina also got sixteen," I commented. "Did anyone solve it a different way?" More hands waved.

Lorena took a deep breath. She spoke hurriedly as if to get all her information out in one breath. "I saw the five and the five and that makes ten and then four and two is six and ten and six is sixteen."

I used the large bead board to model her thinking. I slightly separated the five and four on the top, to show where each number came from. Then I slightly separated the five and two on the bottom. "These are the pieces that Lorena saw," I said, and I wrote:

Lorena

$$5 + 4 + 5 + 2$$

"Lorena knows that five and five makes ten," I said. "She just knows that, and used it to help her." On the side I wrote:

$$5 + 4 + 5 + 2 =$$
$$10 + 6 = 16$$

"It's like the game *Roll and Add*," said Alejandra, smiling. "We do that."

"I see what you mean," I said. "Did anyone do it that same way?" A few children raised their hands.

"How does it help you to put the fives together?" I asked. I wanted to highlight this strategy and how it is particularly efficient.

Victoria spoke up. "It's like you don't have to count all the beads. Your eyes look and they tell you there's five red ones and you see the five red ones under and you can tell there's ten. Then you put on the other six."

"Did anyone do it a different way?" I asked. Alfredo wanted to share.

"I counted by fives," he said. "Five, ten, fifteen, then sixteen." He showed his thinking with his bead board, which I showed the group with my large bead board. I separated the top into a five and four, writing the numbers under each group. I did the same with five and two on the bottom. "Alfredo then saw another five by adding one from the bottom to the four on the top. Then he said five, ten, fifteen, and one more is sixteen." I wrote:

Alfredo

$$⑤ + 4 + ⑤ + 2 =$$
$$⑤ + 1$$

$$5, 10, 15, 16$$

"Can you follow his thinking?" I asked. "He sees fives like Lorena. Why is that a good idea?"

"You don't have to count them all," Juanita explained. "It's faster."

"Did anyone use a different strategy?" I asked.

Heriberto had an idea. "You put one extra on the top and take one off the bottom. Then you have ten on the top and six more makes sixteen."

I again used the large bead board to model his thinking. "Why did you put one more on the top?" I asked.

"Because tens are easy," he answered.

"Why did you take one off the bottom?" I inquired.

"Because," Heriberto said, "You have to keep all of them the same."

I rephrased his thinking to make it clearer for the group. "You have to keep the total number the same, so you get the same answer. But you can move around the little groups to make it easier to figure out." I wrote:

Heriberto

$$9 + 7 = 10 + 6$$
$$10 + 6 = 16$$

When I read the first equation I said, "Nine plus seven is the same as ten plus six." I like the children to see equations with subsets on both sides of the equals sign. Not only does this represent Heriberto's thinking, it also helps the children understand the equals sign in a way different from "the answer is." Many older children don't have this experience and in later years arrive at algebra class with a limited and incorrect understanding of the equals sign.

I could tell that the children's attention span could accommodate only one more strategy. Sereslinda had a different way.

"It was really easy, because I know there's twenty beads and I saw that we didn't use four and twenty take away four is sixteen."

A ripple of understanding went through the room. "Hey, I like that!" exclaimed Juanita. "It's easy!"

And it was. I wondered if this subtractive kind of thinking would serve them in mental math without the bead board. I wrote:

Sereslinda

$$20 - 4 = 16$$

Then I pointed to the large bead board as I read parts of the equation, and ended the session. "So Ashley and Courtney must have sixteen stuffed animals on their beds in all. And look at all the different ways you figured it out!"

Linking Assessment and Instruction

You may wish to make the following observations:

- How did the children construct the problem on their bead boards? Did they count beads one at a time? Did they move groups of five beads over and then count on? Or did they move over an entire ten and then subtract to make the number they wanted?
- How did the children solve the word problems?

  - Did they count each bead by ones? This is a beginning strategy.
  - Did they add the two sets of five red beads to make ten? If so, how did they manage the other numbers? Did they count on from ten or did they just know a "ten-plus" combination?
  - Did they find doubles and then count on? For example, for $7 + 6$, did they group six plus six and then add one?
  - Did children use compensation? For example, for $9 + 7$, did they add a bead to the top and take a bead away from the bottom to make $10 + 6$, as Heriberto did? If so, did they just know the "ten-plus" combination, or did they count on?
  - Did the children look at the number of beads not included, and subtract that number from ten or twenty?

Counting Buttons

CHAPTER 17

OVERVIEW

This activity gives children an opportunity to count by groups, an idea that is foundational to place value. The children hear the story Corduroy, *about a bear who lost a button, and then figure out how many buttons everyone in the classroom is wearing. They begin by counting the number of buttons they themselves are wearing, and make a Unifix train of that length. They compare their trains at their tables, and then estimate how many buttons there are in the room. After putting all the cubes together to make a class train, the children count the cubes by ones, twos, fives, and tens.*

MATERIALS

- Unifix cubes, about 12 per student
- *Corduroy*, by Don Freeman (New York: Viking, 1968)

TIME

- one class period

Teaching Directions

1. Read *Corduroy* to the class. Talk about the number of buttons Corduroy was wearing, and how many he should have had. Ask the students to count the buttons they themselves are wearing. Have them estimate how many buttons the people in the room are wearing in all. Write their estimates on the board.

2. Have a volunteer stand up. With the class's help, count the student's buttons. Get that many cubes, and match each cube to a button, so that the students remember what the cubes stand for. Then connect the cubes into a train. Do this with several students.

3. Stop to compare the trains that you've made so far. Figure out which train has the most cubes and which has the least. Put the trains in order, from smallest to largest. Figure out how many more buttons one student is wearing than another, by holding two trains together and counting any extra cubes.

4. Have four more students count their buttons and make a train out of that number of cubes. Again have those students compare their trains.

5. Have all of the other students count their buttons, get that number of cubes, and connect their cubes into trains.

6. Ask the students to join their cubes to make a train that stands for all the buttons in the room. Remind the children of their estimates, and see if they want to change any of them.

7. Count the cubes by ones. Periodically check the estimates and see if the students think it could still be that number. After you find out how many buttons in all, think about which estimate was closest. Write the total on the board, and circle it.

8. Explain that counting by ones can take a long time. (This articulates a reason for counting by other numbers.)

9. Discuss what would happen if the students count the cubes by twos. Break the train apart into twos. Ask how many cubes they will find when counting by twos. (Some students will think that the total changes when we count by different

numbers.) Count the cubes by twos and compare the answer with the total when counting by ones. Discuss why the numbers are the same.

10. Reconnect the cubes to make the original train. Repeat the procedure, counting by fives and then tens. Discuss why the numbers turned out the same.

11. Have the students discuss whether they would get a similar number if they did the activity again tomorrow. What if they did it at the end of the year? When might they have a large number of buttons? When might they have a smaller number of buttons?

12. Repeat the activity throughout the year to test their predictions and to let the children revisit the mathematics.

Teaching Notes

Place value is based on the idea of making equal groups of ones, tens, hundreds, and so on. But in order to manage groups of ten, children have to first understand what equal groups are. Children learn this more easily when they work with smaller groups, such as two and five.

This activity also challenges children's understanding of conservation of number. At first children may think that breaking apart a quantity into different sizes of groups changes the total. Over time they learn that the quantity doesn't change when the grouping changes. This ability to conserve numbers is necessary for understanding place value.

Children enjoy exploring their world numerically. They are interested in how many buttons they have. Some children may be wearing no buttons, and they contribute an important number—zero. During the activity these children pretend to "hold" cubes, but in fact, hold nothing. I want the children to know that zero is a numerical concept—an empty set.

Revisiting the lesson allows the children to confront these basic ideas over and over again, letting them dig deeper into the mathematics that is occurring. It's fun to see how the total number of buttons changes from day to day. You may see a sharp rise in buttons as the children try to wear their most "buttony" clothing!

The Lesson

The children sat on the rug in a circle around me. I read them the story *Corduroy*, an old favorite. Then I asked them to find out how many buttons they were wearing.

"I have three," said Gerardo.

"What if you were missing one button, like Corduroy?" I asked him. "How many buttons would you have?"

"Two," he answered immediately.

Robert showed us four buttons on his jacket and two buttons on his pants. "There's six. They're snap buttons," he explained. So we decided to count snaps as buttons during this activity.

"I wonder how many buttons we would find if we counted all the buttons in this room," I mused out loud.

"Four," said Heriberto.

"There's five," said Armando.

I rephrased my question to make sure they understood what I was asking. "If we counted all the buttons that all of us are wearing altogether, Robert's and Cristina's and Armando's and *all* of us, how many buttons would we count?" I asked. "Do you think there are a million?"

The children laughed. "No."

"Do you think there are only two in the whole room?" I continued.

The children shook their heads "no."

"Then how many buttons do you think there are?" I asked.

"There's a hundred," said Victoria. I wrote *100* on the board.

"There's maybe like thirteen," said Cristina. Thirteen was probably a large number to her. I wrote it under the 100.

"There's five," said Jennifer. I wrote *5*.

"There's something like eight thousand and eight," said Armando, smiling.

"How do you write that?" I asked.

"It's eight and a thousand," he answered. I wrote an *8* and a comma, saying, "That means eight thousand. And then no hundreds and no tens and just eight left." As I did so, I wrote *8,008*.

"I think it's more than a hundred but not much," said Armando, and I wrote *100+*. "It could be twenty-eight," said Gerardo. I wrote *28*.

"We have a lot of estimates," I said. "Let's find out for sure how many buttons we're wearing altogether."

I checked my clothing for buttons as the children watched. "None here," I said, looking at my jacket. "And none on my pants or my shirt!" I laughed to myself. I had forgotten to wear clothing with buttons! "I guess I need to get that number of cubes," I said, reaching into the tub with cubes. I held up my empty hand. "There," I said. "This shows how many buttons I have."

"Zero!" answered the children.

I asked for a volunteer, and chose Miguel to stand up. "How many buttons is Miguel wearing?"

Miguel showed us his shirt button. "There's three," he said.

"He had more right here," said Victoria, pointing to his waistband. We found a clasp.

"It's another way to attach clothes, but it's a clasp, not a button," I said. I took out three cubes and matched each cube to a shirt button as the children counted. I wanted to make a clear connection between the cubes and the buttons so the children would remember what the cubes stood for. We counted the cubes out loud. Then Miguel connected his cubes into a train.

"What does this train mean?" I asked.

"Three buttons," the children chorused.

I had five children stand up one at a time and we did the same thing. Carlos had six buttons, Juanita had one, Amanda had two, but neither Erin nor Omar had buttons. I gave both children their handful of "no buttons," again reinforcing the role of zero in our number system.

Six children stood in front, holding their trains. "Who has more buttons, Miguel or Carlos?" I asked.

"Carlos," the children chorused. The boys were standing side by side. I had them hold their cube trains up.

"How many more cubes does Carlos have?" I asked. I held the cube trains side by side. "These two are together, and these cubes match and these cubes match," I said. "How many extras does Carlos have? How many more does Carlos have than Miguel?" We counted the extras: One, two, three. Then we compared Carlos and Amanda's trains in the same way.

Next I asked the remaining children to come up and get the number of cubes that matched their buttons. After the children were seated again in the circle I asked for their attention. I held up my imaginary cube train. "See my cubes? This shows how many buttons I'm wearing," I continued. "Hold up your train if it shows that you have more buttons than I do. Which of you is wearing more buttons than me?" I said, restating the question. Most of the children held up their trains.

"How many buttons are you wearing?" I asked Cristina.

"Four," she said.

We counted her train and found four. "Four is more than zero," I said. We also checked Victoria's train.

"Hold up your train if it shows that you have fewer buttons than I do," I said. "Who has a train that has less than mine?" Carina held up her train and then quickly lowered it. "Why doesn't anyone have a hand up?" I asked.

"It's because," Miguel said seriously, "that you don't have any buttons and you can't have a littler number."

"We all have more," offered Juanita.

"Not me," objected Erin.

"What do Erin and I have?" I asked. We both held up our imaginary trains. "Is mine more than hers, less, or the same?"

"The same," the children chorused.

Erin sat down, and I refocused the children on the original question. "We made a lot of estimates about how many cubes we have in all. Let's take turns bringing up our trains and hooking them together." Before long our class train snaked across the circle. I pointed to the estimates. Then I said, "Think about how many buttons there are altogether: one hundred, thirteen, five, eight thousand and eight, one hundred plus, or twenty-eight."

"It can't be five," said Jennifer. "I think one hundred." So I erased the 5 and wrote 100 in its place.

"How can we find out?" I asked.

"Count them," said Laura.

As we counted them by ones, the children counted at different speeds. "I'm confused," I said. "I guess we need to start all over with one. This might take a long time."

We began again and I stopped about halfway. "We're at fifteen," I said. "What numbers do you think could be close to our answer?" I asked. I repeated the numbers and listened to the children's responses. "It's not thirteen because we're already at fifteen. And it can't be eight thousand and eight," said Armando.

"It can't be five either," said Erin.

"Do you think we have one hundred?" I asked.

Some children weren't sure. "It can't be, no way," said Navin.

We continued counting and found thirty. "The twenty-eight is the closest," said Victoria.

I wrote 30 on the board and circled it.

Counting by Other Numbers

"Now," I continued, "It takes a long time to count by ones. And if you make a mistake you have to count all over from one, just like we did. How else can we count the cubes?"

"By twos," said Juanita.

"How many will we get if we count by twos?" I asked.

"A hundred," answered Heriberto.

"No, maybe thirty-three," said Miguel.

"It's still the same," said Sereslinda. Many of the children weren't sure. So I quickly broke the train into twos. As we counted by twos I moved the small trains to one side. We got thirty. I pointed to the 30 I had circled.

"That's interesting!" I said. "We counted by ones and got thirty. Then we counted by twos and still got thirty. Were we just lucky, or did that happen for a reason?" I wanted to challenge the children's abilities to conserve number. I imagined that some children thought that changing the configuration of the same cubes would change the number. I wanted to find out which children thought this. I paused to give them time to think.

"Thirty and thirty," said Victoria. There seemed to be no connection between the numbers to her.

"It's two and two and two and two," said Nina.

I couldn't tell what she meant. So I restated my question. "When we counted the cubes by one, two, three, four, and on and on, we got thirty. Then we took the same cubes and broke them into twos and counted thirty. Why did that happen?"

"Well it's like you count by ones and you get thirty and it's still thirty," said Heriberto.

"Why did that happen?" I probed.

"Well it's still the cubes," he said. "There are thirty."

Sereslinda had an idea. "There's only thirty so you get thirty," she said. It seemed that Heriberto and Sereslinda were conserving this amount. I would know more when they made predictions for counting by fives.

I reassembled the long train. "What if we count by fives?" I asked. "How many cubes will we have?" There was a short discussion with more voices agreeing with Sereslinda that it would be the same.

"But five is more than two," protested Jennifer. "It'll be fifty." Miguel guessed that there would be twenty-five, because the groups were bigger. And many children weren't sure.

I broke the long train into fives and we counted, and we again got thirty. Gerardo seemed surprised, but more children joined the chorus: "It's the same!"

I reassembled the train once more. "Now," I said, "What if we count by tens? How many cubes will we find?" Most of the children said thirty, but I didn't think for an instant that all the children "had" conservation. Some children still had a fragile understanding of the concept. If we repeated the activity the next day, they might change their minds. We did count the cubes by tens, though, and we did find thirty.

I returned to the large train of cubes. "Each cube stands for what?" I asked, wanting to refocus them on the meaning of the symbol that we were using.

"It's a button," Victoria told us.

"How many buttons would we get if we did this again tomorrow?" I asked. "Do you think it will be more, less, or the same?" I wanted to prepare the children for revisiting the problem the next day. I suspected that they would wear as many buttons as they could, and that the number would increase. I wrote the day's date and *30 buttons* on the board as a reference.

Linking Assessment and Instruction

You may wish to make the following observations:

- Were the children's estimates reasonable? Did they alter their estimates in reasonable ways as they gathered more information? This is evidence of good number sense.
- How did the children compare cube trains? Did they easily identify shorter and longer trains? Could they identify trains that were "two more than four" or other specific differences? Did they do this confidently and consistently? These are indications of good number sense.
- Did the children recognize that they can count a quantity in different ways, and that the total will remain the same? This idea of conservation is important in place value: grouping in tens and ones will still yield the same total.
- Did the children know the number sequence of counting by twos, fives, and tens? If not, where did the pattern break down for them? This "skip-counting" and the patterns that result will become a tool for children in later years, as they explore the number system and the operations of multiplication and division.

A Candy Shop

HOW MANY CANDIES?

OVERVIEW

In this investigation, the class becomes a candy shop. The children learn how the base ten system functions as they package candies in groups of ten to give to many other classrooms. Then the children find out how many candies they have packaged altogether.

Later, the children use the packs of ten to play a guessing game. One child puts out some ten-packs and some loose candies. The other children guess how many candies there are without counting each candy. Then they count each candy to check.

MATERIALS

- store-bought bags of hard, individually wrapped candies—enough so that each person in the classes that will receive candies gets 1 candy
- containers to hold candies, enough for each table where the children will work
- 2 or 3 larger bowls, to hold 100 candies in each
- 3-by-5-inch index cards

TIME

- three class periods

Teaching Directions

Day 1
Introducing the Lesson and Making Ten-Packs of Candies

1. Explain that the classroom will temporarily become a candy shop. Decide on a name for the shop.

2. Show the students the large store-bought bags of wrapped candy. Ask them to predict how many candies they have altogether. Discuss how they might easily count the candies such as by counting by twos, fives, and tens.

3. Explain that they'll work in partners to make packages of ten candies. Show the students how to make the ten-packs by grabbing a handful of candies, then making sure there really are ten. Explain that you want them to check each other's counts to make sure that there really are ten.

4. Show the students how to line the candies up close together, so that the pack is as short as possible. Show how they will tape the line of candies, first on the front side. Then turn the line of candies over and tape the back to make a solid "ten-pack." (See the illustration on page 103.)

5. Place baskets of candies at each table. Keep aside about thirty "loose ones" so that you can play the guessing game and complete the candy bags in the next lesson.

6. As the students complete lines of ten candies, circulate from table to table to provide them with strips of clear adhesive tape. Tear off a strip of tape about the length of the candy line. One student presses down the tape firmly and then turns the candy line over. Tear off another strip of tape so the student's partner can tape the other side.

7. When the table has completed as many ten-packs as possible, have those children figure out how many candies they have at their table.

Day 2
Counting All the Candies

1. Gather the students in a circle on the rug to examine how the candies look now. Count the

candies by their groups of ten. As you do so, record on the board the multiples of ten: 10, 20, 30, 40, 50, and so on. When you get to one hundred, group them in a bowl, call it "a hundred," and label it *100*. Make new groups of ten, recording multiples of ten (110, 120, 130, etc.), until you have another hundred. Place them in another bowl and label it as well. Continue until all the candies, including the ones set aside as loose ones, are counted.

Day 3
Playing the Game How Many Candies?

1. Gather the students in a circle on the rug. Ask the students to close their eyes. Put out a few ten-packs and some single candies.

2. Have the students open their eyes. Ask them to tell how many candies they think there are and why they think that. Write the number on the board. Count by ones to check to see if it's right. Encourage discussion and different ways that students can explain their guesses. When students have trouble shifting from counting by tens to counting by ones, count again, supporting the students with the appropriate transition.

3. Invite a student to take on your role by putting out the ten-packs and loose candies.

4. Watch to see if students notice the pattern in two-digit numbers, that the first number matches the number of ten-packs and the second number matches the number of loose ones. If this comes up, investigate whether this happens a lot, by checking a few other numbers. If it doesn't come up, leave this conversation for the next lesson.

Teaching Notes

Many mathematical ideas can be elusive for young children, but place value is one of the most difficult. This is because we are asking children to think in a new way about number. First graders have learned to count only recently. To the children, "five" has always meant a set of five individual objects. Each individual object is assigned a number when we count. Suddenly "five" can mean five *groups* of objects; we no longer count each item, but instead we count a group, or "unit." This idea is sometimes called "unitizing."

In this lesson, children's fragile understanding of unitizing becomes evident. When counting groups of

tens and ones, they have trouble understanding when to use the pattern of counting by tens and when to switch to counting by ones. It takes time and many experiences for children to understand this process.

How the units relate to each other is a complex idea as well. There are ten individual items in "a ten," there are ten "tens" in "a hundred," and one hundred items in "a hundred." If you've ever tried to work in the base five system, or any other base system, you know how difficult these relationships can be.

To make place value even more complex, five's meaning changes according to where the number is written in a sequence. Sequence is difficult for first graders. They often reverse letters or numbers; they might not distinguish 71 from 17. Yet place value requires that children not only write the numeral in the correct place but that they also attach a specific value to the numeral occupying a particular place.

True understanding of place value requires "multiplicative" thinking. The values of numerals change. For example, the 7 in 71 really means seven groups of ten, or 7×10. The 7 in 17 means 7×1. And when we write 714, the 7 means 7×100. Multiplicative thinking is abstract, and difficult for young children.

The Lesson

Day 1

Introducing the Lesson and Making Ten-Packs   The children sat in a circle on the rug, eyeing with interest the two large bags of hard, wrapped candies. "We're going to become a candy shop today," I announced. "Since the children in the second through fifth grades are taking tests this week, they each need something to cheer them up. I think we have enough in this bag of candies for each child to have one candy. But we need the shop to package the candies for each classroom."

"Can we have some too?" Erin asked.

"Of course!" I answered. "We'll make a bag for ourselves. And I think when we make the bags for the classrooms that we should include the teachers and the teacher assistants, don't you?" The children agreed.

"We need a name for the candy shop," I said. "What name should we have?" After a bit of discussion and a quick vote, we decided on Candy Land Candy Shop. I wrote the name on the board.

I held up the two large bags of candy and said, "How many candies do you think we have?" I wrote the children's predictions, partly so they could see how these larger numbers are written. Soon we had listed: *2,000   100   76   700   299.*

"There's a lot," said Victoria.

"It's gonna take a long time to count them," added Alfredo.

I showed the children the label on one of the bags. "The bag says that there are about one hundred twenty candies in it and I have two bags. How many candies should we have altogether?"

I wrote *120* on the board and said, "This means that it has one hundred and twenty." I wrote *100 + 20.* Then I wrote another *100 + 20* for the other bag. "How much is this altogether?" I asked. "How many hundreds do we have?"

"Two hundreds," said Juanita.

"And forty," added Carina.

"Right," I said, "Two hundred and forty." I wrote *200 + 40 We should have 240 candies* on the board.

I emptied the candies in front of me on the rug. "Let's find out how many candies we do have," I suggested, and I began to count each candy by ones. "One, two, three, four . . ." I paused and sighed, looking at the huge pile. "This is going to take forever. Is there a quicker way to count?"

"Yes," said Robert. "Ten, twenty, thirty . . ."

This melody of numbers was familiar to the children.

"There's so much," answered Cristina.

"We could get mixed up," said Heriberto.

"Let's count by tens," said Gerardo. He remembered the times we had done this.

"Or twos," said Laura.

"Or we could count by fives," added Alicia.

"Why would it help to count by groups?" I asked. I wanted to establish the reason for this.

"Like you don't have to say every number," said Carina. "It's easier.

"And it goes faster so if you make a mistake you don't have to start all over," said Brittney.

"We're going to make groups of ten today," I said. "I'm going to put a basket of candy at each table. You and your math buddy are going to see if you can grab ten candies. Take them out and check that there really are ten, because we're a company and we don't want any mistakes." Having children try to grab ten would engage their sense of number, and adjusting the quantity would invite children to make use of number relationships.

"Then," I continued, "put the ten candies close together in a line. Make sure you rotate the candies so they're as close together as possible," I said. "We're going to tape them together and we don't want to

waste tape." I put the candies together as close as possible, showing the children what I meant:

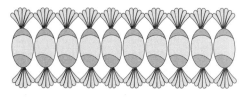

"I'll walk around and tear off strips of tape," I explained. "I'll put the tape lightly on your candies. You'll push the tape down firmly and turn the candy strip over. I'll tear off another strip of tape. You'll push it down firmly. That way the candy pack will stay together." I showed the children what I meant:

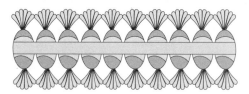

"Keep going until you've made all the ten-packs that you can. Then figure out how many candies you have at your table."

I poured candies into five plastic baskets, reserving some for the "loose ones" that we'd need to fill our orders. I placed the baskets on the tables and we got started.

Making Ten-Packs   The children got busy trying to grab ten candies, adjusting their counts, and laying out the candies. I walked around quickly tearing off strips of tape. It was a bit hectic, but I liked the bustling feeling of all of us working together. In the past I've devised easier ways to make ten-packs, such as giving children aluminum foil to make packets. But I realized it's very important that the children be able to see each individual candy, so I generally use this lively way of making ten-packs.

The children were happily engaged in counting and adjusting their lines of candy. Heriberto and Robert counted the candies they had grabbed. "I got nine and one more is ten," Robert said.

Raymond counted his candies by ones and got eleven. "I have to put one back."

The children were clearly using number relationships to adjust their candy counts.

At one table all the children had made personal piles of candy and each child had completed a ten-pack. They didn't think of combining their leftovers. "Make sure that your math buddy checks your groups of ten," I reminded them so that they would work together. "And I wonder if there's any way you can make more ten-packs at your table." Later Heriberto told me, "Mrs. Confer, there's another one! We got Juanita's and mine and we made another one! But there's three we can't use."

As children completed all the ten-packs they could, they began to figure out how many candies were at their table. "It must be a hundred," guessed Heriberto.

"Look," said Juanita, matter-of-factly putting all five ten-packs in a line, leaving the three loose candies on the side. "It's ten, twenty, thirty . . ." She hesitated and her voice trailed off, and others joined in, "Forty, fifty, sixty, seventy, eighty."

"It's not that much," Carina stated firmly. "You can't go by tens." I watched this discussion with interest. The idea of unitizing, counting individual items, and counting groups of items, was emerging. This is a difficult concept for young children to understand.

Heriberto tried: "One, two, three, four, five, six, seven." He pointed to ten-packs and loose candies alike.

"It's not one, it's ten," said Carina. "There's ten in here. It's ten, twenty, thirty, forty, fifty, fifty-one, fifty-two, fifty-three."

"Carina," I said, "help us understand what you're doing. Why do you say ten for the first pack?"

"'Cause there's ten," she said. It was obvious to her, but not to all the others.

"And then you go on to twenty?" I asked.

"It's ten more," Carina explained.

"And then you keep going by tens, to thirty and forty and fifty," I said, moving aside ten-packs as I counted.

"Now you have just the loose ones," I said. "Is it sixty?"

"No, now you count by ones," she explained. "It's not ten anymore." We continued counting by ones to fifty-three.

While I knew that all the children did not follow Carina's thinking, it was good for them to hear her describe what she did. Over time, with more experiences, they would develop understanding about unitizing.

Day 2

Counting All the Candies The children sat in a circle on the rug next to their math buddies. "It's so many!" said Gina enthusiastically.

"It's a lot, lot, lot of candy! It's enough for the whole school!" Victoria said.

"At least a hundred," Miguel added.

I showed the children their predictions from the day before for how many candies there were in all, and we read them out loud. "How should we count them?" I asked the children.

"By tens!" they answered. So we began to count the packs by tens, pushing a ten-pack aside each time. "Ten, twenty . . ."

Then I heard some children continue, saying "Twenty-five, thirty, thirty-five . . ." This interested me. They had reverted to the pattern for counting by fives.

I stopped. "Let's begin again. Why can I just say 'ten' at the start?"

Heriberto spoke up. "'Cause you got ten so you just say ten."

"Oh," I said, "I just know there's ten in this pack, so I can just say ten instead of counting the candies." I wrote *10* on the board.

I picked up another ten-pack. "Now how many do I have?" I asked. Some children said twenty and others said eleven. "Check in with your math buddy," I suggested. "Do we have eleven candies now or do we have twenty?"

I waited for the children to talk for a bit and then asked for their opinions.

"It's eleven, because you go ten, eleven," said Robert.

"But you got twenty," Juanita interrupted him.

"Let's see," I said. We counted each candy from one, and indeed found twenty. I wrote *20* on the board under the 10.

We continued this way, adding another ten-pack and predicting how many candies we had then. We frequently had to count from one to check. Soon we had this list of numbers on the board: 10, 20, 30, 40, 50, 60, 70, 80, 90, 100. I put ten ten-packs in a bowl and wrote *100* on an index card and taped it to the bowl.

I lifted up another ten-pack. "If we keep going and count these, how many will we have?" I asked. Some children thought there were 200, others thought we had 201, and Heriberto told us he thought we had 110. I picked up a single candy. "How many would this make?" I asked. The children agreed that it made 101. I kept adding another single candy until we got to 110. "That's like another ten-pack," I said, and I wrote *110* on the board.

We continued this way, making another sign for the second bowl of a hundred, until we had counted all the ten-packs. Then we found that we could make another ten-pack with some of the loose ones that the children had left. And I showed them the thirty loose candies that we would need to fill our orders. Finally we found out that we had 238 candies in all.

"The label told us we should have two hundred and forty candies," I said. "Do we?" The children shook their heads. "Do we have more than two hundred and forty or less than two hundred and forty?" I asked. "Talk to your math buddy and see if you agree. And see if you can figure out how many more or how many less we have."

The buzz of children talking filled the room. Miguel and Armando poked each other and Cristina stared out into space. I could tell that it was almost time to stop. But first I asked the children to answer my question.

Armando raised his hand. "It's not enough. We should call the store and tell them."

Juanita thought we had more than 240. "It's the eight that's more," she said.

I wrote these numbers on the board: *238, 239, 240.* "We have two hundred and thirty-eight, one more is two hundred and thirty-nine, and one more is two hundred and forty. We're missing two candies."

"The store man ate some," Robert guessed.

Day 3

Playing the Game *How Many Candies?* Half the class sat around me on the rug while the other children did math workshop. I wanted the children to revisit the idea of grouping and counting by tens, which is so central to place value.

"I have a game," I said, pouring out the ten-packs of candy and leftover loose ones.

"Ooh! Wow!" were the children's reactions to the pile of wrapped candies.

"You all close your eyes, I'll put out some ten-packs and loose candies, and you can guess how many candies there are. Sound fun?"

The children agreed enthusiastically, and closed their eyes. I put out two ten-packs and three loose candies:

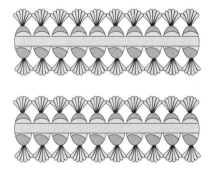

"Open your eyes!" I said. "How many candies do you think there are?"

I waited for the children to think. Many were pointing and trying to count by ones. "There's twenty-four," said Juanita.

"Why do you think there are twenty-four candies?" I asked her.

Juanita counted each candy from one and got to twenty-three.

"How many candies are there?" I asked the group. They answered twenty-three.

"How do I write twenty-three?" I asked. The children answered, "A two and a three."

"Can anyone explain that there's twenty-three candies in a different way?" I asked.

The children had scooted forward in their enthusiasm and I asked them to scoot back so that everyone could see.

Victoria came and counted the ten-packs and single candies, saying, "Ten, twenty, thirty, forty, fifty." She looked around, unsure of her answer.

"You think it might not be fifty?" I asked her.

Victoria shook her head and shrugged. "Maybe," she said.

I wrote *50* on the board next to the 23. "What's going on?" I asked the children. "Are there twenty-three candies or are there fifty? Please talk to your math buddies. What do you think and why do you think that?"

"There's twenty-three," said Alfredo after awhile. "You can't have fifty. It's too much."

"We saw there's twenty-three and we counted it," said Sereslinda.

I wanted the children to confront the mechanics of shifting from counting by tens to counting by ones. I held up one ten-pack. "This is ten," I said. "How much do I have now?" I asked, holding up a second ten-pack.

"Twenty," the children answered.

Then I picked up a single candy. "Now how many do I have?" I asked.

I heard mixed replies, thirty and twenty-one.

We counted from one to check. "I knew it!" said Navin.

Then we continued counting the last two loose candies, and got to twenty-three. "Two ten-packs and three loose ones is twenty-three," I said, circling that number on the board.

Some children were clearly in a state of confusion, or as Piaget would say, *disequilibrium.* They were in the fog that is at the cusp of new understandings. These children were trying to make sense of counting by groups versus units, counting by tens and shifting to ones, all part of place-value understandings. And the children might remain unsure for some time, as they build beginning, fragile concepts. These new ideas would solidify through more experiences.

But I was happy that these children were on the journey toward making sense. Too often classroom activities, and especially workbook pages, mask misunderstandings that are never dealt with. They produce the veneer of learning rather than true foundational understanding. These children were on an important path, and I was pleased.

"Let's play the game again," I said. "Close your eyes!" I put out four ten-packs and seven loose ones. "Open your eyes! Please talk to your math buddy. How many candies do you think there are?" The children pointed and talked.

After a moment Jennifer shared her thoughts. "There's forty-seven." She'd counted by ones.

"How do I write forty-seven?" Martin advised me, and I wrote *47* on the board. "Who can explain how many there are in a different way?" I asked.

Alfredo tried to count by tens but got mixed up. I encouraged him to count again in his native language, Spanish, and he counted more consistently by tens, but then forgot to switch to ones for the singles. I wrote *110* on the board.

"Which is it, forty-seven or one hundred and ten?" I asked.

"Alfredo passed forty-seven, it's too much," said Victoria.

We counted together by tens, beginning with the first ten-pack, the second, and so on. When we passed forty and came to the first single candy, I heard a chorus of "Fifty" mixed in with "Forty-one."

"What is this one?" I asked, pointing to the first loose candy.

We counted all the candies from one and found that it was forty-one.

"We did it again!" laughed Heriberto. "It's not fifty. You have to count different for the little ones!"

And when we kept counting we found that there were, indeed, forty-seven candies.

We played this game frequently that week. Sometimes I put out the candies, and sometimes children would take on my role. Over time I noticed more and more children being able to shift appropriately from counting by tens to ones. But few children connected the ten-pack organization to the numerals that we wrote.

Then one day, when I asked how to write thirty-eight, Raymond told us, "A three and a eight. Just like the candies."

"What do you mean?" I asked.

"There's three like the big ones and eight like the little ones," he explained. Raymond was noticing the pattern of place value in two-digit numbers, that the ten-packs matched the first digit and the loose ones matched the second digit.

I articulated this for the children. "Raymond says that this three matches the ten-packs." I held them up. "And this eight matches the eight loose ones." I held the eight single candies up.

"Do you think we were just lucky or would it happen again?" I asked.

Alejandrina and Navin thought it was always like that, but many children didn't understand why this happened.

I put out two ten-packs and one loose candy. "How many candies do we have?" I asked. When the children said twenty-one, we found that there were two ten-packs and one loose one. "It's the same!" said Jennifer. "Two and one."

"Do you think we were lucky again, or is something happening?" I asked. "Let's try this one." I put out four ten-packs and two loose ones.

"It's forty-two, just like the numbers!" Navin said.

Some children realized that the pattern was somehow connected to the ten-packs, others didn't. But I knew that when we packaged candies for the classes in the next lesson, this pattern would emerge once again. The children would have more chances to hold the candies themselves, think about relationships, record, and discuss their ideas.

Linking Assessment and Instruction

You may wish to make the following observations:

- Did the children recognize that they can count a quantity by tens or by ones, and that the total will remain the same? This conservation idea is basic to place value.
- Did the children know the number sequence of counting by tens?
- When the children tried to get a handful of ten candies, and then adjusted their counts to make ten, did they use number relationships to made the adjustment? For example, did they say things such as, "I have twelve and I know that it's two too many so I have to put two back"? Or did they just continually count, and then take out or add one more until they had ten?

- How did the children count ten-packs and loose ones? Did they only trust counting by ones? Did they count by tens and switch to counting by ones correctly? Did they do this confidently and consistently? Or were they inconsistent, as was the case for many of the students?

- Did the children notice the relationship between the digits in the written numbers and the number of ten-packs and loose ones? How did they explain this relationship?

CHAPTER 19

A Candy Shop

PACKAGING CANDY BAGS

OVERVIEW

This investigation builds on the preceding one, and continues to develop children's place-value understanding. Children fill candy orders for classrooms by reading order forms for each class and putting ten-packs and loose candies in zip-top bags. Then the children make a "packing slip" for each bag.

The children use the packed bags in a guessing game called What's in the Bag?, *which helps them make the connection between the ten-packs and the tens place in the written numeral. The children are told how many candies go to that class, and the children guess how many ten-packs and how many loose candies are in the bag and how they look. The children then open the bag to check. Finally the children deliver the candy bags to the classrooms.*

MATERIALS

- container of candy ten-packs and loose candies made during the preceding investigation
- half-sheets of copy paper for each classroom, on which are written the teacher's name and the number of students in that class (Use one order form and one bag for classes that often work together, and include an order form for the office staff. This will provide smaller and larger numbers for the children to explore.)
- gallon-size zip-top bag, 1 for each classroom that will receive candies
- large 1–100 chart

Mrs. Valencia's Class

22 Students

TIME

- two class periods

Teaching Directions

Day 1
Packaging Candy Bags for Each Classroom

1. Show the students the "order forms," with each teacher's name and the number of students in that class. With their help, figure out how many candies each bag will need, taking into account the teachers and any support personnel. Write the equation and the total number of candies needed for that classroom on each order form. (For example, if a class of twenty-two students has a teacher and a teacher assistant, write $22 + 2 = 24$.)

2. Show the students the tub of ten-packs they made the other day, and loose candies that you kept aside to fill the orders. Place these in a central spot, such as on the rug.

3. Explain that packing slips describe the candies that each class needs, and that the children will make a

packing slip for each class. On the board, write a list of what each packing slip needs: The name of the candy shop, the classroom teacher's name, number of people, number of ten-packs, and number of loose ones. You may wish to make a sample packing slip. A packing slip might look like this:

Candy Land Candy Shop

Class <u>Ms. Sanchez</u>

Number of Candies <u>24</u>

Number of Ten-Packs <u>2</u>

Number of Loose Ones <u>4</u>

---

4. Give each pair of students an order form. Ask the students to read the order form and fill the class bag, using as many ten-packs as possible, and then loose candies.

5. Have them make a packing slip for each bag by writing the necessary information on a sheet of copy paper.

6. Have them check each other's bag to see that the correct amount of candies is included, and that the packing list is accurate. (This provides the children with additional practice.)

Day 2
Playing What's in the Bag?

1. Gather the students on the rug, seated next to their math buddies.

2. Have one student select a bag and read the teacher's name. Write the name of the teacher on the board. Have the student read the total number of candies in the bag. Write that number next to the teacher's name. Have the other children guess how many ten-packs and how many loose candies are in the bag.

3. Leave that information on the board, and do the same with other bags.

4. Ask the students what they notice about the numbers on the board. They will probably see that the number of ten-packs matches the first digit, and the number of loose candies matches the second

digit. Wonder aloud whether this always happens. Discuss why this happens.

5. Challenge the children's thinking in as many ways as you can. For example, you might say things such as "We have twenty-three candies, and we have two ten-packs and three loose ones. I thought two plus three makes five. But we have more than five candies here." Or ask the children to find where the numbers are in the candies. Point to the 2 in 23 and say, "Where are these?" (They are the two ten-packs.) Then hold up two loose ones and say, "Is this what the two means in the numbers?" Let the students explain where the 2 actually is. Then point to the 3 and say, "Where are these in the candies?" (the three loose ones). Some children will not make this connection easily.

6. Have the students play *What's in the Bag?* with partners.

7. Repeat this game, perhaps as a morning routine, or make it part of math workshop time. In this way students receive additional practice. Deliver the candy packages to each classroom.

Teaching Notes

This activity continues the place-value investigation. The children focus on the ten-pack and single arrangements of the candies, and how this relates to how we write two-digit numbers.

The place-value understandings that underlie this pattern are complex. The children still have emerging abilities to "unitize," or see ten objects as a *group* of ten that can be counted in the same way that they count individual objects. A child's ability to count by tens and then shift to counting by ones is often not consistent.

In this activity the children encounter the fact that a number's meaning changes according to where it is placed in the number. For example, "two" can have different meanings: two ten-packs or two single candies. The discussions between children, and the "disequilibrium" that the teacher introduces into the conversation, uncover any fragile and emerging place-value understandings.

Simply telling children about place value does not work. Children must construct these complex relationships for themselves, through talking about them, and through confronting complexities and confusions. It takes many experiences for children to make sense of place value.

This activity can be extended even further. Once the bags are packed, you can ask children to solve various problems, such as "How many candies are in Ms. Johnston's and Mrs. Dominguez's bags altogether?" or "How many more candies are in Mr. Kelsey's bag than in Mrs. Dominguez's bag?" The actual bags offer a way for children to check their answers.

The Lesson

Day 1

Preparing Order Forms   "Can we eat the candy?" asked Carlos.

"How about at the end of math time today?" I answered. "Today someone's going to make a bag for our class."

The children erupted into "Hurray!" and "Yes!"

"Let's get started," I said. "We have a lot to do first."

I showed the children the half-sheets of paper that listed each teacher's name along with the number of students in that class. "These are our order forms, to tell us how many candies to pack for each class. This number tells us how many children are in the room. But we should give a piece of candy to the teacher and teacher assistant as well," I said. "Mr. Ortiz has twenty-one children. He has one assistant, Mrs. Lopez. How many candies will we need to pack for that room?"

"Twenty-three," said Gerardo. "It's twenty-one for all the kids, then twenty-two and twenty-three."

"It's twenty-two," said Miguel. He tried to count on with his fingers. "Twenty-one, twenty-two." He held up two fingers. "That's for Mr. Ortiz and Mrs. Lopez."

"Let's check on our hundred chart," I suggested. Counting on can be difficult, and children sometimes get confused about where to start counting. "All these numbers, one, two, three, four, all the way to twenty-one, stand for the kids," I said, pointing to the chart. "And the twenty-two is for Mr. Ortiz. And twenty-three is for Mrs. Lopez, who helps him."

Next to the 21 on the order form, I wrote + 2 = 23. Then I circled 23. "This tells us how many candies we need for that room."

We did all the order forms the same way, mentally adding two to the number of students, checking our thinking on the hundred chart, and writing the equation on the order form. Each time I circled the total number that we'd need. The children were getting a lot of practice with counting on mentally, as well as using the hundred chart as a tool for addition.

Packing Candies   "Now we're ready to start packing," I announced. I showed them the order form for Ms. Dominguez, which had 18 on it. "How can I pack this?"

I heard several children count out loud, "One, two, three, four, five, six, seven . . ."

"I'd like us to use as many ten-packs as you can," I said. "How many ten-packs will I need?" I asked. "I'd like everyone to think about this." I paused.

"Two," said Heriberto. I picked up two ten-packs. To check, we counted the candies from one, and got to twenty. "It's too much," Heriberto told me.

"Use a ten and then get eight," suggested Victoria. I got these out and Victoria checked them by counting on, "Ten . . . eleven, twelve, thirteen, fourteen, fifteen, sixteen, seventeen, eighteen."

"Victoria didn't even have to count the candies in the ten-pack," I commented, articulating her strategy. "She knows there are ten and just said 'ten.'"

I continued. "I'm going to give you and your partner an order form. Pack that number of candies, using as many ten-packs as possible. Then you and your partner need to make sure that you've packed the right number of candies for that room. Both of you need to check. After all, we're a candy shop and we can't make mistakes. Then you need to make a packing slip."

"What's that?" asked Alicia.

I explained. "A packing slip is a piece of paper that tells what's inside. When you buy things there's often a packing slip in the box. Our packing slip has to say the name of our company." We read the name on the board that we had picked yesterday, *Candy Land Candy Company,* and in Spanish, *Compañía de Tierra Dulce.*

"You also need to write the number of candies that are in the bag," I continued. "Then you need to write how many ten-packs and how many loose ones you put in."

As a reference I wrote on the board:

Name of the candy shop	*Nombre de la tienda de dulces*
Teacher ____	*Maestro* ____
Number of candies ____	*Número de dulces* ____
Number of ten-packs ____	*Paquetes de diez* ____
Number of loose ones ____	*Cuántos sobran* ____

I quickly made a sample packing slip on a piece of blank copy paper, so the children could see what it would look like. "You can make it look any way you want, as long as this information is on the paper. We'll hand the bag to Ms. Dominguez, and she'll open the bag and think, 'I wonder what's inside this.' Then she'll open the packing slip and read it and say, 'Oh, there's one ten-pack of candies and eight loose ones for our class.'"

I left the tub with ten-packs on the rug, and placed the loose candies on the rug next to the tub. The math buddies went to the tables with their order forms and a blank sheet of paper. I left the pile of ten-packs on the rug as well as the loose candies I had saved back from the start of the project.

I circulated around the tables. "Let's see how many candies you need to pack, Gerardo," I said. He showed me the 45 that was on his order form. "How many ten-packs do you think you'll need?" I asked.

"Um, three?" he said questioningly.

"How many loose ones do you think you'll need?" I asked.

"I think, I think, I think maybe . . . five," he answered.

"No, no. No," said his partner Alfredo. "Let's go count them."

The boys went to the rug to gather and count candies. I moved on to another table, observing the busy bustle in the room of children engaged in an activity that interested them.

Erin and Juanita were reading the teacher's name on their form. "Mar-Mar-tin-ez," they sounded it out.

"What number of candies does Mrs. Martinez need?" I asked.

"Twenty-three," they read.

"Hmmm," I said, "I wonder how many ten-packs will be in her bag."

"Um, two," answered Erin. "'Cuz I need twenty. Ten and ten is twenty."

"How many loose candies will you need?" I inquired.

"How many other candies?" she asked. "Maybe one loose one."

"Let me know what you find out," I said as I moved on to another table. I find this chance to hear how individual children are thinking about this new idea of "unitizing," counting units as well as groups of units, to be of critical importance. I watch children move in and out of understanding this complex idea, which is so very different from the kind of counting that they had done before.

I returned to Gerardo and Alfredo, who were working on forty-five. They had six ten-packs. They counted the candies in the ten-packs from one and by ones, Alfredo in Spanish and Gerardo in English. Children often count more consistently in their native language. Gerardo counted, "thirty-eight, thirty-nine, forty, forty-one, forty-two, forty-three, forty-four, forty-five, forty-six, forty-seven, there's too many." He stopped counting, and took away two ten-packs, leaving only four.

"Can I cut the ten-packs?" asked Alfredo. He was demonstrating his understanding of inclusion, that the five he needed was inside a ten-pack.

"I'm afraid the candies will fall apart if you do that," I answered. "Can the loose ones on the rug help you?" I said. "How many will you get?"

"Five," said Alfredo as he hurried away.

Carlos and Robert were hard at work on their bag of twenty-one candies. They had put in one ten-pack and had gone back to get more candies. They dropped a pile of loose candies on the table, counting on from their ten-pack: "Eleven, twelve, thirteen, fourteen, fifteen, sixteen, seventeen, eighteen, nineteen, twenty, twenty-one."

"That does make twenty-one," I agreed. "But could you have done it with more ten-packs?"

"I told you so," said Robert. The boys exchanged their loose candies for another ten-pack and two single candies.

"One, two, three . . ." Carlos counted all the twenty-two candies one at a time.

"It's too much," Robert said. "Let me do it." He pushed aside a candy and counted to twenty-one from one by ones.

Laura and Nina called me over to their pile of two ten-packs and three loose ones. "We're working on twenty-three," Laura said. "It's twenty . . . twenty-one, twenty-two, twenty-three, right?" she said. She knew that two tens are twenty and then could count on from twenty by ones. "Let me check," she said again. "Ten, twenty, thirty, I mean twenty-one, twenty-two, twenty-three." Clearly they were finding it difficult to shift between counting by tens and ones. They would need many chances to confront and reconfront their confusions over time.

I checked in on Alfredo and Gerardo, who had four ten-packs and five loose candies in front of them. They had written *45* on their slip next to *ten-packs*.

"How many ten-packs do you have?" I asked the boys.

"Forty-five," they answered, confusing ten-packs with individual candies. I helped them count the ten-packs, reinforcing what they were counting by saying, "One ten-pack, two ten-packs, three ten-packs, four ten-packs." Alfredo took over, again counting each candy from one, ending with "Thirty-nine, forty, forty-one, forty-two, forty-three, forty-four, forty-five, forty-five ten-packs." He was still confused.

I tried again. I swung a ten-pack back and forth in front of the boys. "What's this?"

"A ten-pack," they answered.

"How many of these things do you have?" I asked.

"Four," answered Gerardo.

"Oh, so you have four ten-packs, not forty-five," I said.

The boys' confusion reflected the struggle that was central to the lesson: Sometimes you count individual items and sometimes the units you count are groups of the individual items. I well knew that the boys' correct final answer did not indicate that they "understood" it, but that they were merely on the journey toward constructing this new idea.

I found Lorena stuffing a bag with many ten-packs. "We need eighteen," she said. It looked like she had eighteen ten-packs in her bag. I tried to emphasize the context to encourage Lorena and Cristina to make sense of the problem. "How many candies does Mrs. Dominguez need?" I asked.

"Eighteen," Lorena answered. Cristina nodded.

"Check to see if you have eighteen candies," I suggested.

Lorena and Cristina began counting ten-packs. "One, two, three," they began. I interrupted them. "Do you have three candies?" I asked. Lorena nodded, uncertain, but Cristina had a different idea. "No, it's one, two, three, four, five, six, seven, eight, nine, ten," she said, counting a ten-pack, then continuing on to count the other candies by ones. Lorena joined in and together they got to thirty. The difference between counting individual items versus counting groups was also hazy for these two. They, and all children, would get to count and recount the candies in the bags, and have many chances to use the candy bags to solve problems before we actually handed the candies out to classrooms.

As children finished packing their bags, I asked them to put the bags on the rug. Then I encouraged these children to check each other's bags. This would give them another chance to think about place value concepts.

When all the children were finished, they gathered on the rug next to their math buddies.

"That was fun," commented Cristina. The others nodded.

I showed the children our class candy bag. "Our packing slip says we need to have twenty-five candies in it." I wrote *25* on the board. "Before we eat our candies, how many ten-packs do you think we have in our bag? And how many loose ones? Check with your math buddy to see if you agree."

After a moment I called on Armando. "It's easy," he said. "There's two of the tens and five little ones."

Alicia wasn't so sure. "How do you know?" she demanded.

"The first number is the big ones and the other number says the little ones," he explained.

I asked Miguel to explain his thinking to the group.

"There's ten and ten and five loose ones," Miguel told us.

Then we took out the candies, and the children chorused, "I was right!"

We passed out the candies to the children.

"Amanda isn't here," said Cristina, explaining why one candy was left over. We put it in her cubby.

Day 2

Playing *What's in the Bag?*   The next day, the children sat by their math buddies, in a circle around the rug. The completed bags, stuffed with candies and packing slips, lay before me. "Our Candy Land Candy Company is going well!" I said. "The kids are really going to like these bags. We'll deliver them to the classes in a few days. Today we'll check the bags by playing a game called *What's in the Bag?*"

Sereslinda picked up a bag and read the teacher's name. "Mrs. Hernandez. She needs twenty-seven candies." I wrote *Mrs. Hernandez* and *27*.

"How many ten-packs and how many loose candies do you think should be in the bag?" I asked. "Talk with your math buddy to see if you have an idea." I paused while most of the children talked.

In a moment I got their attention.

"It's twenty-seven," said Juanita. "Two ten-packs and seven loose ones."

"Why do you think that?" I asked her.

"It's two, seven in the candies and two, seven for the ten-packs," she explained. "I just know."

"So you see a two in the number twenty-seven, and you know it's two ten-packs and seven loose ones. Can anyone else explain what Juanita is talking about?"

"They both are the same," observed Robert.

"It's two, seven and two, seven," added Victoria.

Sereslinda checked the bag. "Yup, two long ones and seven loose ones," she announced, laying them on the rug.

Carlos chose a bag next, saying, "Let's look at Mr. Hennessey's." He got out the packing slip and read the number of candies. "It's twenty-three," he said.

I wrote *Mr. Hennessey* and *23*. "How many ten-packs and how many loose ones would you expect?" I asked.

Carlos said, "It's two, three, two, three."

I wanted to attach some numerical meaning to his comment. "How many students does Mr. Hennessey have?" I asked.

The students answered, "Twenty-three."

"What's this two for?" I asked, pointing to the next column.

"Two ten-packs," answered Juanita.

"What's the three for?" I asked. The children chorused, "The loose ones." We checked the bag, and the children were right.

I decided to push the children's thinking. "So the numbers are the same, like Carlos said. Why is that?" I asked.

"It's like tens and ones," Armando said.

"It's two packs with ten in it and three leftovers," said Laura.

"But why does two and three make twenty-three?" I asked. "I thought two and three made five." There was a silence in the room.

Heriberto ventured an idea. "It's different. We're showing what we did to the candy. It's like how many ten-packs we made and how many more we needed."

I taped the two ten-strips up on the board as well as the three loose candies. There was some more silence.

"You can count them," said Armando. "It's twenty-three. I did it."

So we counted each candy and got to twenty-three. "But I thought two and three made five," I repeated. I wanted to keep the confusion alive. It was only through this kind of discussion that the children would come to understand and then articulate the complex idea that the first numeral meant groups of ten and the second numeral meant single items.

"You've got ten-packs and you've got loose ones," said Victoria. "The first number shows you the ten-packs and the other one is the loose candies."

"Talk to your math buddy," I said, "and see what you both think." This would allow more children a chance to articulate their ideas.

FIGURE 19–1 Mrs. Dominguez's packing slip.

I moved the discussion on and asked Cristina to choose a bag (see Figure 19–1). She got Mrs. Dominguez's bag and read "Eighteen." I wrote *Mrs. Dominguez* and *18* on the board.

"Think about what should be in her bag," I said. "Eighteen. This should be in the bag." I reached for the extra ten-packs that the children didn't use. I began counting the ten-packs, "One, two, three, four, five, six . . ."

Navin interrupted me. "That's not right. It's too many."

"What?" I asked inquiringly, looking around, inviting other children to participate in the discussion.

"That's just too many," agreed Cristina.

"I don't see why," I said. "You have eighteen there. I need to keep going."

"That's not right!" Some children were pretty definite, although others seemed to have no problem with what I was doing.

"Talk to your math buddy," I said again. "What do you think about how I'm making eighteen?"

Armando shook his head. "It's the ten-packs," he said. "You need one ten-pack or you have too much."

"It's a ten-pack and then eight loose ones," agreed Heriberto. "That's how you get eighteen."

"So the bag should have one ten-pack and eight loose ones and that makes eighteen?" I asked. Heriberto nodded. I opened the bag and held up exactly what Heriberto said we'd have. A few children looked surprised.

"Let's count the candies here," I said.

Alicia raised her hand. She counted the loose ones, saying, "Ten, twenty, thirty, forty, fifty, sixty, seventy, eighty."

"Is this eighty candies?" I asked, holding up the eight loose ones.

"Yes," said Alicia.

"This is a very interesting question," I told the group. "Please talk to your math buddy: How many candies are in my hand: is it eighty or eight? And how do you know?"

I waited while the children talked to each other. They continued to be interested in this important question: When do we count by tens and when do we count by ones?

Then we continued the discussion. "Who has an idea: Are there eighty or eight candies and how do you know?" Hands went up. I called on Juanita.

"There's eight, 'cause you count one, two, three, four, five, six, seven, eight," Juanita said.

"I know it's not eighty 'cause eighty's a lot," offered Kayla.

I called on Heriberto. "It's not ten, twenty, thirty. That's not a ten-*pack*."

Miguel said, "If you had like a ten-pack and another and another you could count by tens. But you only have the loose ones and they're one each time."

I wanted many different children to explain their ideas. I often find that children understand each other better than they understand how I word things. And I knew that Alicia and many others might be confused about unitizing for some time. I hoped to surround them with the opportunity to confront the idea many times in different contexts, to explain their own thinking and to hear the ideas of many other children.

We continued with this kind of conversation for more teachers' bags. When we got to Ms. Lee and Ms. Alene, who team-teach, we found that we needed forty-five candies. I wrote the teachers' names and *45*. We discussed what might be in the bag. Then I opened the bag and took out the four ten-packs and five loose ones. "Yes!" said Miguel excitedly.

I asked the children a new question. First I pointed to the 4 in 45. Then I said, "Show me where the four is in the candies."

Hands went up immediately, and Jesse held up the four ten-packs.

I held up four loose candies. "Is this what the four means?" I asked.

"It could be four," said Juanita.

"But not now," Heriberto said. "That number goes with the ten-packs."

I wanted more children engaged in the question, and asked the children to talk to their math buddies about what the 4 means in 45. More children were sounding firm about the 4 standing for four ten-packs.

"It's the ten-things, I mean the big ones," Brittney told us. She showed us where the 4 was in the number on the board.

"So the four tells us how many ten-packs," I said. "Mrs. Dominguez has eighteen. How many ten-packs does she have?"

"It's one," answered Andrei.

Playing the Game with Partners   Not all the children were making this connection, although more had than the previous day. "Let's play this game with partners," I suggested. This would give the children more hands-on practice with the meaning of the digits in place value. I put the bags in the center of the rug with the math buddies sitting in pairs around the bags.

Victoria and Brittney sat together. Victoria reached for a bag and took out Mr. Urrea's packing slip. She said, "Mr. Urrea's got twenty-six candies. You tell me how the candies are." Victoria hid the bag from Brittney.

Brittney closed her eyes and then said, "There's, um, two ten-packs and four, I mean six loose ones." She went on to explain, "Ten and ten is twenty and that's two ten-packs and then three and three is six so there's six loose ones."

Victoria peeked into the bag. "You're right," she said, spilling the candies on the rug. She held up the two ten-packs for Brittney to see. Then together they counted the loose ones.

"It's my turn," said Victoria. "I get to guess."

Brittney returned Mr. Urrea's bag to the center pile and got out another one. She read the packing slip and said, "Mrs. Udall has twenty-six people who need candy. What's in the bag?" Brittney hid the bag behind her back.

"You say twenty-six?" asked Victoria. "A two and a six?" Brittney nodded.

Victoria thought. Then she said, "It's two ten-packs because ten and ten is twenty and then twenty-one, twenty-two, twenty-three, twenty-four, twenty-five, twenty-six." She counted on using her fingers. "It's six loose ones."

What's in the Bag? became part of math workshop. This gave the children more chances to connect the arrangement of the candies with place value. And I had more opportunities to observe different pairs of children to watch them guess and check their idea. Over time more children made the connection between the digits and the ten-packs.

Extensions

An extension of this lesson is to have children draw how the candies are arranged in specific bags. For example you might tell them, "Mr. Urrea's bag has twenty-six candies in it. Can you draw what the candies look like? How many ten-packs will be in the bag, and how many loose candies?" Just as children think about the numbers in different ways, they also approach this problem in different ways, depending on their facility with unitizing.

For example, Alicia consistently drew each item, one at a time, never grouping them at all. Jennifer also drew individual items, but then went back and counted and circled ten candies to show the ten-packs. Sereslinda was thinking about tens as she worked, and drew candies in lines of ten, making a rectangle around each ten-pack that she completed. She wrote *10, 20, 30, 40* above each ten-pack. Carina just made circles with the numeral 10 inside to denote ten-packs.

Another extension is to have the children figure out how many candies there will be if we combine two teachers' bags. The children have an opportunity to use the ten-pack/loose candy organization (or tens and ones) to help them think about two-digit addition problems.

Linking Assessment and Instruction

You may wish to make the following observations:

- When packing the bags, how did the children figure out how many ten-packs and how many loose ones they needed? Did they immediately know, indicating a good sense of place value?
- When packing the bags, did some children get some candies, count them, and then adjust the total? This means they used number relationships to solve the problem.
- Did the children count by tens and then switch to counting by ones appropriately? Did they do this consistently? If not, their understanding is still fragile.
- Did any children count only by ones? This may indicate that the children don't yet trust that counting by tens will give the same answer as counting by ones.
- Did the children confuse counting ten-packs with counting loose ones, as Alicia did? This indicates fragile place-value understandings.
- Did the children notice the relationship between the digits in the written numbers and the number of ten-packs and loose ones? Did they use this pattern to help them when they played the game? How did they explain it?
- Were children firm in their beliefs when you asked questions to challenge them? This indicates solid place-value understandings. Children who waver or become unsure are still making sense of place value.
- Could children reverse their thinking, and explain how the candies are arranged in the bag when given the total number of candies? This is evidence of place-value understanding.

Blackline Masters

Estimate and Count Recording Sheet   **119**

More and Less Recording Sheet   **120**

Pattern Block Cutouts   **121**

Spill and Compare Recording Sheet   **127**

What Do You See? Cards   **128**

Shake and Spill: 5   **131**

Shake and Spill: 6   **132**

Shake and Spill: 7   **133**

Shake and Spill: 8   **134**

Estimate and Count Recording Sheet

Name _____

☐ Estimate _____

     Count _____

- -

☐ Estimate _____

     Count _____

- -

Name _____

☐ Estimate _____

     Count _____

- -

☐ Estimate _____

     Count _____

More and Less Recording Sheet

Container _____ holds _____ cubes.

Container _____ holds _____ cubes.

Which container holds more?

Which container holds less?

Or are they the same? _____

- -

Container _____ holds _____ cubes.

Container _____ holds _____ cubes.

Which container holds more?

Which container holds less?

Or are they the same? _____

From *Teaching Number Sense, Grade 1* by Chris Confer. © 2005 Math Solutions Publications.

Pattern Block Cutouts

Pattern Block Cutouts

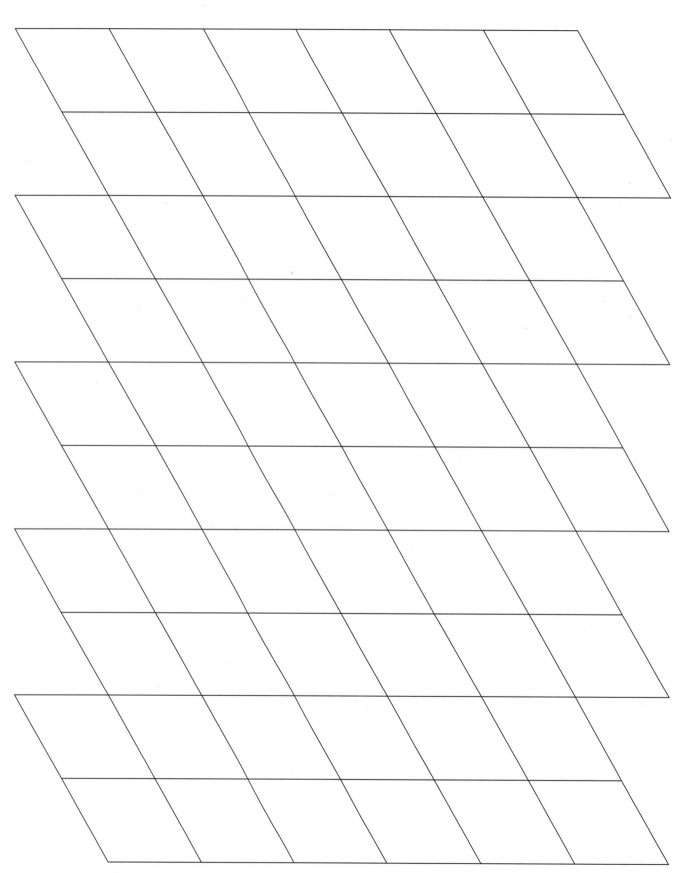

From *Teaching Number Sense, Grade 1* by Chris Confer. © 2005 Math Solutions Publications.

Pattern Block Cutouts

Pattern Block Cutouts

From *Teaching Number Sense, Grade 1* by Chris Confer. © 2005 Math Solutions Publications.

Pattern Block Cutouts

Pattern Block Cutouts

From *Teaching Number Sense, Grade 1* by Chris Confer. © 2005 Math Solutions Publications.

Spill and Compare Recording Sheet

Names: _____ Our Number [ ]

More Reds	More Yellows	The Same Number of Reds and Yellows

- -

Names: _____ Our Number [ ]

More Reds	More Yellows	The Same Number of Reds and Yellows

What Do You See? Cards

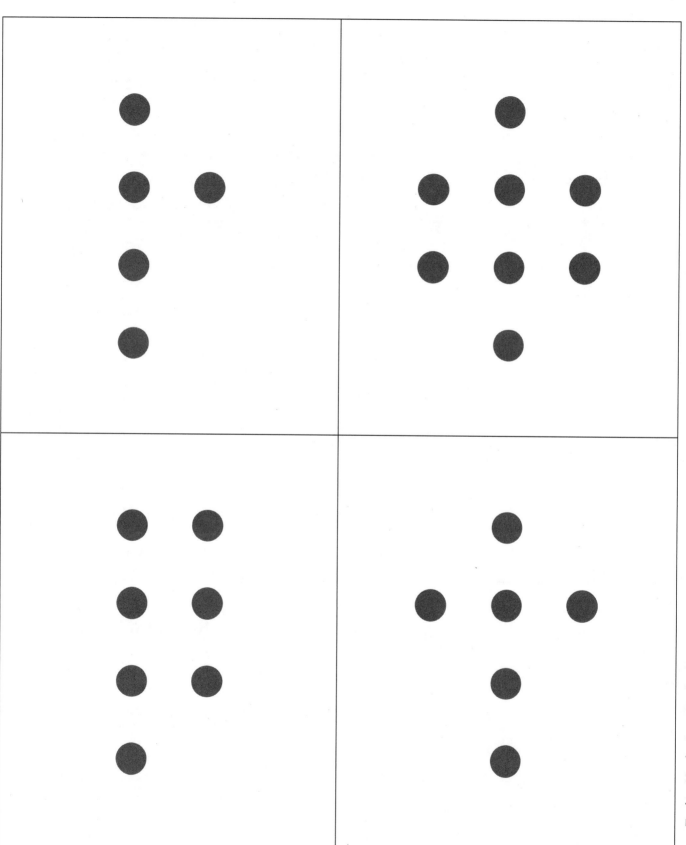

What Do You See? Cards

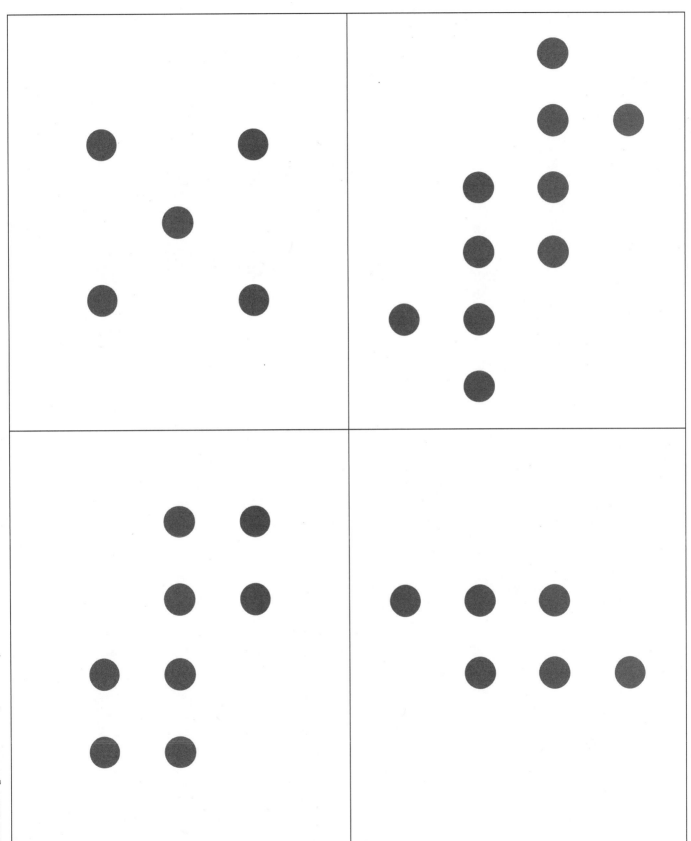

What Do You See? Cards

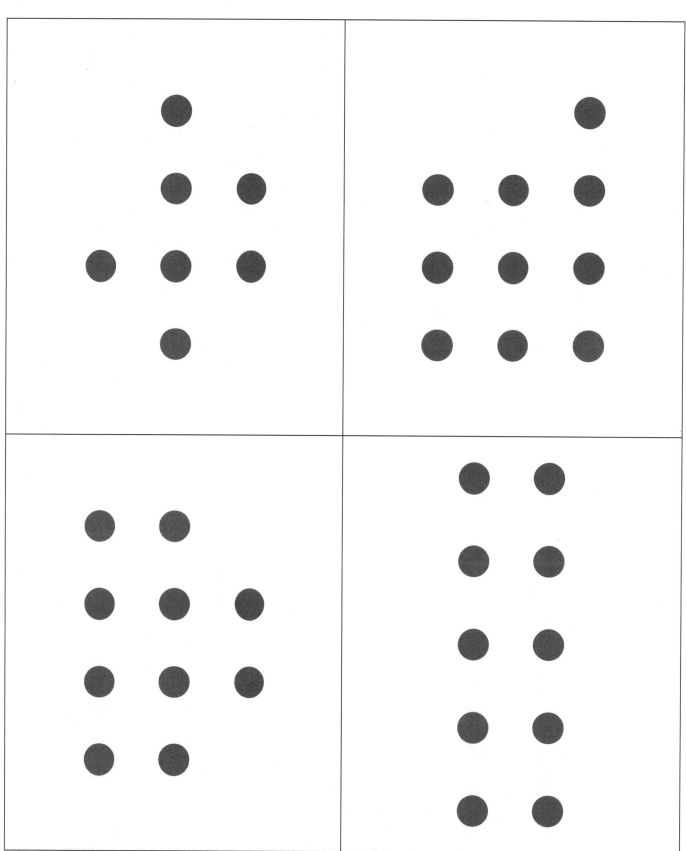

From *Teaching Number Sense, Grade 1* by Chris Confer. © 2005 Math Solutions Publications.

Shake and Spill: 5

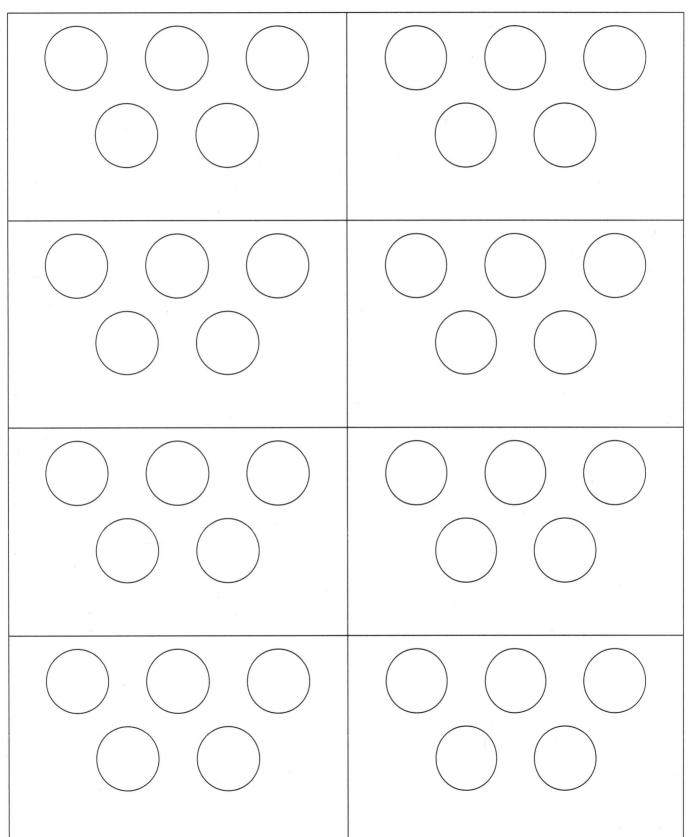

Shake and Spill: 6

From *Teaching Number Sense, Grade 1* by Chris Confer. © 2005 Math Solutions Publications.

Shake and Spill: 7

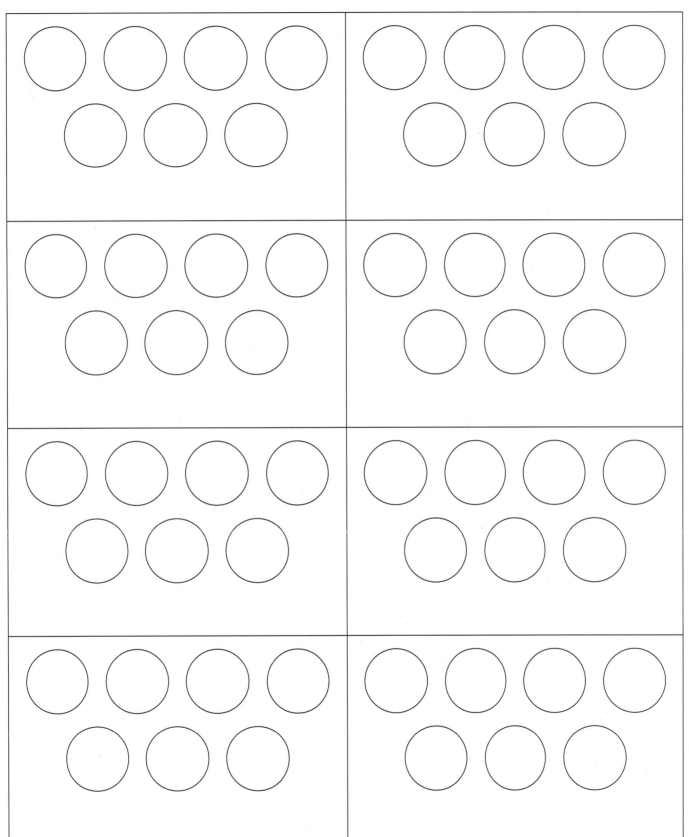

Shake and Spill: 8

From *Teaching Number Sense, Grade 1* by Chris Confer. © 2005 Math Solutions Publications.

Index

addition
  in bead board lesson on combinations
    of numbers, 67–72
  equations, activity on developing and
    solving, 73–79
  equations describing groups of dots,
    lesson with, 40–44
  making number sentences from larger
    numbers, lesson, 61–66
  number of feet and tails of animals,
    lesson, 80–86
  story problems with numbers less than
    ten, lesson with, 93–96
  strategies for, xiv, 73–76
  target numbers, activities for adding
    parts of, 45–51
  ten, lesson on adding numbers to
    make, 52–60
animals, addition lesson on total number
  of feet and tails of, 80–86
assessment
  with addition equations, activity on
    developing and solving, 79
  with bead board lesson on
    combinations of number six, 72
  with bead board lesson on
    decomposing into 5s and 10s, 92
  with counting by groups activity, 100
  with counting by tens, activities,
    106–7, 115
  with decomposing ten, lesson, 59–60
  with estimating and comparing,
    lesson, 20
  with estimating length, activity, 15–16
  with lesson on making number
    sentences from larger numbers, 66
  with looking inside numbers for
    smaller groups, lesson, 44
  with naturally-occurring problems, 5
  with number comparison
    investigation, 34
  numbers of feet and tails of animals,
    addition lesson, 86
  with pattern block numbers, lesson, 25

  with real-life problem-solving
    activities, 5, 10
  with smaller/larger number-guessing
    game, 38–39
  with story problems using numbers less
    than ten, lesson, 96
  with target number decomposition
    lesson, 50–51
  with voting activity, 9–10

base ten system, lesson investigating,
  101–7
bead boards
  combination of number six, lesson,
    67–72
  instructions for making, 68
  introducing, 67, 68–69
  secret numbers, counting 5s and 10s
    routine, 87–92
  Secret Numbers, routine, 87–92
  Six Birds, lesson, 67–72
  Story Problems, lesson, 93–96
  story problems with numbers less than
    ten, lesson, 93–96
bigger. *See* larger
Blackline Masters, 117–34
  Estimate and Count Recording
    Sheet, 119
  More and Less Recording Sheet, 120
  Pattern Block Cutouts, 121–26
  Shake and Spill, 131–34
  Spill and Compare Recording Sheet, 127
  What Do You See? Cards, 128–30
Bruno Bruin, 7

Candy Shop, A
  How Many Candies?, investigation,
    101–7
  Packaging Candy Bags, investigation,
    108–15
Carle, Eric, 7
comparing
  more and less, lesson, 17–20
  odd/even, investigation, 26–34

compensation strategy, 94, 95
composing numbers, in number
  sense, xiii
computation, strategies for, xiv–xv
conservation of number, 23, 98
Containers: More and Less,
  lesson, 17–20
Corduroy, 97, 98
counting
  by groups, activity, 97–100
  with number comparison,
    investigation, 26–34
  in number sense, xii–xiii
  with pattern block numbers, lesson,
    21–25
  by tens, activities, 101–15
counting all, 73–74, 89
  as strategy for computation, xiv
counting back, as strategy for
  computation, xiv
Counting Buttons, activity, 97–100
counting on, 73–76, 89
  as strategy for computation, xiv
counting what remains, as strategy for
  computation, xiv
Cuenta Ratones, 53

data
  addition lesson on number of feet and
    tails of animals, 80–86
  frequency of two-color counters
    appearing, lesson, 61–62
  frequency of two-color counters
    appearing, lesson on, 64–66
decision-making, activities requiring
  mathematical, 6–10
decomposing numbers
  looking inside numbers for smaller
    groups, lesson, 40–44
  making number sentences from larger
    numbers, lesson, 61–66
  in number sense, xiii
  with pattern block numbers, lesson,
    22–23

decomposing numbers (*continued*)
  into 5s and 10s with bead boards, 87–92
  target number, activity for decomposing, 45–51
  ten, lesson on decomposing number, 52–60
  Ways to Make problems, 53, 54
designs, lesson for making pattern block, 21–25
dice, activity on developing and solving addition equations using, 73–79
disequilibrium, 109
doubles
  finding, 73–74, 76
  in number comparison, investigation, 28, 32–34
  as strategy for computation, xiv
Dragons, Dragons, 7, 8, 9
Dream Snow, 7, 8, 9

Eight Blocks, 24
equations
  addition equations, activity on developing and solving, 73–79
  with bead board lesson on combinations of number six, 67, 69–72
  looking inside numbers for smaller groups, lesson, 40–44
  story problems with numbers less than ten, lesson, 93–96
  target numbers, writing equations for decomposed, 46
equivalence
  conservation of number and, 23
  place value and, 98
Estimate and Count, activity, 11–16
  Blackline Master, 120
  recording sheet (Blackline Master), 119
estimating. *See also* predicting
  in counting by groups, activity, 97–100
  counting by tens and, 101–7
  length, activity, 11–16
  more/less, lesson, 17–20

Fire Race, 7, 8, 9
5s (fives)
  bead board lesson, 67–72
  counting by, 27
  counting by, with bead boards lesson, 87–92
  counting by groups, activity, 97, 100
  place value and, 102

games
  counting by tens, 101–7
  Guess My Number game, 35–39
  number-guessing game, 35–39
  Roll and Add dice game, 73, 76–79
  What's in the Bag?, 108, 109, 112–15

graphing frequency of two-color counters, lesson, 64–66
Guess My Number game, 35–39

Heckedy Peg, 7, 8, 9

Just Another Ordinary Day, 7, 8
Just Like Daddy, 7, 8

Koala Lou, 7, 8

landmark numbers
  in bead board lesson, 87–92
  in number sense, xiii
larger
  looking inside numbers for smaller groups, lesson, 40–44
  in smaller/larger number-guessing game, 35–39
length, estimating activity, 11–16
less
  estimating and comparing, lesson, 17–20
  number comparison, investigation, 26–34
  with smaller/larger number-guessing game, 35–39
little. *See* smaller
Little Penguin's Tail, 7, 8

Making Classroom Decisions, activity, 6–10
mathematical decision making, activities requiring, 6–10
money, activities, 7–10
Moon Lake, 7, 8
more
  estimating and comparing, lesson, 17–20
  number comparison, investigation, 26–34
  in smaller/larger number-guessing game, 35–39
Mouse Count, 52
Mouse Count, lesson, 52–60
multiplicative thinking, 102
My Rotten Redheaded Older Brother, 7, 8

number facts, strategies and, xv
number-guessing game, 35–39
number lines
  as models for computations, xiv
  with smaller/larger number-guessing game, 35–39
number patterns
  doubles (*see* doubles)
  plus one, lesson using, 80–86
number relationships, xiii
numbers
  changing of meaning, 109–10
  complexity of, xii

defined, xii
  importance of experiences with, xi–xii
  making sense of numbers, importance of, xv
  young children and, xi
number sense
  counting, xii–xiii
  decomposing and composing numbers in, xiii
  defined, xii–xiii
  landmark numbers in, xiii
  number relationships and, xiii
number sentences from larger numbers, making, 61–66

odd/even comparison, investigation, 26–34
Over in the Grasslands, 80
Over in the Grasslands, lesson, 80–86
"Over in the Meadow," 80

pairs, real-life problem-solving activities with, 2–5
parties, problem-solving activities for, 2–5
Pattern Block Numbers, lesson, 21–25
  cutouts (Blackline Masters), 121–26
place value, 97, 98, 102, 109–10
  Candy Shop, A: How Many Candies?, investigation, 101–7
  Candy Shop, A: Packaging Candy Bags, investigation, 108–15
  counting and grouping by tens, introductory activities, 101–15
plus one number pattern, lesson using, 80–86
predicting. *See also* estimating
  counting by tens with, 101–7
  with more/less, lesson, 17–20

real-life problems, investigations for solving, 1–10
  naturally-occurring problems, activities with, 1–5
  voting, activity, 6–10
Roll and Add, activity, 73–79

Salt in His Shoes, 7, 8, 9
same number comparison, investigation, 26–34
school libraries, mathematical activities with purchasing books for, 6–10
Secret Numbers, routine, 87–92
Shake and Spill, lesson, 61–66
  Blackline Masters, 131–34
Six Birds, lesson, 67–72
6s (sixes), with bead board lesson on combinations of numbers, 67–72

smaller
  looking inside numbers for smaller groups, lesson, 40–44
  in smaller/larger number-guessing game, 35–39
Snap It!, activity, 45–51
Solving Real-World Problems, activity, 1–5
Spill and Compare investigation, 26–34
  recording sheet (Blackline Master), 127
Story Problems, lesson, 93–96
strategies, encouraging, 94
subtraction, strategies for, xiv

10s (tens)
  bead board lesson, 67–72
  counting and grouping by, lessons, 101–15
  counting by, with bead board lesson, 87–92
  counting by groups, activity, 97, 100
  decomposing number ten, lesson, 52–60
  making tens, as addition strategy, xiv, 73–74
  place value and, 102
  taking away, xiv
Thank You, Brother Bear, 7, 8, 9
2s (twos)
  counting by groups, activity, 97–100
  real-life problem-solving activities with, 2–5

unitizing, 102, 109

Very Busy Spider, The, 7
volume, lesson on estimating and comparing, 17–20
voting, activity, 6–10

Walsh, Ellen Stoll, 52
Way Out in the Desert, 81, 82
Ways to Make problems, 53, 54
What Do You See?, lesson, 40–44
  cards (Blackline Master), 128–30
What's in the Bag?, game, 108, 109, 112–15
Williams, Karolyn, 6–10
Wilson, Anna, 80
Wood, Audrey, 7
Wood, Don, 7